Gathered in My Name

†

STUDIES IN WORLD CATHOLICISM

Michael L. Budde and William T. Cavanaugh, Series Editors
Karen M. Kraft, Managing Editor

Other Titles in This Series

Beyond the Borders of Baptism: Catholicity, Allegiances, and Lived Identities. Edited by Michael L. Budde. Vol. 1, 2016. ISBN 9781498204736

New World Pope: Pope Francis and the Future of the Church. Edited by Michael L. Budde. Vol. 2, 2017. ISBN 9781498283717

Scattered and Gathered: Catholics in Diaspora. Edited by Michael L. Budde. Vol. 3, 2017. ISBN 9781532607097.

A Living Tradition: The Holy See, Catholic Social Doctrine, and Global Politics 1965–2000. A. Alexander Stummvoll. Vol. 4, 2018. ISBN 9781532605130.

Fragile World: Ecology and the Church. Edited by William T. Cavanaugh. Vol. 5, 2018. ISBN 9781498283403.

Love, Joy, and Sex: African Conversation on Pope Francis's Amoris Laetitia *and the Gospel of Family in a Divided World.* Edited by Stan Chu Ilo. Vol. 6, 2019. ISBN 9781532618956.

The Church and Indigenous Peoples in the Americas: In Between Reconciliation and Decolonization. Edited by Michel Andraos. Vol. 7, 2019. ISBN 9781532631115.

Pentecostalism, Catholicism, and the Spirit in the World. Edited by Stan Chu Ilo. Vol. 8, 2019. ISBN 9781532650352.

Gathered in My Name

Ecumenism in the World Church

EDITED BY

William T. Cavanaugh

CONTRIBUTORS

Paul Avis

Elias Kifon Bongmba

Mark Chapman

Michael L. Cooper-White

Chukwumamkpam Vincent Ifeme

Grace Ji-Sun Kim

Paul D. Murray

Teresa Okure, SHCJ

Juan Sepúlveda

Vimal Tirimanna, CSsR

Justin K. H. Tse

Felix Wilfred

Philip Wingeier-Rayo

 CASCADE *Books* · Eugene, Oregon

GATHERED IN MY NAME
Ecumenism in the World Church

Studies in World Catholicism 9

Cascade Books
An Imprint of Wipf and Stock Publishers
199 W. 8th Ave., Suite 3
Eugene, OR 97401

www.wipfandstock.com

PAPERBACK ISBN: 978-1-5326-8558-3
HARDCOVER ISBN: 978-1-5326-8559-0
EBOOK ISBN: 978-1-5326-8560-6

Cataloguing-in-Publication data:

Names: Cavanaugh, William T., 1962–, editor.
Title: Gathered in my name : ecumenism in the world church / edited by William T. Cavanaugh.
Description: Eugene, OR : Cascade Books, 2020 | Studies in World Catholicism 9 | Includes bibliographical references and index.
Identifiers: ISBN 978-1-5326-8558-3 (paperback) | ISBN 978-1-5326-8559-0 (hardcover) | ISBN 978-1-5326-8560-6 (ebook)
Subjects: LCSH: Christian union. | Ecumenical movement.
Classification: BX8.3 .G34 2020 (print) | BX8.3 .G34 (ebook)

Manufactured in the U.S.A.   DECEMBER 28, 2020

Table of Contents

Contributors

Paul Avis is a priest of the Church of England and honorary professor in the Department of Theology and Religion at Durham University, UK. He has served as general secretary of the Council for Christian Unity (1998–2011), theological consultant to the Anglican Communion Office (2011–12), subdean and canon theologian of Exeter Cathedral and as a chaplain to HM Queen Elizabeth II. He is editor-in-chief of *Ecclesiology*, and his publications include *Reshaping Ecumenical Theology: The Church Made Whole?* (2010); and *The Vocation of Anglicanism* (2016), both published by T&T Clark.

Elias Kifon Bongmba is the Harry and Hazel Chavanne Chair in Christian Theology and professor and chair of the Department of Religion at Rice University in Houston. He holds a PhD from the University of Denver's Iliff School of Theology and an MDiv from North American Baptist Seminary in Sioux Falls, SD. He serves as president of the African Association for the Study of Religion, and his publications include *Facing a Pandemic: The African Church and the Crisis of HIV/AIDS* (Baylor University Press, 2007). He is also the editor of *The Wiley Blackwell Companion to African Religions* (2012) and *The Routledge Companion to Christianity in Africa* (2015).

Mark Chapman is professor of modern church history and theology as well as vice principal and academic dean at Ripon College Cuddesdon in England. He is also professor of the history of modern theology at the University of Oxford. A Church of England priest, he is canon theologian of Truro Cathedral, a member of the General Synod for the Diocese of Oxford and its Council of Christian Unity, and co-chair of the Meissen Theological Conference. His recent publications include *The Fantasy of Reunion: Anglicans, Catholics, and Ecumenism, 1833–1880* (Oxford University Press, 2014) and the edited volumes, *Costly Communion: Ecumenical Initiative and Sacramental Strife in the Anglican Communion* (Brill, 2019) and *Hope in Ecumenical Future* (Palgrave Macmillan, 2017).

Michael L. Cooper-White, DD, is an ordained Lutheran minister who served from 2000–2017 as president of the Lutheran Theological Seminary at Gettysburg. He holds an MDiv from the Seminary and completed his internship with the Lutheran Church in Chile at the height of the repression by Augusto Pinochet's military junta. He is currently president emeritus of United Lutheran Seminary (a consolidation of Gettysburg and Philadelphia seminaries), and president of The Gettysburg Group, a consulting collaborative that serves ecclesial and other entities in organizational and leadership development. He also holds a certificate in dispute mediation from Philadelphia's Good Samaritan Center.

Chukwumamkpam Vincent Ifeme is a full professor at the Pontifical Lateran University of Rome's Istituto Superiore di Scienze Religiose's "Redemptoris Mater" campus, where he has taught since 2007. He is also director of the Office for Ecumenism and Dialogue in the Diocese of San Benedetto del Tronto-Ripatransone-Montalto, Italy, where he is very active in practical ecumenical initiatives under the direction of the Italian Episcopal Conference's National Office for Ecumenism and Interreligious Dialogue (UNEDI). He holds a PhD in systematic theology from the Pontifical Urbaniana University in Rome.

Grace Ji-Sun Kim is an ordained Presbyterian (USA) minister of word and sacrament and professor of theology at Earlham School of Religion. She holds a PhD from the University of Toronto. A past member of the board of directors for the American Academy of Religion (AAR), she also sits on the editorial board for the *Journal of Religion and Popular Culture* and blogs regularly for The Huffington Post. She is co-editor of the Palgrave Macmillan Book Series, Asian Christianity in Diaspora, and her publications include *Reimagining Spirit: Wind, Breath, and Vibration* (Cascade, 2019) and the co-authored *Healing Our Broken Humanity: Practices for Revitalizing the Church and Renewing the World* (IVP, 2018).

Paul D. Murray has served as professor of systematic theology on the faculty of Durham University's Department of Theology and Religion since 2002 and as director of Durham's Centre for Catholic Studies since 2008. In 2011, Pope Benedict XVI appointed him to the third phase of the Anglican-Roman Catholic International Commission (ARCIC III) and, in 2012, as a consultor to the Pontifical Council for Justice and Peace. He holds a doctorate from Cambridge, and his dissertation was published as *Reason, Truth, and Theology in Pragmatist Perspective* (Peeters, 2004). Among his other publications are "Roman Catholicism and Ecumenism" in *The Oxford Companion to Catholicism* (Oxford University Press, 2018) and the edited volume, *Receptive Ecumenism and the Call to Catholic Learning: Exploring a Way for Contemporary Ecumenism* (Oxford University Press, 2008).

Teresa Okure, SHCJ, is a sister of the Society of the Holy Child Jesus and the first African to join the congregation. She earned her doctorate at Fordham University and is professor of New Testament and gender hermeneutics at the Catholic Institute of West Africa in Port Harcourt, Nigeria, where she has also served as academic dean and head of the Department of Biblical Studies. From 2011 to 2018, she was a member of the Anglican-Roman Catholic International Commission (ARCIC III) and is the current founding president of the Catholic Biblical Association of Nigeria. Co-editor of *Global Bible Commentary* (Abingdon, 2004), she has many other publications to her name, including *Rethinking Martyrdom* (Orbis, 2016), co-authored with Jon Sobrino and Felix Wilfred.

Juan Sepúlveda is a Pentecostal pastor and theologian who served from 1997 to 2018 as planning director of SEPADE (Evangelical Service for Development) based in Concepción, Chile; currently, he is a member of SEPADE's board of directors. He teaches courses on Latin American church history and mission and ecumenism at CTE (Evangelical Theological Community of Chile) and other theological institutions. He was invited as a Pentecostal observer at the May 2007 Fifth General Conference of the Latin American and the Caribbean Bishops (CELAM) in Aparecida, Brazil, and served from 1992 to 2002 as a member of the Advisory Group for the Office of Ecumenical Churches and Relationships within the World Council of Churches. He holds a doctorate from the University of Birmingham in England.

Vimal Tirimanna, CSsR, is a professor of systematic moral theology at the Pontifical Alphonsian Academy, Rome, and the National Seminary of Our Lady of Lanka in Sri Lanka. He served for five years as the official representative of the Sri Lankan Catholic Bishops to the Office of Theological Concerns of the Federation of Asian Bishops' Conferences and for ten years as executive secretary of this same office. Appointed in 2010 by the Pontifical Council for Christian Unity, he is a member of the Catholic delegation to the Anglican-Roman Catholic International Commission (ARCIC). He has published in journals such as *New Blackfriars* and *Concilium*, and his books include *Vatican II and Official Catholic Moral Teachings* (Dharmaram, 2015).

Justin K. H. Tse is assistant professor of humanities (education) at Singapore Management University and previously served as visiting assistant professor in Northwestern University's Asian American Studies Program. He is secretary of the Society for the Philosophical Study of Education and a steering committee member of the American Academy of Religion's Chinese Christianities Seminar. He holds a PhD in geography from the University of British Columbia and is the author of various articles and book chapters, including "Spiritual Propositions: The American Evangelical Intelligentsia and the Supernatural Order," in *Spaces of Spirituality* (Routledge, 2018). He is also the lead editor of *Theological Reflections on the Hong Kong Umbrella Movement* (Palgrave MacMillan, 2016).

Felix Wilfred is emeritus professor of the State University of Madras in Chennai, India, where he also served as president of the Faculty of Arts and chair of Philosophy and Religious Thought. Currently, he is the founding director of the Asian Centre for Cross-Cultural Studies in Chennai and editor-in-chief of the *International Journal of Asian Christianity.* Past president of *Concilium,* he is also editor of *The Oxford Handbook on Christianity in Asia* (Oxford University Press, 2014). He has been a visiting professor at several universities, including the University of Frankfurt, Boston College, Ateneo de Manila University, and Fudan University in China. He was a member of the Vatican's International Theological Commission and served ten years as executive secretary of the Federation of Asian Bishops' Conference's Theological Commission.

Philip Wingeier-Rayo was appointed dean in 2018 at Wesley Theological Seminary and also serves as professor of missiology and Methodist studies there. He holds a PhD in theology, ethics, and culture from Chicago Theological Seminary, an MTS from Garret-Evangelical Seminary, and an MTh from Seminario Evangélico de Teología in Matanzas, Cuba. His publications include *La Evangelización y la Misión de Dios: Una Teología Bíblica* (Wesley's Foundery, 2020) and *Where are the Poor? A Comparison of the Ecclesial Base Communities and Pentecostalism* (Pickwick, 2011). His academic work is informed by fifteen years of missionary service in Nicaragua, Cuba, Mexico, and the Rio Grande Valley in south Texas.

Introduction

WILLIAM T. CAVANAUGH

NOTHING DIVIDES LIKE DIVISION. Formal divisions among Christian bodies —Chalcedonian/non-Chalcedonian, Orthodox/Catholic, Catholic/Protestant—have complex origins, often in doctrinal disagreements, but also in political and cultural differences. Whatever the origins of the divisions, the divides, once made, take on a life of their own, and the original disagreements can fade in importance relative to the simple fact that we are now divided, and *we* are not *they.* This dynamic of otherness and rivalry has had a profound effect on Christianity in the global South, where many churches are the result of post-Reformation missionary activity under conditions of competition among the various Christian bodies. In the gold rush for souls in colonial Africa, for example, Catholics competed with Anglicans in Uganda and Methodists with Presbyterians in South Africa. There is no doubt that missionaries regarded doctrinal differences as important and wanted Africans to get their salvation from the true Church in its purest form. But it is also the case that missionaries were motivated by the desire to gain more souls for *our side.* Differences in doctrine and discipline are important, but in many cases such differences are accentuated by the divisions themselves. What may not have been an insuperable difference can become one once the rivalry between churches causes the rivals to exaggerate the differences: *they* are to be avoided because *they* believe in abominable heresies. Doctrinal differences can cause division, but division can exacerbate doctrinal differences, especially where missionaries compete.

In many ways, I think the ecumenical movement that has gained momentum since the latter part of the twentieth century can be understood as

1

a recognition that one of the principal causes of division is division. Differences in doctrine, church structure, and discipline are real and will not simply disappear with a healthy dose of goodwill. But the ecumenical movement seems to have recognized that division itself is a problem, and the chances of coming to something like agreement on doctrines and structures are greatly improved by taking a new attitude toward division. Division is not necessarily evidence of *their* depravity and the error of *their* ways. Division—or at least the spirit of division, of *us* versus *them*—is rather evidence of *our* sin, of the kind of fractiousness that makes differences insuperable when they need not be. Division is not evidence of our righteousness but rather of our unrighteousness; division is therefore to be overcome not simply by demanding change from others but by an examination of ourselves and our own motivations and blind spots. Once the spirit of division is identified as a problem in *me* or in *us*, then the door is open for seeing the other's differences not as threats but as potential gifts from which we can benefit. The spirit of division is overcome by seeing differences as gifts we have to offer one another. Full unity is good, but it might not be incompatible with a diversity of gifts that need not, in every case, divide us.

The essays in this volume are the result of a conference at DePaul University on the occasion of the five hundredth anniversary of the Protestant Reformation in 2017. The annual World Catholicism Week conference of the Center for World Catholicism and Intercultural Theology gathers scholars from around the world to examine a theme from the lens of the global South—Africa, Asia, and Latin America primarily. By way of contrast, many of the commemorations of the Reformation's quincentennial—along with scholarship on ecumenism more generally—have been focused on Europe and the Western world more generally. Ecumenism in the West has advanced under conditions of an increasingly secularized society and declining church attendance. With less to defend as Christianity has lost its hegemony in the West, shrinking churches have turned to one another as natural allies in the face of secularized indifference or secularist hostility. In the culture wars in the United States, the old denominational differences have faded in importance compared to differences in politics and culture. White evangelicals—who, in the recent past, would have dismissed Catholics as unsaved—have made alliances with conservative Catholics over issues like abortion and gay marriage. Similar alliances unite liberal Catholics with mainline Protestants over issues like the environment and immigration. Political and cultural differences cut across denominational boundaries, and in many ways the former are more determinative than the latter. Conservative Catholics may feel they have more in common with conservative Anglicans or evangelicals than with liberal Catholics. Ecumenism takes on new dimensions under such circumstances.

This volume shifts the focus to the global South, where the situation is different from the West and circumstances vary widely. The promises and challenges of ecumenism are different in postcolonial and post-missionary Africa, where the churches continue to expand, competition among denominations is lively, and Christian rivalry with Islam is a reality in many countries. Ecumenism takes another form in Latin America, where Protestants have severely eroded the hegemony once exercised by the Catholic Church, a hegemony originally forged in the zeal of the Counter-Reformation to combat the perceived errors of Luther and Calvin. Ecumenism means something different again in India, where the Christian churches are a tiny and beleaguered minority facing an increasingly militant Hindu nationalism. This volume pays close attention to the different contexts of intra-Christian relationships across the world, that is, the actual situation on the ground. If it will succeed, in whatever way ecumenical "success" is measured, ecumenism cannot be simply a matter of experts in a conference room attempting to come to agreement about doctrines abstracted from the contexts in which the doctrines were forged, the contexts in which doctrinal disagreements caused ecclesial ruptures, or the contexts in which Christians continue to live out our divided existence. All ecumenism must be sensitive to the lived experience of Christians in whatever part of the world they find themselves.

The stories told in this volume about the lived experience of relations among different types of Christians in the global South exhibit a complex interplay of competition and cooperation. There can be no doubt that, despite goodwill ecumenical efforts across the globe, competition continues to mark relations among different Christian bodies. In Africa, Christians continue to compete to convert the remaining adherents of African traditional religions, a competition that sometimes recalls the ambiguities and cultural imperialism of the European missionaries who long ago ceded control to African leadership. In Latin America, aggressive Protestant proselytization attempts to convert Catholics to Christianity, since Catholics, as one Honduran pastor told me, are really just pagans covered with a thin "varnish" of Christianity. The narrative is rarely as simple as these examples sound, however. For instance, even in such circumstances of competition in Latin America, Catholics may owe a debt of gratitude to their competitors. As Todd Hartch has argued, building on empirical studies by Rodney Stark and Buster Smith, competition from Protestants has awakened the Catholic Church in Latin America and made it more effective. Stark and Smith have found that, in many areas, the rate of active Catholic participation has increased where Protestants have had success at converting significant numbers of nominal Catholics. It has long been recognized that the charismatic movement is a gift to the Catholic Church in Latin America that was received in large part from the practices of the Protestant Pentecostal movement. Hartch makes the further claim that it was competition itself from Protestant churches that breathed life into the Catholic Church in many parts of Latin America.[1] This dynamic certainly cannot be generalized to all forms of competition everywhere. Sometimes competition brings out the worst, not the best, in the competitors. But it does indicate the complexity of competition for ecumenical relations.

Cooperation, of course, is more obviously prized by the ecumenical movement, but cooperation does not always result from an intentional effort to join forces. Often, cooperation grows out of hardship and opposition. Where Christians face aggression from governments or members of other faiths, they often discover that what divides them is overwhelmed by what unites them. This is most obvious in the extreme cases that Pope Francis has labeled the "ecumenism of blood." According to Francis, the martyrs of today "are witnesses to Jesus Christ, and they are persecuted and killed because they are Christians. Those who persecute them make no distinction between the religious communities to which they belong. They are Christians and for that they are persecuted. This, brothers and sisters, is the ecumenism of blood."[2] The essays in this volume contain examples of this ecumenism of martyrs. In Chile under the Pinochet regime, for example, Catholics and Lutherans forged an ecumenical response to the torture and disappearance of the regime's opponents. Catholics and Lutherans found that taking risks together in the name of same crucified Prince of Peace brought them together in ways that dialogue could not.

As inspiring as such extreme circumstances can be, however, Pope Francis has asked that we see the ecumenical possibilities in the more quotidian emergency facing the world, the everyday need of the world for the Gospel in both its spiritual and material forms. In his homily for the Week of Prayer for Christian Unity in 2015, Francis not only appealed to Christian unity based on the plight of persecuted Christians—the "ecumenism of blood"—but also on the plight of the "many men and women around us who are weary and thirsting, and who ask us Christians to give them something to drink."[3] The Pope indicates that Christians must find unity in responding

1. Hartch, *Rebirth of Latin American Christianity*. See also Stark and Smith, "Pluralism and the Churching of Latin America," 35–50.

2. For the full text of Francis's remarks, see "Pope Francis Says 'Ecumenism of Blood' Is Uniting Christians."

3. "Pope Francis Says 'Ecumenism of Blood' Is Uniting Christians."

to this call together, treating it as an emergency in which all must work together, not stopping first to quibble over the finer points of doctrine. "For this to be effective, we need to stop being self-enclosed, exclusive, and bent on imposing a uniformity based on merely human calculations. Our shared commitment to proclaiming the Gospel enables us to overcome proselytism and competition in all their forms."[4] Francis adds:

> So many past controversies between Christians can be over-come when we put aside all polemical or apologetic approaches, and seek instead to grasp more fully what unites us, namely, our call to share in the mystery of the Father's love revealed to us by the Son through the Holy Spirit. Christian unity—we are con-vinced—will not be the fruit of subtle theoretical discussions in which each party tries to convince the other of the soundness of their opinions. When the Son of Man comes, he will find us still discussing! We need to realize that, to plumb the depths of the mystery of God, we need one another, we need to encounter one another and to challenge one another under the guidance of the Holy Spirit, who harmonizes diversities, overcomes conflicts, reconciles differences.[5]

The first section of this volume, "Competition and Cooperation," be-gins with Elias Bongmba's examination of the notion of "comity" among Protestant missionaries in Africa, whereby denominations agreed to avoid territories in which other denominations were already established. Analyz-ing the cases of Cameroon and Uganda, Bongmba shows how such "gentle-men's agreements" broke down into competition among Christian bodies, in part because the faithful do not necessarily stay put in the same territory over time, so their pastors tend to follow them, and in part because of com-petition from Catholics and Pentecostals. Bongmba surveys the often-fierce competition among Christian bodies but ends on a hopeful note, citing ecu-menical progress over the last few decades. Bongmba argues for an under-standing of ecumenical collaboration that is deeper and richer than merely dividing up territory and promising to avoid one another.

The section on competition and cooperation ends with Philip Wingei-er-Rayo's examination of the competition between Pentecostals and Catho-lic base communities in Mexico. Wingeier-Rayo gives a helpful historical overview of the establishment of the Catholic Church in Latin America and the later Protestant challenge to Catholic hegemony, with an emphasis on Mexico. Wingeier-Rayo then tells the story of Pentecostals and Catholic

4. "Pope Francis Says 'Ecumenism of Blood' Is Uniting Christians."
5. "Pope Francis Says 'Ecumenism of Blood' Is Uniting Christians."

base communities in Mexico, situating the latter within a broader account of liberation theology and the "option for the poor" in the Catholic Church. He then lays out his findings from field work in Cuernavaca, illustrating the similarities and differences between grassroots Pentecostal and Catholic communities. Wingeier-Rayo finds that the similarities often outweigh the differences, and that the stereotypes—Catholic base communities are leftist fronts, Pentecostals are apolitical fundamentalists—do not hold. He concludes that the two groups may be catering to different, non-competing spiritual needs, and that the two groups may be making each other better Christians.

The second section, "Ecumenism of Blood," begins with two detailed examinations of the Chilean experience. Juan Sepúlveda provides a brief overview of Protestant growth in traditionally Catholic Chile and notes the minimal ecumenical engagements prior to the 1970s, when dramatic events would force more direct cooperation. Cooperation was spurred first by an atheist president, socialist Salvador Allende, who asked that the traditional Catholic *Te Deum* to ritualize the president's inauguration be opened to non-Catholic religious leaders. Polarization under Allende brought ecumenical efforts to promote social harmony. And then, two days after the first ecumenical prayer for peace, the military coup brought a fresh urgency to ecumenical cooperation, now to aid the victims of the military regime. Ecumenical efforts to address poverty and social marginalization under the Pinochet regime also led to ecumenical prayer and Bible study on the grassroots level. Unfortunately, Sepúlveda concludes that the ecumenical energy provided by the emergency has not been sustained post-Pinochet, and ecclesial bodies have returned to "normal," inward-looking pastoral strategies.

In his contribution, Michael Cooper-White tells the story of the collaboration between Cardinal Raúl Silva and Lutheran Bishop Helmut Frenz in the wake of the military coup in Chile on September 11, 1973. Drawing on his own personal recollections of having worked with Frenz, Cooper-White recounts the early days of the ecumenical Committee for Peace which, led by Silva and Frenz, rescued many of those marked by the regime for death. In the midst of these gripping stories, Cooper-White asks if such ecumenism can be sustained in more ordinary times, and he ends on a note of cautious hope.

Mark Chapman's contribution to this section explores some of the complexities and ambiguities of the "ecumenism of blood" by probing the example of the Ugandan martyrs, both Catholic and Anglican. Papal statements about the Uganda martyrs have emphasized the ecumenism of martyrdom since Pope Paul VI's visit to Uganda in 1964. Chapman nevertheless investigates some of the potential problems attached to narratives of martyr-dom. The Uganda martyrs have been used as a key moment in the advance of European Christian civilization over "primitive" culture. More recently, the Uganda martyrs' resistance to King Mwanga's advances have been used to mark authentic African culture against homosexuality, which is identi-fied with Western influence in the Ugandan culture wars. Chapman argues that the language of martyrdom carries baggage from colonialism and can be used in the demonization of gays, Muslims, and others as much as it can be used to unite Christians.

The third section of the volume, "Ecumenical Engagement with So-cial Issues," explores ecumenical action with regard to family, immigration, and climate change. Justin Tse offers a fascinating case study, based on his own fieldwork, of ecumenical relations between Catholics and Anglicans in Hong Kong. Leaders of both ecclesial bodies have joined forces in la-menting strains on family life and advocating that people avoid political and ideological squabbling which weakens family bonds. Tse argues that what appears to be ecumenism in this case is really the result of the bishops of both communities attempting to curry favor with the authorities con-trolled by the People's Republic of China. At the same time, there is grass-roots cooperation between Catholics and other Christians on the basis of conservative "family values" that presents itself as democratic resistance to the imposition of liberal values by the PRC-linked authorities. Ecumenical cooperation at both the elite and grassroots levels is motivated, in opposing ways, by the burning question of Hong Kong's autonomy from the PRC.

Chukwumamkpam Vincent Ifeme then looks at the phenomenon of ecumenism amidst the new reality of immigration in Italy. This tradi-tionally homogeneous Roman Catholic country has seen in recent years a large influx of non-Roman Catholic Christians, primarily from Africa, the Middle East, and Eastern Europe. After reviewing some major milestones of official Catholic ecumenical efforts in Italy and more broadly, Ifeme focuses on ecumenism at the local level, including Caritas welcome centers for im-migrants, the use of Catholic churches by non-Catholic communities for worship, and local ecumenical celebrations. Ifeme shows how, in a country where Catholicism has long been the establishment, immigration offers an opportunity for a double welcome, to those who are outsiders both to the culture and to the Catholic Church.

Grace Ji-Sun Kim approaches ecumenism through the lens of the global climate crisis, arguing that this issue is one on which all Christians should be able to unite. After laying out the evidence for the urgency of addressing climate change, Kim discusses some ecumenical theological resources for care of God's creation. She also examines some ecumenical efforts to address ecological issues, including those by the World Council of Churches and the Ecumenical Water Network.

The fourth section of the volume, "Receptive Ecumenism," considers some more formal questions about how ecumenical dialogue and action should proceed. One of the conference's keynoters, Paul Murray, addresses the usefulness of Receptive Ecumenism in the context of the global South. Murray dismisses the idea that formal ecumenical dialogue is irrelevant in the South and seeks instead to see how the diverse experiences of Christians in the global South can have an impact on formal ecumenism. After summarizing the basic vision of Receptive Ecumenism—"ask not what others should learn from your tradition; ask rather what your own tradition can learn from these others"—Murray shows this vision in practice in Roman Catholic–Anglican dialogues. He then argues that Receptive Ecumenism can work across both denominational and geographical boundaries. The growth of Pentecostalism in the South, for example, can teach the Catholic Church as a whole much about the personal role of the Spirit and the renewing of church charisms.

Paul Avis seeks, in his chapter, to move beyond the mere celebration of differences to the agreement toward which he says ecumenical efforts must advance. The question Avis addresses is, "To what degree must we agree, and how can we achieve that agreement?" Avis lays out a sophisticated account of an "emergent differentiated consensus" between two lines of thinking that have a common intention and a common object, even if they don't agree on all the details. Ultimately, Avis argues, such a consensus cannot merely be taught but must be lived in all its messiness and in recognition of the need for further work.

Vimal Tirimanna considers the question of whether divisions among Christians need to be considered as entirely negative. Tirimanna argues that, although such divisions can never be considered as positive in and of themselves, a providential God could be using divisions among Christians as part of God's plan to save the world. Tirimanna shows how, throughout salvation history, God has used the negative acts of free human action to achieve God's purposes. Tirimanna then draws upon Receptive Ecumenism to argue that God can use Christian divisions to facilitate the exchange of gifts and wisdom among different bodies of Christians. We need repentance and conversion to be able to receive those gifts.

In the fifth and final section of the volume, "Plurality and Unity," two of the keynote speakers from the conference, one from Asia and the other from Africa, put forth their own programmatic and somewhat different approaches to ecumenism. Felix Wilfred notes that ecumenism tends to be linked to the magisterium in official documents of the Catholic Church. In

Asia, however, ecumenism has taken place from the bottom up. Christians in Asia have attempted to move beyond denominational differences brought by colonial authorities and missionaries toward a more indigenous expression of church that is more inclusive. The need to confront caste divisions, the persecution of Christians, and geopolitical tensions have brought new forms of ecumenical cooperation. In Asia, the inclusiveness of ecumenism has been widened to include inter-religious cooperation, and Wilfred argues that broader conceptions of truth gained from interreligious dialogue have enriched ecumenical dialogue. Wilfred argues that ecumenism should be viewed from the lens of difference and plurality rather than the restoration of unity.

Teresa Okure, by way of contrast, considers ecumenism from the point of view of Jesus' call for unity. Okure lays out four hermeneutical principles for reading the scriptures on unity—self-inclusion, life, appropriation, and reformulation of the question based on the concerns of the global South—and argues that we must gather in Jesus' name, not in the name of our various churches and denominations. Drawing on a wealth of scriptural passages, Okure argues that the church is God's work, not ours, and we therefore need to purify our motives of possessiveness and partisanship. Each party to ecumenical engagements must change and become like a little child, trusting as Jesus admonished us to do. We become friends when, trusting God, we each leave the safe confines of our ecclesial homes and go out into the world on mission together.

These fourteen essays are by no means exhaustive of the topic of ecumenism in the world church. There are many topics and regions that we have not covered, and the accent is heavily on Catholic-Protestant relations, to the neglect of the Orthodox. With regard to these limitations, I can only lament a limitation of space and resources. I hope, nevertheless, that this volume goes some way toward highlighting the voices of the global South and the increased importance of making the ecumenical conversation truly one of the whole *oikoumenē*, the whole of the inhabited earth.

Bibliography

Hartch, Todd. *The Rebirth of Latin American Christianity*. New York: Oxford University Press, 2014.

"Pope Francis Says 'Ecumenism of Blood' Is Uniting Christians." *Catholic Herald*, January 26, 2015. https://catholicherald.co.uk/pope-francis-says-ecumenism-of-blood-is-uniting-christians/.

Stark, Rodney, and Buster Smith. "Pluralism and the Churching of Latin America." *Latin American Politics and Society* 54 (2012) 35–50.

PART ONE

Competition and Cooperation

I

From Comity to Competition: What Prospect for Ecumenism?

ELIAS KIFON BONGMBA

IN THIS PAPER, I discuss competition in African Christianity and argue that, with ecclesial independence and the growth of new forms of revival in Pentecostal-Charismatic Christianity, the old mission and ecclesial practice of comity has given rise to competition. I illustrate my argument with case studies from Cameroon and Uganda. This essay is based on a critical analysis of the current literature on African Christianity.[1]

Definition and Scope of Comity in Christian Missions

This essay has three parts to it. I begin by discussing the notion of comity, pointing out that the goodwill gesture intended to facilitate world evangelization did not work well because mission agencies competed for space and influence. In the second section, I discuss the emergence of competition in contemporary African Christianity, not so much to make the point that comity was absent but rather to highlight a different motive for competition among churches. In the final section, I return to the witness of the church today and argue that, despite their differences, ecclesial groups can collaborate in the practice of their Christian witness in a pluralistic world.

1. I would like to thank Bill Cavanaugh and Karen Kraft for giving me critical feedback on this paper.

Comity was largely a "Protestant principle" because it was promoted by Protestant missiologists and denominational leaders who would also promote the practice of ecumenism.[2]

The term and practice referred to friendly and polite agreements between two different parties. In legal terms, comity refers to the respect countries give each other when they agree to respect each other's laws. The idea of comity in mission and evangelism circles grew out of the quest for unity among Protestants in different mission contexts. The Centenary Mission Conference, held in London in 1888, gave concrete form to comity, the idea of which had been around for most of 1800s.[3] In mission practice, comity referred to arrangements that divided territories or spheres of influence in mission and evangelism, thus producing what Beaver famously described as "denominationalism by geography."[4] Comity was put in place "to prevent wasteful duplication, competition, and presentation of variant forms of worship and polity which might confuse non-Christians and hinder communication of the gospel."[5] Stephen Neill described it as "a delimitation of territories, and a gentleman's agreement among the missions not to work in the territory where another mission was already established."[6]

The first comity agreement was signed in July 1830 between the London Missionary Society (LMS) and Wesleyan missionaries; it designated Tonga and Fiji as Wesleyan areas of influence and Samoa as an LMS territory. This type of verbal agreement was ratified by various churches and organizations that supported these mission endeavors. However, it was also understood that each organization could not prevent others from entering the area if they did not evangelize that area after a certain period. According to Beaver, urban areas were exempt and, in some cases, the government of Australia assigned mission groups to specific areas of the country. Beaver further claims that this practice was so highly regarded that some American mission organizations accepted the arrangements before they set out for the Philippines.[7] However, the system faced challenges because some Lutheran groups and the Latter-day Saints did not participate in it. Since comity also involved rules about boundaries, membership transfers, and

2. I am indebted to Michael Goheen for this insight. See Goheen, "Mission and Unity," 83–91; Beaver, *Ecumenical Beginnings in Protestant World Mission*; Hutchinson, *Errand to the World*; Neill, *History of Christian Missions*; Corwin, "Comity," 212; Clark, *True and False*.

3. Beaver, "Comity," 123.

4. Beaver, "Comity," 123.

5. Beaver, "Comity," 123.

6. Neill, *History of Christian Missions*, 401.

7. Beaver, "Comity," 123.

other practicalities of mission operations, national arbitration groups were set up to monitor the practice.

At the heart of comity was an ecumenical spirit which gave ecclesial bodies an opportunity to carry out evangelism in a noncompetitive manner. The idea of churches working together for the cause of the gospel was so important that well-known figures like Jonathan Edwards called for such union among Christians. The full title of his tract on the topic is telling: "A Humble Attempt to Promote Explicit Agreement and the Visible Union Among God's People, in Extraordinary Prayer for Revival of Religion, and the Advancement of Christ's Kingdom on Earth, Pursuant to Scriptural Promises, and Prophecies Concerning the Last Time."[8] During the turbulent World War II period, Archbishop of Canterbury William Temple reaffirmed the hope of unity represented by the global mission endeavor at the time when he said:

> As though in preparation for a time like this, God has been building up a Christian fellowship which now extends into every nation and binds citizens of them all together in true unity and mutual love. No human agency has planned this. It is the result of the great missionary enterprise of the last hundred and fifty years. . . . Almost incidentally, the great world fellowship has arisen; it is the great new fact of our era.[9]

The arrangements started to fall apart soon after their inception, but Neill argued that, in the case of India, keeping Christians and mission groups in one geographical locale made it possible for the agreements to work. However, as people became educated and some moved in search of work, it was not possible for the mission groups to follow them. In some cases, the Lutherans and Anglicans followed their members around, but Free Church missionaries thought Christians could join a faith community of their choice. "It became clear that comity was no solution and could not be more than a palliative in a situation which itself was indefensible."[10] According to Neill, that was the situation at the time of the Edinburgh Conference of 1910, which would usher in the conciliar movement of missions. Some mission agencies continued to work together, but by World War II, comity was all but gone. The reason for this was that the disruptions of the war era relocated and dislocated many people; the thought was that, if a church participated in comity, members leaving one church would be welcomed into the new churches in the area where they moved, but that was

8. Edwards, *Humble Attempt*.
9. Temple, *Church Looks Forward*, 4.
10. Neill, *History of Christian Missions*, 401.

not the case. Comity did not mean dissolution of theological groundings for the church; what many denominations did was to establish their churches in the regions where their members had moved. Such was the case in the Philippines, when Christians from Protestant churches moved from the Luzon region to Mindanao; rather than lose their members to another Protestant church that subscribed to comity, the denominations started churches in those new areas.[11]

On October 3, 1951, *The Christian Century* reported:

> Word from the Philippines reveals that following a visit by Methodist Bishop Jose L. Valencia to Mindanao, seventeen Methodist churches have been organized in that area, which under a comity agreement has been regarded as territory of the United Church of the Philippines. During recent months, Methodist farmers from the Huk-infested sections of central and northern Luzon have migrated to Mindanao, and the Methodist conferences determined to follow their members thither. So far, this departure from accepted comity policy has created little discord within ecumenical circles—mainly because all Christian workers are overburdened with new responsibilities incident to the "open door" situation that Protestantism finds today in the Philippines.[12]

The mission society, rather than other ecclesiastical institutions, has been the basis of unity. One of the most exciting debates of the twentieth century was the question of the moratorium on missions. This debate was interesting for several reasons. First, in calling for such a radical step, John Gatu wanted to give the African church space to develop and assume responsibility for its ecclesial vision and support. What was clear at that time, but not discussed critically, is the fact that while missionaries represented Western Christian churches, a large chunk of the mission work was already being done by agencies and through ecumenical initiatives. Protestant ecumenical bodies, like the International Missionary Council (IMC) and the Commission on World Mission and Evangelism (CWME), affiliated with the World Council of Churches because they had a great stake in world missions at the time. These organizations made the notion of Western churches a broad designation which in and of itself heightened the stakes in the operation of the idea of comity itself.

In his review of the Bangkok mission of the IMC and CWME of 1972–1973, John V. Taylor pointed out that one of the things that was evident in

11. "After Comity, What?," 677–78.

12. Townsend, "Break Comity Agreement," 1139–40.

that assembly was that, although inner reorganization of the mission agencies was surely needed, international organizations and mission agencies still had a role to play.[13] However, the churches also sent a clear signal to ecumenical groups like the World Council of Churches that they wanted a new type of relationship, which included concerns over whether theological studies in the West and mission structures would adapt and meet new demands. Taylor concluded:

> The fact remains that much of the vitality and onward march of the Christian faith still resides in the traditional structures of the churches in all the continents. If the World Council and its related bodies are tempted to regard some of these slow-moving structures as peripheral to its concerns in the future, it may condemn itself to a peripheral position about the actual life of the churches themselves. That would be a tragedy. The CWME would be ill-advised to disenfranchise altogether the Western mission boards and societies, or the structures that link the different member churches of confessional families, in its advocacy of newer and more genuinely ecumenical patterns. The value of the Bangkok Assembly is that of a ferment, a leaven.[14]

From Comity to Competition

In 1984, the influential missionary to India and ecumenical leader Lesslie Newbigin argued that the idea of unity and hence comity was collapsing. He cited four reasons: (1) the desire of religious institutions and organizations to preserve their traditions (in missions); (2) new fundamentalisms that wanted to turn away from old ways of doing things; (3) the urgency of a focus on peace and justice questions; and (4) the idea that there was a wider ecumenism which was more useful than the ecumenical movement as understood by church groups involved in that movement.[15] Despite the good intentions of the comity agreements, violations were recorded in different parts of the world because mission agencies faced competition from other mission organizations. What I call violation of the comity spirit is the manifestation of competition on the so-called mission field, and this was intense in many places. Competition grew between Catholics and Protestants and within each of those traditions. In Uganda, Protestant

13. Taylor, "Bangkok 1972–1973," 370.
14. Taylor, "Bangkok 1972–1973," 370.
15. Newbigin, *Reunion of the Church*, 2–4.

missionaries from the Church Missionary Society (CMS) arrived in 1877, and two years later, Catholics arrived in the region.[16] The new missionaries assumed an honored place in society, were seen as pseudo-chiefs, and recruited a clientele. Following a series of conflicts—which included the rejection of homosexuality by court pages and fighting which deposed the king of Buganda, Kabaka[17] Mwanga II—Britain reasserted control. However, to succeed in dominating, Lord Frederick Lugard[18] instigated rivalries between Catholics and Protestants through his support of the Protestants in achieving the domination of Buganda.[19] The Protestants took advantage of this and fought alongside the Kabaka against the Banyoro people in the wars of 1894–1896. Mwanga was later restored as the Kabaka and would be followed by the installation of his two-year-old son. In the case of Uganda and particularly the Buganda Kingdom, competition between the Catholics and Protestants was motivated by colonials.

In Nigeria, from the 1900s on, the Roman Catholic missionaries competed with the Church Missionary Society among the Igbo.[20] F. K. Ekechi has argued that, as in Uganda, some Christian towns in the Igbo community received preferential treatment from the colonial leaders, and many people of Igboland decided to become Christians in order to reap some of the benefits that new status carried in the colonial society. Indeed, this was a situation which made many people flock to the churches. Missionaries themselves were aware of this preferential treatment and wrote about it.[21] Ekechi points out that there was a serious rivalry between the Catholics and Protestants about establishing a foothold in the city of Calabar, but the initial attempt by the Catholics failed because the Primitive Methodist Missionary Society had been in the area since 1846. The Roman Catholics would later have access to Calabar in 1905, and missionary Fr. Joseph Shanahan (who would later become a bishop) promised that he would use education to "strike the last blow at the Presbyterians."[22] Ekechi illustrates that there was a scramble described by some as a state of war between competing missions as all the mission organizations practiced "mutual exclusivism."[23] Ekechi asserts: "While

16. Wrigley, "Christian Revolution in Buganda," 33–48, 41.

17. *Kabaka* is the title of the king in Buganda.

18. Lugard was a British administrator who played a major role in the British colonies between 1888 and 1945. See Perham, "Frederick Lugard."

19. Wrigley, "Christian Revolution in Buganda," 44.

20. Ekechi, "Colonialism and Christianity in West Africa," 103–13.

21. Ekechi, "Colonialism and Christianity in West Africa," 105.

22. See Paris, "Shanahan to the Directors," as cited in Ekechi, "Colonialism and Christianity in West Africa," 107n23.

23. Ekechi, "Colonialism and Christianity in West Africa," 108.

it is true that the Protestant denominations haggled among themselves for the occupation of certain towns and villages, they seemed, however, united in their opposition to the expansive propensities of the Roman Catholics."[24] In 1911, Protestant mission groups met in Calabar and agreed to cooperate (comity). However, this was not put into effect, and the Roman Catholic Church succeeded in challenging the Protestants' territorial dominance in the Calabar region. Fr. Shanahan claimed: "Les protestants . . . ont vu leur jours s'évanouir. Leur influence est nulle et leur oeuvres son en decadence [The Protestants . . . have seen their days vanishing, their influence is non-existent and their services are in decline]."[25] Roman Catholics won the battle because they vigorously promoted education, using schools to attract a large number of people from the region; this validated Fr. Shanahan's claim that the ones who had the schools also had the country, the religion, and the nation's future. Later, to ensure this, Catholics offered free admission to some of their schools, something the Protestants could not match. Catholic numbers grew in its schools and churches, and the Protestants conceded that they had more to fear from what they called the "Romanist menace than [from] the Muslims."[26] The competition that took place between the Roman Catholics and Protestants in this part of Nigeria reflects the general loss of comity in Christian missions.

Carl E. Olivestam and Christina Thornell have also demonstrated that in Central Africa, the Swedish Mission faced competition in their work with the Église Evangélique Baptiste (EEB).[27] The Swedish Evangelical Free Church began its work in the Central African Republic in 1923, establishing local churches and service institutions, such as schools and health clinics. Their work with the EEB was governed by cooperative agreements which they reviewed and renewed as needed; the church and its leaders believed that they were in a "competition-free zone."[28] The church had been organized with a leadership vision inspired by the Swedish Evangelical Church, a doctrinal position which emphasized a personal conversion experience, regular participation in church life for growth, and other teachings that encouraged members to meet the needs of one another. These ideas were also communicated in the preaching ministry of the church and, in the larger context, guided the selection and training of church leaders.

24. Ekechi, "Colonialism and Christianity in West Africa," 109.
25. Ekechi, "Colonialism and Christianity in West Africa," 110 (my translation).
26. Ekechi, "Colonialism and Christianity in West Africa," 115.
27. Olivestam and Thornell, "Exposure of the Swedish Mission," 371–95.
28. Olivestam and Thornell, "Exposure of the Swedish Mission," 373.

Competition among Protestants

The spirit of competition was not limited to a struggle for space between Roman Catholics and Protestants but even among Protestants and, on the eve of the twenty-first century, among Pentecostal churches. Africa has experienced more than a century of religious innovation, reformation, and revitalization in the Christian tradition. For example, early literature on African Initiated Churches (AICs) demonstrated their vitality in the sheer number of their churches and ministries.[29] And the Pentecostalization of Africa has been equally marked by a growing body of research that would lead one to think, if one were unaware of what is going on in African Christianity, that the mainline church is dead. However, that is not the case. The mainline churches have survived by incorporating practices from AIC and Pentecostal churches, something C. G. Baëta discussed several years ago.[30] In the wake of comity's collapse, Protestant churches in Africa have structured ecumenism under the rubrics of the All Africa Conference of Churches (AACC) and the Association of Evangelicals of Africa and Madagascar (AEAM), as well as other national organizations.

Studies abound about new forms of competition in African Christianity today. While the historical and mission-affiliated churches continue to compete in different ways, more recent studies have focused on the Pentecostal churches, which comprise the fastest and most significant Christian population on the continent. We have seen disregard for comity and the introduction of vicious competition, particularly in the Pentecostal tradition. I use the term "tradition" mostly because Pentecostal-Charismatic churches belong to different denominations or are independent, stand-alone churches which their ministries and evangelism programs. Studies show that Pentecostal pastors use different strategies to compete with other Christian denominations as well as among their own churches for membership.[31]

There are several reasons for such increased competition in the current Pentecostal context. First, Pentecostalism has emerged in Africa through an independent model because many of the churches are not linked to a major denomination. Although some have established branches and organized into large ecclesial institutions (e.g., the Redeemed Christian Church of God), Pentecostal churches are largely megachurches run by a high-profile pastor who has adopted the "big man of God" model.[32] The

29. Sundkler, *Bantu Prophets in South Africa*; Turner, *Black Africa*.

30. Baëta, *Prophetism in Ghana*, 135.

31. Gifford, *Ghana's New Christianity*.

32. Kalu, *African Pentecostalism*, 113–14; Maxwell, "Delivered from the Spirit of Poverty?," 1–12.

big-man-of-God pastors have successfully cultivated a clientele relationship with their churches' members and, in an ironic twist, depend on those members to promote both their power and their livelihood.

A second reason competition has grown is that the stakes are high for pastors in terms of gaining wealth and recognition on the local, national, and international levels as well as in relationships with political leaders. The perception is that the "big man of God" can do anything. Thus, the very nature of ministry is being redefined in Pentecostalism today as competitive. A. Olalekan Dairo has argued that "all over the world and in Nigeria in particular, 'marketing' God is fast becoming a top bracket business."[33] Third, competition grew as Pentecostal leaders began to see themselves as mediators of the growing social and economic crises that have plagued the postcolonial state. While supporting and in many ways promoting political dictatorships, some Pentecostal pastors believe that, as leaders, they are chosen or anointed by God and, as such, should not be resisted.

Fourth, competition has been deepened by a lack of theological depth in some Pentecostal circles. Early Pentecostals (and I must stress the word "early") approached evangelism as a pragmatic solution to what they perceived as the urgent needs of the times rather than from a well-thought-out theology of missions or through well-structured mission organizations like the London Missionary Society, Church Missionary Society, Paris Evangelical Fellowship, or American Board of Foreign Missions, which dominated mission work in Africa from the nineteenth century onwards. Willem Saayman has argued that Pentecostals developed a perspective of missions which was "not the result of some thought out theological decision, and so policy and methods were formed mostly in the crucible of missionary praxis."[34]

Competition in Cameroon and Uganda

Competition has been reported in Cameroon and Uganda and, in this section, I discuss the competition that has taken place in both countries beginning with the case of Cameroon. Dr. Zacharis Tannee Fomum began his journey in Cameroon as a crusading preacher who called on people to be born again and would later compete with the Presbyterian Church in Cameroon (PCC). His father was a PCC pastor of the PCC, the largely Anglophone historic church founded in 1886 by missionaries from the Evangelical Missionary Society of Basel, generally known as the Basel Mission. The PCC is distinct from the Église Presbyterienne du Cameroon (EPC),

33. Dairo, "Privatization and Commercialization of Christian Message," 195.
34. Saayman, "Some Reflections," 46.

which was founded by the American Presbyterian Church. The PCC has its headquarters in Buea, in southwest Cameroon. Its services and institutions include hospitals, community development projects, and educational institutions ranging from nursery schools to a theological seminary and a Protestant university in Bali. In the past, the PCC settled refugees from southern Africa, especially Namibia, when some of the countries were fighting for liberation from white minority regimes. One of its former moderators, the Right Reverend Dr. Nyansako-Ni-Nku, served as president of the All African Conference of Churches from 2003 to 2008. Although the majority of PCC churches are located in Cameroon's two Anglophone regions, the PCC in Yaoundé (which began its work in the 1970s) was housed at the Église Presbyterienne in Djongolo. It was here in the Djongolo PCC church that Fomum started preaching his "born again" message.[35]

Elected to the church's evangelism board, Fomum used that position to begin the New Life Campaign, a move which launched competition. Members of the New Life Campaign identified with Fomum and his exclusive message that a person must be born again to be called a Christian and then live a life committed to Christ. Robert Mbe Akoko argues that his followers set themselves apart from other Christians, and tensions arose in the PCC in Yaoundé between Fomum and the PCC church's pastor, the Reverend Dr. Michael Bame Bame.[36] Fomum criticized the PCC and also claimed that his father, a PCC pastor, was not a Christian. Fomum also invented new rituals for his followers, insisting on baptism by immersion instead of the Presbyterian practice of sprinkling. Sanctioned by the PCC, Fomum chose to leave and join the Full Gospel Mission where, for more than seven years, he continued a growing evangelistic ministry. In 1975, he formed Christian Missionary Fellowship International (CMFI) and opened a temporary worship center at Obili in Yaoundé. Tensions remained in the PCC because many of its members left and joined Fomum's church, and Dr. Bame Bame, who had worked hard to strengthen the PCC's spiritual profile in Yaoundé, was very deeply disappointed.

I arrived in Yaoundé to serve as the first full-time pastor of Etoug-Ebe Baptist Church there in 1982, seven years after Fomum founded CMFI. From its beginning, the church claimed and declared a vision to reach two hundred nations of the world with the Gospel by the year 2065. It would later describe its vision in the following words:

> The grip of what this meant has come to us increasingly, and the
> burden has come increasingly. By the work of the Holy Spirit in

35. Kor, *Revival Palaver in Bastos.* See also Akoko, *Ask and You Shall Be Given*, 146.
36. Akoko, *Ask and You Shall Be Given*, 147.

us, we are now a group of brethren who are laying our all at the
feet of Jesus and stretching out increasingly

- to love the Lord,

- to love each other,

- to love all believers,

- to love all human beings.

We feel compelled to use any means available to modern
man to

- proclaim repentance towards God and faith in the Lord Jesus
  Christ to every human being,

- Contribute to other brethren in the effort to reach every human being with the gospel.

We feel compelled to make disciples of the Lord Jesus and
help others in their effort to make disciples of the Lord Jesus
and, by the grace of God, make a contribution to God's global
purposes in our generation.

We are a community bonded to the Lord Jesus and bonded
to one another, reaching out to those who are yet to be bonded
to the Lord Jesus Christ.[37]

One cannot doubt the seriousness of the church's vision (unfortunately, in very gender-specific terms), but its establishment introduced a
new level of competition centered on the idea of faith, the nature of the
ecclesial community, and its global outreach. During my days in Yaoundé,
this distinction reflected a vision nurtured through Fomum's crusades and
preaching. Many Christians continued to debate the appropriation and significance of the "born again" message, but the intense competition for souls
had divided the PCC.

In addition to his duties at the PCC in Djongolo, Dr. Bame Bame
was also a professor at the Protestant Faculty of Theology in Yaoundé. He
had a Bible study and prayer fellowship with an interdenominational circle
of friends that included Dr. Solomon Nfor Gwei, a former Baptist pastor
who, at that time, was the Vice Minister of Agriculture. I attended some of
these prayer meetings, and their focus was on church unity and love among
Christians even if they belonged to different denominations, because they
believed that such a spirit of love would be a good example of Christian
witness in the city and the rest of the country. Dr. Bame Bame combined
strong scholarly and pastoral skills. He and I rotated hosting and preaching on the Cameroon radio program, "Morning Meditation." Broadcast on

---

37. Fomum, "On Our History," paras. 1–4.

Sunday morning, the program was a service of the then Federation of Protestant Churches and Missions of Cameroon (FEMEC), whose predecessor, the Evangelical Federation of Cameroon and West Africa, was founded in 1943. Today, the organization is called the Council of Protestant Churches of Cameroon. Robert Mbe Akoko's excellent study of Pentecostalism in Cameroon maps out this competition between Pentecostals and the PCC.[38]

Tensions remained between Bame Bame and Fomum. However, Fomum's ministry attracted new members, especially youths, and was also heavily criticized. Many people in Yaoundé, where Fomun's ministry was based, felt that some of his followers displayed a holier-than-thou attitude. Fomum's followers spread their message very vigorously throughout the city of Yaoundé; at Etoug-Ebe Baptist Church, where I served as the first resident pastor, we lost a few members. In one family, the husband remained a member of the Deacon's Board, but his wife attended CMFI. She no longer came to our church and would not even join us if we organized a Bible study in their home. I met with Fomum sometimes when I was in Yaoundé, but these were mainly courtesy visits; we did not discuss anything substantial, although he was always very complimentary of our work in Yaoundé.

The great irony is that Bame Bame, who fought against Fomum's approach to ministry, became a Pentecostal Christian himself and launched an equally severe competition that led to a split between the PCC and his ministries. Bame Bame claimed that he received a new vision on a 1987–1988 visit to the Democratic Republic of Congo with his wife. And in 1990, he started a revival ministry within the PCC church in Yaoundé.[39] He stressed the presence and role of the Holy Spirit in the life of the believer, and he named the new ministry the Pilot Revival Prayer Group in Cameroon. Its activities, which spread to other churches within the PCC, had ingredients similar to those of Pentecostalism.[40] Akoko reports that Bame Bame instituted practices such as possession by the Holy Spirit, healing exorcisms, and speaking in tongues as well as music, dance, and verbal utterings associated with Pentecostals. The revival was also driven by what followers claimed were uplifting prayers, and, in all of these ways, it demonstrated a marked difference from the PCC.[41]

Also in 1990, the PCC appointed the Reverend Isaac Sakwe Elangwe to replace Bame Bame at the Djongolo PCC Church. It was not long before

38. Akoko, *Ask and You Shall Be Given*. In addition to my own observations from the time I lived in Yaoundé, I follow Akoko's account here closely.

39. Akoko, *Ask and You Shall Be Given*, 149.

40. Konings, "Religious Revival in the Roman Catholic Church," 31–56.

41. Akoko, *Ask and You Shall Be Given*, 149–50.

disagreements began to surface on theological and stylistic approaches to ministry. Bame Bame and his group also held afternoon revival services in the same church building, and they attracted a large following. During those services, Bame Bame wore a white garment and walked barefoot; he created a new approach to the liturgy which baffled and mystified some Christians. Some PCC members preferred that ceremonies like baby dedications and marriages be conducted during the afternoon revival services. Bame Bame's strong supporters started paying their tithes to the new revival group, confirming the PCC's fears that this was a separate, competing church. The church sent out a pastoral letter in January of 1993 warning that the revivalists were now acting like a separatist group. Bame Bame rejected those claims, arguing that his aim was to revive and unite the church. In 1994, the Synod of the PCC called on the revivalists to abandon their practices by December 31, 1995, or be removed from the PCC membership rolls. But Bame Bame did not change. The PCC held a synod meeting in Kumba in 1997 and decided to ban the group. The Synod also transferred Bame Bame to the Presbyterian Theological Seminary in Kumba to teach as a professor. Instead, Bame Bame terminated his membership with the PCC and joined the Mission of the Evangelical Church in Cameroon, started by Korean missionaries.[42] Bame Bame later started his own church in Yaoundé, calling it The Church Patmos, after the Isle of Patmos, where John the Beloved Disciple preached until the end of his life.

Competition in Uganda

The second example of competition focuses on questions of morality, and the best example we have comes from Uganda. Uganda has a history of strong, principled positions on faith that dates back to the stand taken by the pages who served in the court of the Kabaka. The pages were killed for refusing to continue their homosexual relationship with the Kabaka. The Catholic Church would later canonize them as saints, and today, Uganda Martyrs University stands as a symbol of this massacre. The Protestant churches in Uganda witnessed the *Balokole* ("the saved ones") movement, in which people made a public confession of their faith; it had begun among members of Church Missionary Society churches in Rwanda and spread in East Africa. With many church leaders taking part, this revival made an

42. Akoko, *Ask and You Shall Be Given*, 153. Konings, "Religious Revival in the Roman Catholic Church," 33.

impact on all churches in the region and reshaped East African Christianity.[43] The climate was right for a new religious experience.[44]

Aspects of comity in *Balokole* have been eviscerated by some Pentecostal leaders. In a recent study, Caroline Valois has presented a rich discussion of competition between two Pentecostal pastors in Uganda. There
is a climate of intense debate on homosexuality in this country, created
by Pentecostal pastors and resulting in some members of their congregations seeing others as less than fully Christian.[45] The intense competition
in Uganda has been played out in a hazardous way. Pastor Martin Ssempa
of One Love Church allegedly accused Pastor Robert Kayanja of Miracle
Centre Cathedral of being a homosexual. It was alleged he had "sodom-
ized" six boys in his church in Kampala. In an anti-gay context, this accusation nearly destroyed Pastor Kayanja's church, and he sued. The accusation
against Kayanja was made in a context of competition over who was holy, or
an authentic Pentecostal pastor. The pastors who made the accusation were
found guilty of "conspiring to tarnish the reputation of Pastor Kayanja."[46]
The competition in Uganda has introduced what Valois argues comes close
to the blackmail of oher Christian leaders, especially on the question of
homosexuality in Uganda, a debate in which Pastor Ssempa played such a
leading role, painting homosexuality as unbiblical, foreign, and unnatural.

In a vast landscape where people have tried to respond to economic
and political hardships as well as live with significant health issues, each
Pentecostal church in Uganda has presented itself as an authentic Christian
church, offering its services to address every need and defect among people
and society.[47] As a way of overcoming the economic crisis African countries
have faced, Pentecostals have also created a social and spiritual bonding
and intricate pragmatic relations that scholars have described as networks
which are not only local but global.[48] Valois argues that, while Miracle Centre Cathedral has tapped into the global success market approach, One Love
Church sees Pentecostalism as a vehicle for transforming the nation. The
two differ on how they see homosexuality. At Miracle, it is a matter of one's

43. Bruner, "Public Confession," 254–68; Ward and Wild-Wood, *East African
Revival*.

44. Maseno and Owojaiye, "African Women and Revival."

45. I am indebted to the background discussion of this account of competition in
Uganda. See Valois, "Scandal Makers," 39.

46. Valois, "Scandal Makers," 38.

47. Engelke, "Discontinuity and the Discourse of Conversion"; Meyer, "Make a
Complete Break."

48. Marshall, "Mediating the Global and Local in Nigerian Pentecostalism,"
278–315.

salvation. At One Love, it is a national menace that must be fought severely; therefore, One Love's fight against homosexuality in Uganda reflects its worldview.[49] Valois argues that both churches believe that transformation depends on the presence and power of the Holy Spirit.

However, One Love's Pastor Ssempa believes he must call Uganda and Africa back to God because culture and morality have broken down. Valois concludes: "The Pentecostal movement is reeling from that, those two sides of Pentecostal expression."[50] For Ssempa, accountability is framed as a church cornerstone. When Ssempa was convicted of conspiring to tarnish Pastor Kayanja's reputation, he was made accountable for the allegations he leveled against Kayanja, when the court found him and five other defendants guilty.[51] In a moment, the competitive spirit came to a head. After being found guilty, Ssempa left the courthouse, donning his ubiquitous black robes. Kayanja's supporters rejoiced in song, and one stated that "whoever is against Pastor Kayanja is against the Miracle house of prayer . . . [but] we are the winners."[52] It remains to be seen if Kayanja will recover fully and restore the integrity of his ministry or if the two pastors can work together given the bitterness generated by this unnecessary competition.

Beyond Competition to Collaboration

The review I have just presented demonstrates that one could have described the notion of comity as dead on arrival, even though the idea, its virtues, and its dreams reflected a common Christian concern: obey the command to make disciples of nations. While Protestants and Roman Catholics competed in the different areas where they served, post-Vatican II Catholicism has demonstrated a greater understanding of Protestant churches and, more importantly, the common witness of the church. In *Lumen Gentium*, the ecclesial community is called to recognize and accept the gift of the Holy Spirit, who gives life and lives in the hearts of believers, because he is the advocate of each Christian and the Church. The Holy Spirit has gifted the Church:

> The whole company of the faithful, who have an anointing by
> the Holy Spirit, cannot err in faith. They manifest this distinc-
> tive characteristic of theirs in the supernatural instinct of faith

49. Valois, "Scandal Makers," 41.

50. Ssempa interview, May 2012, cited in Valois, "Scandal Makers," 41.

51. Ndagire, "Six Pastor Kayanja Sodomy Accusers Convicted."

52. Valois, "Scandal Makers," 48.

(*sensus fidei*) of the whole people when, from the bishops to the most ordinary lay person among the faithful, they display a universal agreement on matters of faith and morals.[53]

The Spirit enables the ecclesial community to remain faithful. It sanctifies and guides the faithful through the sacraments and ministries, "enriches it with virtues," and endows each person with a special grace and gifts to equip the Church for all responsibilities that would benefit the household of God. The presence of the Holy Spirit continues to revitalize the ecclesial community in Africa, and one cannot say that it is a monopoly of the Pentecostals as some would have us think. The task of the Church is to forge paths of collaboration within the diversity of the Church.

It is important for two reasons that ecclesial communities forge new collaborations. First, the ecclesial community must come to grips with the signs of the times. The shift of gravity in missions and the center of Christianity is old news now. The same can be said of what was once called "Third World Missions," which today refers to missions from the global South to the Northern Hemisphere, even if such missions today are dominated by "asylum pastors." Regarding the task of the contemporary Church and the important question of whether the global ecclesial community can think as the body of Christ on the imperatives of today, I think the competition in Cameroon and Uganda underscores two things: a brief assessment of what has been called the new evangelism and a new way of being "church."

The New Evangelization is a term made popular by Saint John Paul II.[54] And it was Pope Benedict XVI who created the Pontifical Council for Promoting the New Evangelization on June 28, 2010, on the eve of the feasts of St. Peter and St. Paul, to promote the work of evangelization in the wake of growing secularization. The Church's mission is to proclaim the Gospel at all times, especially now. In *Evangelii Nuntiandi*, Pope Paul VI said that "first proclamation" was imperative because of "the frequent situations of de-Christianization in our day," in which many live without the basic foundations of the faith and as if they have not received the sacrament of Baptism.[55] It was already clear on the eve of the twenty-first century that new, collaborative efforts across denominational lines would be needed to promote evangelism as a practice. Following the great Protestant push to evangelize the world in a generation, a statement that received great support from the delegates at the 1910 Missionary Conference, the Protestant World Council of Churches introduced new efforts to collaborate in world evangelism

53. Paul VI, *Lumen Gentium*, 4, 12.

54. Benedict XVI, *Ubicumque et Semper*.

55. Paul VI, *Evangelii Nuntiandi*.

through its Commission on World Evangelism as well as evangelical groups like the Billy Graham Evangelistic Association and the Lausanne Movement. Another collaborative effort is the Church Growth Movement, a programmatic, new approach to planting and growing churches started by Donald McGavran and his colleagues at Fuller Theological Seminary in Pasadena, California.

In 1991, the World Council of Churches (WCC) met in Canberra, Australia, for its Seventh General Assembly with the prayerful theme, "Come Holy Spirit—Renew the Whole Creation." If Vatican II was called to open the windows and let fresh air into the Church, the WCC invoked the Spirit's presence to do more than renewing the Church alone; it prayed that the Spirit renew all of creation. This is not a contradiction or rejection of *Lumen Gentium;* it is a logical extension of the faith in the Spirit's role at a time when we have recognized the interconnection of the created order. What is needed is a new spirit of discernment that explores how the ecclesial community can contribute to reshaping the created order in a new spirit of comity. In other words, the challenges we face today invite the ecclesial community to re-conceptualize comity in order to address the evangelical mission and the spiritual and social needs of the day. This is important for several reasons.

First, the ecclesial community has a theological mandate to promote collaboration. Churches have been called to make disciples, not only to add to the membership rolls but also to make the reign of God a reality. In that process, it does not make sense to fight and undercut one another. While we celebrate the phenomenal growth of the Church in Africa today, it must be noted that the Church still needs to apply its Christian message to justice and human rights in the postcolonial era. One must also note that, as imperfect as the evangelical witness has been, the Christian tradition has walked with and stood with millions affected by HIV/AIDS, the Ebola Virus Disease (EVD), the massive refugee crisis, and gender discrimination.[56]

The magisterium and the documents of both the WCC and the Evangelicals demonstrate that the practice of evangelism continues to be the Church's marching orders; it is complicated and challenging, not primarily because of secularism but rather our inability to appropriate and live with pluralism. And that is why the late twentieth-century evangelization that dawned in Africa—championed as in the past by African evangelists—responded to deep social crisis and turmoil, to redefine the Church's notion that we are all going to hell if we do not change. In the process, the significant

56. Bongmba, *Facing a Pandemic;* Azetsop, *HIV and Aids in Africa;* Haddad, *Religion and HIV and AIDS;* Dube, *HIV/AIDS and the Curriculum;* Phiri et al., *African Women, HIV/AIDS, and Faith Communities;* Chitando, *Mainstreaming HIV and AIDS.*

revolutions in ecclesial expansion—education, social services, and development programs—ushered in by the historic churches were easily dismissed, even by those who benefitted from those revolutions, as the competition in Cameroon illustrates. Therefore, the ecclesial community stands at the crossroads again in our time.

It is interesting that we do not have a clear definition of what we see at that crossroads. Isn't it interesting that the ecclesial community sees less and less of the devil who historically has been defined as the enemy who comes to destroy and kill? Instead, we see secularism; secular humanism; socialism and communism (neither of which seem to occupy the church very much these days); or other religious traditions of the world. At one time, missionaries in Africa thought the Gospel's two great enemies were heathenism and Islam. Indigenous African religions have not been eviscerated, despite the scorn heaped on them by present-day Pentecostals. I think that we live at a time when it is clear that worrying about Islam is not a fruitful approach to growing the church because Islam as a religion is also seeking to grow its religious communities.

The Pew Research Institute has shown that, due to an increase in birth rate and numerical group, by the year 2060, Muslims will make up 31 percent of the global population, just behind Christians, who will make up 32 percent.[57] What do you do when confronted with such data? What the ecclesial community needs to rekindle is a proclamation of the Good News and a message of justice in a collaborative manner. Collaboration is essential because all churches are part of the lifelong practice that proclaims the love of God. The proclamation and lifestyles that form each ecclesial practice have been shaped by history and a host of traditions which must always be updated. The Church has now become a space where its members have been saturated with revelation (and there are new revelations every day in Africa), and the nasty competition we see stems from the fact that we continue to proclaim, predict, and proscribe everything that does not fit into individual "revelations." However, in playing the cards that we have been dealt—proclaiming the Gospel in a pluralistic world—the ecclesial community is called to ask, "What is the Gospel?" in a new way. The old answer is that the Gospel is the love of God. Therefore, in addition to *kerygma*, the Church is also called to *diakonia*, because the love of God should be extended to all, and *diakonia* opens an expansive space for collaboration.

Second, the ecclesial community has the resources to carry out a new collaboration. These resources include the very teachings of the Church itself and the various charisms given the Church to teach, heal, feed, nurture,

57. Pew Research Center, "Changing Global Religious Landscape."

and encourage one another.[58] These gifts reflect the Church's diversity, which enriches individual churches to play different roles in promoting a practice consistent with teachings of Jesus. Recognizing diversity makes it possible for the ecclesial community to strive to practice what Thomas Stransky described many years ago as "Mission-in-unity" and "unity-in-mission,"[59] even though we cannot see everything the same way.

Paul Collins has argued that the Church must be open to the "other."[60] He grounds concerns for the "other" in the Trinitarian model, where the Holy Spirit is the guarantor of *koinonia*. Thus, the presence of the Holy Spirit opens individuals to the "other" and one ecclesial community to another. The idea of the "other" stresses distinctions which, according to Emmanuel Levinas, must remain that way to avoid totality.[61] The need for a new openness to the "other" is more urgent today because, over the years, the created order has seen the destruction of its inhabitants through wars and brutal acts by dictators, natural and human-made disasters, disease, hunger, gender disparity, human rights abuses, and the lethal battle waged against members of the LGBTQ community perpetrated in the name of religion.

The ecclesial community should consider *diakonia* as a new definition of ecumenism. Working and living out ecumenism calls for sustained ethical thinking and a moral posture which prioritizes and organizes responsibility for others because that is what Jesus has called the Church to do. Another way of thinking about *diakonia* as a marker of ecumenism is to embrace what Paul Avis argues is "a new frontier for ecumenism"; he calls for a differentiated consensus on some of the recent thinking on the question of ecumenism.[62] Avis argues that, even if the ecclesial community were to agree on many issues, there would still be areas of disagreement, especially over issues like sexuality. Avis reminds the Church that, in a time of conflict, it is good to take the time to consult with each other and listen to the Word of God rather than merely use it as window dressing for our particular arguments. "Adopt a patient, charitable, and humble stance and disposition in dialogue."[63] We always ought to act in a way that will not scandalize others. Towards the end of his book, Avis focuses on the Gospel of John where Jesus prays for mystical and visible unity demonstrated by love as well as for missional unity (used in the context of Anglican–Methodist dialogue). We

58. Kekumbu, "Experience of the Holy Spirit," 22–32.
59. Stransky, "Unity in Mission, Mission in Unity," 58–59.
60. Collins, "Church and the 'Other.'"
61. Levinas, *Totality and Infinity.*
62. Avis, *Reshaping Ecumenical Theology,* 164.
63. Avis, *Reshaping Ecumenical Theology,* 182–83.

should emphasize that unity in missions has been a crucial dimension of the work of the WCC and the All Africa Conference of Churches, even as those two ecumenical bodies have wrestled with understanding the relationship between ecclesiology and ethics.[64]

Bibliography

"After Comity, What?" *The Christian Century* 68.23 (1951) 677–78.

Akoko, Robert Mbe. *Ask and You Shall be Given: Pentecostalism and the Economic Crisis in Cameroon*. Leiden: African Studies Center, 2007.

Avis, Paul. *Reshaping Ecumenical Theology: The Church Made Whole?* London: T. & T. Clark, 2010.

Azetsop, Jacquineau, ed. *HIV and Aids in Africa: Christian Reflection, Public Health, Social Transformation*. Maryknoll, NY: Orbis, 2016.

Baëta, C. G. *Prophetism in Ghana: A Study of Some Spiritual Churches*. London: SCM, 1962.

Barret, David B. *Schism and Renewal in Africa: An Analysis of Six Thousand Contemporary Religious Movements*. London: Oxford University Press, 1986.

Beaver, Robert Pierce. "Comity." In *Concise Dictionary of the Christian World Mission*, edited by Stephen Neill et al., 123. Nashville: Abingdon, 1971.

———. *Ecumenical Beginnings in Protestant World Mission: A History of Comity*. New York: Thomas Nelson and Sons, 1962.

Benedict XVI. *Ubicumque et Semper*. Rome: Libreria Editrici Vaticana, 2010. Online. http://w2.vatican.va/content/benedict-xvi/en/apost_letters/documents/hf_ben-xvi_apl_20100921_ubicumque-et-semper.html.

Bongmba, Elias K. *Facing a Pandemic: The African Church and Crisis of AIDS*. Waco, TX: Baylor University Press, 2007.

Bruner, Jason. "Public Confession and the Moral Universe of the East African Revival." *Studies in World Christianity* 18.3 (2012) 254–68.

Chitando, Ezra, ed. *Mainstreaming HIV and AIDS in Theological Education: Experiences and Explorations*. Geneva: WCC, 2008.

Clark, N. G. *True and False Economy in Missions*. Boston: American Board of Commissioners for Foreign Missions, 1891.

Collins, Paul M. "The Church and the 'Other': Questions of Ecclesial and Divine Communion." In *Ecumenical Ecclesiology: Unity, Diversity, Otherness in a Fragmented World*, edited by Gesa Elisabeth Thiessen, 101–14. London: T. & T. Clark, 2009.

Cooper, Barbara M. *Evangelical Christians in the Muslim Sahel*. Bloomington, IN: Indiana University Press, 2006.

Corwin, Gary R. "Comity." In *Evangelical Dictionary of World Missions*, edited by A. Scott Moreau, 212. Grand Rapids: Baker, 2000.

Dairo, A. Olalekan. "Privatization and Commercialization of Christian Message." In *Creativity and Change in Nigerian Christianity*, edited by David Ogungbile and Akintunde E. Akinade, 193–99. Lagos: Malthouse, 2010.

---

64. Sakupapa, "Ecclesiology and Ethics."

Dube, Musa W. *HIV/AIDS and the Curriculum: Methods of Integrating HIV/AIDS in Theological Programs*. Geneva: WCC, 2003.

Edwards, Jonathan. *A Humble Attempt to Promote Explicit Agreement and Visible Union Among God's People, in Extraordinary Prayer for Revival of Religion, and the Advancement of Christ's Kingdom on Earth, Pursuant to Scriptural Promises, and Prophecies Concerning the Last Time*. Boston: D. Henchman, 1747.

Ekechi, F. K. "Colonialism and Christianity in West Africa: The Igbo Case, 1900–1915." *Journal of African History* 12.1 (1971) 103–13.

Engelke, Matthew. "Discontinuity and the Discourse of Conversion." *Journal of Religion in Africa* 34.1 (2004) 82–109.

Fomum, Z. T. "On Our History." *Christian Missionary Fellowship International* (CMFI), November 19, 2016. Online. https://ztfministry.org/index.php?option=com_content&view=article&id=829.

Gifford, Paul. *Ghana's New Christianity: Pentecostalism in a Globalizing African Economy*. Bloomington, IN: Indiana University Press, 2004.

Goheen, Michael. "Mission and Unity: The Theological Dynamic of Comity." In *That the World May Believe: Essays on Mission and Unity in Honor of George Vandervelde*, edited by Michael W. Goheen and Margaret O'Gara, 83–91. Lanham, MD: University Press of America, 2006.

Haddad, Beverly, ed. *Religion and HIV and AIDS: Charting the Terrain*. Scottsville, South Africa: University of Kwazulu Natal Press, 2011.

Hutchinson, William R. *Errand to the World: American Protestant Thought and Foreign Missions*. Chicago: University of Chicago Press, 1987.

Kalu, Ogbu. *African Pentecostalism: An Introduction*. New York: Oxford University Press, 2008.

Kekumba, Yemba. "The Experience of the Holy Spirit in Today's African Contest." *Andover Newton Review* 2.1 (1991) 22–32.

Konings, Piet. "Religious Revival in the Roman Catholic Church and the Autochthony-Allochthony Conflict in Cameroon." *Africa* 73.1 (2003) 31–56.

Kor, Buma. *Revival Palaver in Bastos*. Yaoundé: Cockcrow, 1997.

Levinas, Emmanuel. *Totality and Infinity: An Essay on Exteriority*. Translated by Alphonso Lingis. Pittsburgh: Duquesne University Press, 1969.

Maseno, Loreen, and B. Moses Owojaiye. "African Women and Revival: The Case of the East African Revival." *European Journal of Research in Social Science* 3.3 (2015) 28–36.

Marshall, Ruth. "Mediating the Global and Local in Nigerian Pentecostalism." *Journal of Religion in Africa* 28.3 (1998) 278–315.

Maxwell, David. "Delivered from the Spirit of Poverty? Pentecostalism, Prosperity, and Modernity in Zimbabwe." *Journal of Religion in Africa* 28.2 (1998) 350–73.

McCauley, John F. "Africa's New Big Man Rule? Pentecostalism and Patronage in Ghana." *African Affairs* 112.446 (2012) 1–12.

Meyer, Birgit. "Make a Complete Break with the Past." *Journal of Religion in Africa* 28.3 (1998) 316–49.

Ndagire, Betty. "Six Pastor Kayanja Sodomy Accusers Convicted." *Daily Monitor*, October 2, 2012. Online. https://www.monitor.co.ug/News/National/Six-Pastor-Kayanja-accusers-convicted-/688334-1523898-x9n93m/index.html.

Neill, Stephen. *A History of Christian Missions*. Rev. ed. New York: Penguin, 1986.

Newbigin, Lesslie. *The Reunion of the Church: A Defense of the South India Scheme.* London: SCM, 1948.

Olivestam, Carl E., and Christina Thornell. "The Exposure of the Swedish Mission to Competition in the Central African Arena." *Swedish Missiological Themes* 94.3 (2006) 371–95.

Paul VI. *Dogmatic Constitution on the Church: Lumen Gentium.* Boston: Pauline, 1998. Online. http://www.vatican.va/archive/hist_councils/ii_vatican_council/documents/vat-ii_const_19641121_lumen-gentium_en.html.

———. *Evangelii Nuntiandi: On Evangelization in the Modern World.* Washington, DC: US Catholic Conference, 1976. Online. http://w2.vatican.va/content/paul-vi/en/apost_exhortations/documents/hf_p-vi_exh_19751208_evangelii-nuntiandi.html.

Perham, Margery. "Frederick Lugard: British Colonial Administrator." *Encyclopaedia Britannica*, July 20, 1998. Revised April 8, 2020. Online. https://www.britannica.com/biography/Frederick-Lugard.

Pew Research Center. "The Changing Global Religious Landscape." April 5, 2017. Online. http://www.pewforum.org/2017/04/05/the-changing-global-religious-landscape/#global-population-projections-2015-to-2060.

Phiri, Isabel Apawo, et al. *African Women, HIV/AIDS, and Faith Communities.* Pietermaritzburg, South Africa: Cluster, 2003.

Saayman, Willem A. "Some Reflections on the Development of the Pentecostal Mission Model in South Africa." *Missionalia* 21.1 (1993) 40–56.

Sakupapa, Teddy Chalwe. "Ecclesiology and Ethics: An Analysis of the History of the All African Conference of Churches (1963–2013)." PhD diss., University of the Western Cape, 2017.

Stransky, Thomas. "Unity in Mission, Mission in Unity." *SEDOS Bulletin* 21.2 (1989) 58–59.

Sundkler, Bengt. *Bantu Prophets in South Africa.* London: Oxford University Press, 1961.

Taylor, John V. "Bangkok 1972–1973." *International Review of Mission* 67.267 (1978) 365–70.

Temple, William. *The Church Looks Forward.* London: Macmillan, 1944.

Townsend, Thomas Winburn. "Break Comity Agreement: Philippine Methodists Set up Parishes in the Former United Church Area." *The Christian Century* 68.40 (1951) 1139–40.

Turner, Harold W. *Black Africa.* Vol. 1 of *Bibliography of New Religious Movements in Primal Societies.* Boston: G. K. Hall, 1977.

Valois, Caroline. "Scandal Makers: Competition in the Religious Market among Pentecostal-Charismatic Churches in Uganda." In *Christianity and Controversies over Homosexuality in Contemporary Africa*, edited by Ezra Chitando and Adriaan van Klinken, 38–50. New York: Rutledge, 2016.

Ward, Kevin, and Emma Wild-Wood, eds. *The East African Revival: History and Legacies.* Burlington, VT: Ashgate, 2012.

Wrigley, C. C. "The Christian Revolution in Buganda." *Comparative Studies in Society and History* 2.1 (1959) 33–48.

2

Pentecostalism and Base Christian Communities in Mexico: Similarities, Differences, and Juxtapositions

Philip Wingeier-Rayo

Introduction

I would like to thank Dr. William Cavanaugh and the Center for World Catholicism and Intercultural Theology (CWCIT) at DePaul University for the invitation and the opportunity to participate in the ninth annual World Catholicism Week at DePaul University. Certainly, "Gathered in My Name: Ecumenism in the World Church" is a wonderful theme on the occasion of the five hundredth anniversary of the Protestant Reformation. As professor of evangelism and mission, ecumenism and unity are crucial topics for me as we collectively witness to God's love for the world. I was born to missionary parents in Singapore, where my grandmother was born while my great-grandparents evangelized Muslims in Sumatra and Java. After coming to the US as a boy, I finished growing up just north of here, in Evanston, and graduated from Evanston Township High School before going to college and being called to the mission field myself. I was called to serve in this hemisphere, living and working with my wife for fifteen years in Nicaragua, Cuba, Mexico, and along the US-Mexico border in South Texas.

I arrived in Nicaragua during the Contra War in the late 1980s and had an abrupt entrance into the sphere of Catholic–Protestant relations in Latin America. As if moving from the North Shore to war-torn Nicaragua wasn't enough of a cultural shock, I was also transitioning from a suburban, predominantly white Protestant church to the religious battlefield of Latin America. Nicaragua, in particular, was a fascinating case study. The 1979 Sandinista Revolution victory, with the support of liberation theology and Marxist ideology, was followed by the growth of supposedly apolitical evangelical and Pentecostal sects under attack by the US embargo and the Contra War in the northern mountains. During my two years in Nicaragua, I attended Roman Catholic Masses, middle-class Baptist churches, working-class Church of Christ services, Pentecostal revivals, and base Christian community[1] home Bible studies. It was at the end of my time in Nicaragua that David Stoll published his book, *Is Latin America Turning Protestant? The Politics of Evangelical Growth* (1990).[2] In order to understand the religious competition in Nicaragua, I began an intellectual and spiritual journey into church history, and what I learned is that what had arrived in South America was a different kind of Christianity than what I had been exposed to in North America. This study eventually led me to do ethnographic research in Mexico, which I will describe below.

The Conquest of Mexico and the Protestant Reformation in Europe

Simultaneous with Hernán Cortés's and Francisco Pizarro's conquests of Mexico and Peru was the start of the Protestant Reformation in Europe. On April 2, 1521, Martin Luther defended his ninety-five theses against the Roman Catholic practice of indulgences at the Imperial Diet in Worms, Germany. Seemingly a world apart, these events would soon become entwined, as the Roman Catholic Church felt threatened by Luther's *Sola Scriptura* doctrine and initiated a counter-reformation campaign. These two competing beliefs soon encountered each other in the so-called "New World" with a German Lutheran settlement in Venezuela in 1532 and brief French Huguenot settlements in Brazil and Fort Caroline, Florida, in the 1550s and 1560s. But Spanish captain Pedro Menéndez de Avilés momentarily eradicated the "Lutheran heresy" in Florida in 1556 by slitting the throats of a thousand infidels who did not confess the Catholic faith.

1. Alternatively known by the acronym BCCs as well as CEBs, taken from the original Spanish.
2. See Stoll, *Is Latin America Turning Protestant?*

Hearing reports of French settlements further north and Protestant beliefs from Europe, the Spanish moved to defend their territory and the Catholic faith by establishing a chain of mission systems during the seventeenth and eighteenth centuries in what is today Texas, New Mexico, Arizona, and California. Because there were not enough Spanish soldiers or resources to secure such a vast region, the mission system seemed to be the ideal church-state partnership. The Spanish Crown decided to govern the region as a missionary province supporting the missions with an annual subsidy—a tithe of the taxes charged to the region's residents. Although many priests shared a genuine desire to convert the Native Americans away from their indigenous beliefs to Christianity, the Spanish government supported this mission as a means of introducing Western civilization and bringing the native peoples under submission as subjects. In addition to teaching the tenets of the Christian faith, the missions served to teach the Spanish language, crafts, agriculture, law, and, eventually, European warfare. Within fortified walls, the mission protected the residents from hostile groups such as non-cooperative Native Americans or European Protestant rivals. Internally, the friars governed the mission with a work ethic imported from the European monastic movement. The soldiers also applied Spanish law to runaways and heretics and taught some defensive skills to cooperative residents.

A chain of Franciscan missions was also established further in what is today the State of California. The most famous Franciscan friar was Junípero Serra, who is known as the Apostle of California and was canonized by Pope Francis on September 23, 2015. Serra was born in Petra, Spain, in 1713, and he became a Franciscan in 1730. He taught at Lullian University (Palma de Mallorca, Spain) before coming to Mexico in 1750 to work among the indigenous people. In 1767, he was transferred to Alta California and, in 1769, founded the Mission San Diego, the first mission in what is today the State of California. He died in 1784 after establishing eight more missions in California.[3] His canonization was controversial among Native American rights activists because of accusations against him of mass baptisms. The San Diego mission faced resistance from Native Americans after a reported three hundred forced mass baptisms took place in a period of three months; this provoked an attack on the San Diego mission in 1769.[4] The animosity continued after approximately five hundred baptisms and, in November of 1775, the Diegeños mounted a major attack on the mission.[5]

3. "Saint Junípero Serra."
4. "Libro Primero de los Bautismos."
5. Wingeier-Rayo, "Mission Systems," 372.

The Franciscans were completely taken by surprise, even though there had been warning signs. Fr. Luis Jayme said of the first attack: "No wonder the Indians here were bad when the mission was first founded. To begin with, they did not know why [the Spaniards] had come unless they intended to take their lands away from them."[6]

The mission system thrived until Mexican independence from Spain in 1821 but suffered a serious decline following the annexation of Texas in 1845 and the ensuing Mexican-American war from 1846 to 1848. The missions remaining in Mexican territory were largely dismantled during Benito Juárez's rule as a result of the separation of church and state enacted by the 1857 Mexican constitution. After the approval of the Reform Laws by President Benito Juárez, Mexico became a lay state with separation of church and state. Beginning in 1872, US Protestants were allowed to send missionaries and purchase some confiscated Catholic properties.

Protestants in Latin America

Due to the Roman Catholic control of colonial South America, the Protestants considered this region off-limits until countries began to gain their independence from Spain. However, the 1823 Monroe Doctrine established that European powers could no longer colonize in the Americas, giving the United States more hegemony. Due to Spanish laws preventing non-Catholic beliefs, all Protestant work was in English and began as schools primarily for ex-patriots. The first Methodist Society was established in Rio de Janeiro by Fountain E. Pitts, who traveled to Argentina, Uruguay, and Brazil in 1835. Even after the founding of the Protestant mission boards with more intentional evangelization efforts, Latin America was often considered "Christianized" and left off the list of unreached lands.[7]

The first known Protestant sermon in Spanish was preached in Buenos Aires by Methodist John Francis Thomson on May 25, 1867. After the Spanish colonial laws were rescinded in 1872–1873, Protestant missionary work in Spanish began in Cuba and Puerto Rico. In the case of Mexico, growing US investments under Porfirio Díaz (1876–1911) allowed for greater missionary influence, and Protestantism grew, especially in areas along train routes where the Catholic Church lacked a strong presence. Protestants also began social ministries, such as schools and health dispensaries, and distributed Bibles and other Christian literature.

6. Jayme, *Letter of Luis Jayme, OFM*, 40.

7. Latin America was excluded from the agenda of the 1910 World Missionary Conference in Edinburgh, Scotland.

The Presbyterian Church began its work in December of 1872, and the Methodists followed, purchasing the first Protestant Church in Mexico City on Calle Gante, No. 5. A former Catholic seminarian, Alejo Hernández, converted to Methodism and became the first Mexican Protestant clergy. The *Reforma* of President Benito Juárez reformed the Mexican constitution to allow Protestants to purchase property and begin work with the hope of promoting liberal ideals in the country and counterbalancing the power of the Roman Catholic Church.

The liberal impact of Protestantism was as a voice of reason, democracy, and development. In Mexico, President Juárez received support and encouragement from Protestants and liberals, which eventually inspired a new constitution in 1857, guaranteeing freedom of religion and separation of church and state and officially opening the door to Protestantism.[8] To this day, Mexican Protestants hold Benito Juárez up as a national hero for standing up to the Roman Catholic Church and fighting on behalf of religious pluralism.

One of the soldiers who fought in Juárez's resistance army was Alejo Hernández. He had been a candidate for the priesthood until he heard about Juárez's movement and left the seminary in Aguascalientes, Mexico, to join Juárez's fight against the 1862 French invasion. While in Juárez's army, Hernández read an anti-Catholic treatise left by US soldiers during the Mexican-American War entitled "Nights with the Romanists." Arousing his curiosity, he went to Brownsville, Texas, to find a Protestant Bible; he had a profound religious experience[9] and served as a Methodist pastor from 1871 to 1875. Once the doors were open for Protestant mission work, eighteen denominations arrived, beginning with the Presbyterian missionaries Rev. and Mrs. William Wallace in 1872 and Rev. William Butler, who purchased the Gante Methodist Church where Rev. Alejo Hernández served as pastor, in 1873.

The Protestant values forged during the Enlightenment were based on rationalism, liberalism, and a search for certainty. Jean-Pierre Bastian writes about the role of Protestants in the struggle for democracy in the late nineteenth and early twentieth centuries. He argues that Protestantism is a religion of written, civic, and rational education.[10] The Protestant work in Mexico embodied these ideals in the struggle against the dictatorship of Porfirio Díaz (1830–1915) and was a threat to both the hegemony of the Roman Catholic Church and authoritarian governments. "In the late

8. Velasco, *Mexico*, 37.

9. Velasco, *Mexico*, 46.

10. Bastian, *Protestantismo y Sociedad en Mexico*, 58.

nineteenth and early twentieth centuries," Daniel Miller writes, "Mexican Protestants viewed themselves as advocates of social and political progress in contrast to the Catholic Church which they stigmatized as arrogant and reactionary."[11] Many individuals and congregations broke away from the Roman Catholic Church, and Protestant missionaries began joining forces with liberals in a larger struggle for democracy.[12] In 1910, the Mexican Revolution exploded under the leadership of Emiliano Zapata—in part because of the rational, liberal, and pro-democratic teachings of Protestantism.[13] The spirit of the Mexican revolution was anti-clerical, and many Protestant leaders signed the *Plan de Ayala* with revolutionary demands of *tierra y libertad* (land and liberty) and later became generals or held political posts in the post-revolutionary governments.

Pentecostalism in Latin America

At the same time of the civil explosion within Mexico over the distribution of wealth, land, and human rights, Pentecostalism was exploding around the world. William Joseph Seymour began the Apostolic Faith Mission in Los Angeles on April 14, 1906, when he and seven others fell to the floor in religious ecstasy, speaking in tongues.[14] The congregation immediately grew with gifts of the Spirit and came to be known as the Azusa Street Revival. Early in the revival, there were blacks, whites, Mexicans, Italians, Chinese, Russians, and Native Americans involved, which was unusual for a segregated American society. People came from all around the world to see and experience the revival. The small, forty-by-sixty-foot building was packed with up to eight hundred people and visitors, such as Charles Mason from Memphis, who returned to start the Church of God in Christ—one of the largest black Pentecostal denominations in America. Another visitor was William Durham, who developed the "Finished Work" theology that gave birth to the Assemblies of God.[15] Durham returned to Chicago to start the North Avenue mission, which also drew important visitors, such as physician and Methodist missionary Dr. William Hoover. Hoover experienced a baptism of the Holy Spirit and shared his experience in Valparaiso, Chile, in 1909, leading to the start of the Methodist Pentecostal Church.[16]

11. Miller, "Protestantism and Radicalism in Mexico," 2.

12. Arango, "Evangelical (Protestant) Church in Mexico," 230.

13. Bowen, *Evangelicalism and Apostasy*, 31.

14. Synan, *Holiness-Pentecostal Tradition*, 96.

15. Synan, "William Seymour," 17–19.

16. Wingeier-Rayo, "Hoover C. Willis," 191–92.

Missionaries also left for India, China, Europe, Palestine, and Africa. Early in the twentieth century, mainline Protestant churches did not initially place much importance on Pentecostalism. Even though the Azusa Street revival had already occurred and Pentecostalism was spreading around the world, there was little mention or concern for the movement among Catholics and mainline Protestants during the first half of the 1900s.

The spread of this movement reached Mexico when a couple from Villa Aldama, in the state of Chihuahua, left to avoid the violence of the Mexican revolution. The couple arrived in Los Angeles and began attending a Pentecostal church where they experienced revival, conversion, and baptism of the Holy Spirit. By 1914, when they were well-established in the Pentecostal congregation, the wife, Romana de Valenzuela, began to miss her family and was concerned about their spiritual well-being. In the fall of 1914, she returned home to Villa Aldama to convert them to her new faith.[17] While there, on November 1, 1914, Romana was leading a time of prayer with twelve people when they received a baptism of the Holy Spirit and spoke in tongues.

However, her task would not be complete without baptizing the new believers, so she set out to find an ordained pastor. She reached out to Ruben Ortega, a Methodist pastor in Chihuahua. Rev. Ortega had been exposed to the power of the Holy Spirit by evangelists Dwight L. Moody and Ira Sankey. They taught that believers needed to be baptized in the Holy Spirit, but Romana was asking him to identify the gift of speaking in tongues as evidence of baptism of the Holy Spirit.[18] Ortega had heard about speaking in tongues, but he had never experienced it. However, he was willing to go and pray with Romana's group, where he eventually received baptism of the Holy Spirit and the gift of speaking in tongues. He was then ready to baptize the new converts.[19] The small group begun by Romana de Valenzuela and baptized by Rev. Ortega continued to grow on its own. By 1932, there were Pentecostal missions in the towns of Esperanza, Etchojoa, Chucarit, Empale, San Blas, and Sinaloa in the state of Sonora under the name of Iglesia Apostólica.[20]

As we can see from this brief review of the origins and development of Pentecostalism in Mexico, the history is different from that of mainline Protestantism. This distinctiveness also allowed Pentecostalism to be free from the European and North American influences so deeply ingrained in

17. Gill, *Toward a Contextualized Theology for the Third World*, 43.

18. Gill, *Toward a Contextualized Theology for the Third World*, 43.

19. López, *Historia de la Iglesia Apostólica*, 22.

20. López, *Historia de la Iglesia Apostólica*, 22.

Protestant churches. It had neither the governmental cooperation of colonial Catholicism nor the missionaries and mission boards of Protestantism. Rather, individual faith missionaries shared their experience of baptism of the Holy Spirit and began a series of small revivals in Brazil, Chile, and Mexico, among other places. These revivals often began among the marginalized, who had little formal education or recognition by society.

As mentioned at the beginning of this paper, David Stoll put this movement on the map with the title of his book, *Is Latin America Turning Protestant?* While Stoll included Pentecostals within the larger category of evangelicals, I have argued elsewhere that Pentecostals are a third and distinct phase of Christianity in Latin America.[21] David Martin argued that Pentecostalism best prepares Latin Americans to confront and adapt to modernity. His thesis is that the growth of Pentecostalism is making Latin America more pluralistic because it comes from the roots of Northern European Protestantism rather than the totalitarian, southern European style of Catholicism.[22] Comparing BCCs and Pentecostals in northeast Brazil, Cecília Mariz argued that Pentecostalism helps the poor cope with poverty.[23] In Colombia, Elizabeth Brusco conducted research among evangelicals (including Pentecostals) and concluded that evangelical conversion domesticates men who formerly squandered their salaries on alcohol, gambling, and other women, and this has the latent effect of empowering and raising women's quality of life. In his research on the relationship between Pentecostalism and politics, Douglas Peterson argued that, rather than being an openly political movement, it creates micropolitical change that empowers the poor to learn the skills necessary to participate in a democratic society.[24] Similarly, Edward Cleary and Hannah Stewart-Gambino theorized that Pentecostals are participating more in the Latin American political scene with political parties and candidates for key national positions.[25]

Base Christian Communities (BCCs)

The Roman Catholic Church responded to liberalism and modernity with the Second Vatican Council (1962–1965), allowing for the distribution of the Bible in the vernacular, lay empowerment, liturgical renewal, and

21. Wingeier-Rayo, "Third Phase of Christianity," 1–22.

22. Martin, *Tongues of Fire*; *Pentecostalism*.

23. Mariz, *Coping with Poverty*.

24. Peterson, *Not by Power, Nor by Might*.

25. Cleary and Stewart-Gambino, *Power, Politics, and Pentecostalism in Latin America*.

reading the signs of the times. In the meantime, groups of Christians were already gathering and responding to oppressive conditions, interpreting scripture, and organizing for action. These small groups, called base Christian communities, were spreading throughout Latin America when their theology and practice were made famous by the Peruvian priest Gustavo Gutiérrez, OP, in his book *A Theology of Liberation*.[26] The reconciliation of Catholic belief with the advances of modernity in Vatican II was contextualized by the Conference of Latin American Bishops (CELAM) in their general conference, CELAM II, held in Medellín, Colombia, in 1968; it was here that the church made a "preferential option for the poor." This commitment was reaffirmed at CELAM III in Puebla, Mexico, and BCCs were lifted up as signs of evangelization.

Base Christian communities are lay-led, home Bible studies that emerged in Latin America in the context of resistance to political oppression, economic poverty, and a shortage of priests. Early witnesses believe that these grassroots Bible studies emerged in Brazil in the 1950s and then gained popularity and influence under the military dictatorship between 1964 and 1985.[27] While Protestants had congregations, the Roman Catholic structure had large parishes that had no smaller ecclesial unit where parishioners could study the Bible intimately. In 1962, the Brazilian Council of Bishops met and approved the "Emergency Plan," which created a Joint Pastoral Plan for 1965–1970 that called for the establishment of "basic communities" within the larger parish structure.[28] About the same time, Vatican II (1962–1965) acknowledged the shortage of clergy, allowing for greater lay leadership and also authorizing the translation of the Bible from the Latin vulgate into the vernacular.[29] Vatican II instituted five major changes that opened the doors for BCCs:

1. It affirmed the importance of the laity taking an active role in the church.

2. It called all Catholics, not just the clergy, to be involved in creating a more just world. At the same time, the bishops recognized that the causes for much of the world's misery and suffering could be located in human sinfulness.

---

26. First published in Spanish in 1971 under the title *Teología de Liberación: Perspectivas.*

27. Silva and Hernández, "Personal Experiences," 214–15.

28. Azevedo, *Basic Ecclesial Communities in Brazil*, 28–29.

29. Paul VI, *Lumen Gentium*, 10.

3. It insisted that all Catholics, clergy and laity alike, become more aware of the Scriptures.

4. It called for a careful reading of the "signs of the times," which became the basis for the kind of "bottom-up" theology that has become characteristic of liberation theology and base communities.

5. It set a tone that called for renewal and updating. What resulted was a sense of introspection and self-analysis that flowed into each of the specific documents. This tone also flowed into the church itself in the years that followed. Within this context, church leaders began to question the effectiveness of impersonal parish life and looked for other, more personal structures of church life.[30]

These changes produced by Vatican II created an opening in the Catholic Church for renewal. Moreover, the availability of the Bible in Spanish and Portuguese as well as a very tense socioeconomic and political reality in Latin America were the key ingredients for base Christian communities.

Another key element was Paulo Freire's popular literacy method, which suggested that learning is the process of reflecting on one's reality and gaining consciousness (*conscientizaçao*).[31] While Bible studies are one thing, BCCs involved a specific three-step teaching methodology influenced by Freire: to see, to judge, and to act. The Brazilian Jesuit Marcello de Carvalho Azevedo reflects that "the [base Christian communities] did not arise spontaneously out of the base, out of common people composing them. They were the result of the consciousness-raising activity of clergy and religious, who were helping people to see real elements of their life and historical situation."[32] The BCCs spread from Brazil to Chile, Panama, and Nicaragua and then throughout Latin America. The spread of BCCs did not happen magically or systematically; rather, it was simple human contact, people sharing the methodology from one country to the next. Here is an example of the experience of one priest who traveled from Chile to Mexico.

The French priest, Fr. Pierre Rolland, was a missionary in Chile planning to leave for Cuba when he ran into visa problems. He requested permission from Bishop Sergio Méndez Arceo to work in his diocese in Cuernavaca, Mexico. Supportive of the changes in the Roman Catholic Church, Méndez Arceo was, in fact, ahead of Vatican II in calling for a vernacular translation of the Bible. Prior to Vatican II, he had distributed ten thousand Spanish Bibles and thirty thousand copies of the New Testament,

30. Abbott, *Documents of Vatican II.*
31. Freire, *Pedagogy of the Oppressed.*
32. Azevedo, *Basic Ecclesial Communities in Brazil,* 35.

and his priests were teaching Bible studies—although they still were not considered BCCs.[33]

Assigned by Bishop Méndez Arceo to the working-class parish of La Carolina in 1967, Fr. Rolland recruited married couples to form the parish community. He insisted on married couples to challenge the cultural stereotype that religion was only for women. Even today, the early members of the parish recall how Fr. Rolland visited the poor on his bicycle and encouraged them to think critically about their reality.

Another French priest in Chile, Luis Genoel, had been planning to work in India but was stranded without a visa, so Bishop Méndez Arceo invited him to come work in Teopanzolco, a working-class barrio in Cuernavaca. There, Fr. Genoel also led Bible studies with married couples and added a new level of commitment, requesting that the couples stay for at least one year. Initially, he began with traditional Catholic catechism-themes, such as Eucharistic theology, marriage, Scripture, and morality, but then he introduced the BCC method, "to see, to judge, and to act."

This new Bible study method began to make a difference in people's lives when it addressed real life social issues. Such was the case in Teopanzolco, where the main source of employment was Textiles Morelos, a subsidiary of the Burlington Coat Factory. This textile factory was started and owned by a Roman Catholic Frenchman named Juan Alexis Dubernard Chauveau, who ran a company town. In addition to the factory, he built houses for his employees and the J. F. Kennedy trade school; he also owned other businesses in the city. Although the workers were paid low salaries, they had an affectionate relationship with Dubernard and called him *patrón*. He was a prominent community leader, giving out gifts during the holidays and visiting his workers when they were sick. After serving the parish for a while and teaching Bible studies, Fr. Genoel noticed the social injustices and introduced critical thinking into the lessons, proclaiming to his parishioners: "Look at yourselves! You are all unaware that your religion is a religion of submission to the *patrón;* your belief is the *patrón.* This is not Christian. I didn't have anything against this man. I knew him; we spoke French together. But this man enslaved the people."[34]

Fr. Genoel's Bible studies and encouragement to reflect critically on the reality helped the parishioners and workers to gain critical consciousness. The workers began to organize and went on strike for higher wages and better working conditions. In response, the police were called, and

33. Diocese of Cuernavaca, *Don Sergio*, 33.

34. Interview with Luis Genoel, August 7, 1989. See Emge, "Critical Thinking within a Religious Context," 35.

several parish members were arrested. Bishop Méndez Arceo heard about the incident and came to visit the parishioners in jail; as one of them said, "Twenty-four hours after being detained, they announced that we had a visitor: Bishop Sergio Méndez Arceo. We were all surprised to think that we were deserving enough for a person of that category to visit us in jail. . . . We spent two hours explaining the multiple problems and humiliations that we were enduring."[35] Demonstrating a pastoral presence, Méndez Arceo listened to the parishioners and spoke to the owner, Dubernard Chauveau, to help resolve the differences.

In 1968, the Conference of Latin American Bishops met in Medellín to interpret the meaning of the Vatican II for Latin America. To read "the signs of the times," the bishops appropriated the social sciences in order to understand social injustice in a largely poor continent and then reflected on their role in society. They also used language influenced by Marxist philosophy, liberation theology, and Freireian pedagogy, calling for a just social order where "men are not objects, rather agents of their own history."[36] In the conclusion of their final document, the bishops established the famous "preferential option for the poor" and advocated for social reform.[37]

In 1971, Gustavo Gutiérrez's *A Theology of Liberation* publicized the methodology that had been happening at local levels for nearly a decade. Gutiérrez appropriated the social sciences—for example, Marxist philosophy—to challenge the developmental model of change and the spiritual plane of Christianity. Like Marx, Gutiérrez argues that to have a separate spiritual realm which does not mix with the temporal realm is to make religion an opiate of the people. Liberation theology combines the spiritual and temporal planes so that religion has real, ethical consequences for living out the faith. Therefore, salvation is not some future event that occurs after death or in another place called heaven; rather, salvation occurs here on earth and in time. In other words, salvation is equivalent to liberation. Appropriating the tools of the social sciences, Gutiérrez deconstructs gradual development as merely tinkering with the status quo, where there is gross inequality between the rich and the poor, and he calls for revolutionary change toward a realized eschatology in the here and now.

Juan Luis Segundo published a subsequent book, entitled *The Liberation of Theology*, which further highlights the methodological differences

35. Testimony of Gabriel Muñoz, October 28, 1999 (my translation). See also Chavez and Girardi, *Don Sergio Méndez Arceo*, 117.

36. Segunda Conferencia General del Episcopado Latinoamericano, *Documentos Finales de Medellín*, 2.14.a.

37. Segunda Conferencia General del Episcopado Latinoamericano, *Documentos Finales de Medellín*, 2.14.a.

between traditional theology and liberation theology. He argues that theology is subsequent to action and, thus, a reflection upon action, or praxis. Segundo's book is largely about hermeneutics, or the art of interpretation. He develops the theme of "the hermeneutical circle," borrowing this term from German thinkers Martin Heidegger and Rudolf Bultmann who, in turn, appropriated the tools from the nineteenth-century masters of suspicion, Marx, Freud, and Nietzsche. Segundo defines the hermeneutical circle in the following terms: "The circular character of each interpretation works in such a way that each new reality requires a new interpretation of God, which, in turn, changes reality, and so one must interpret again . . . continuously."[38] This methodology is a radical shift from traditional theology, which works deductively, beginning with universal truths about God and the Bible and then applying them to doctrine. In liberation theology, the methodology is more inductive; one begins with the struggle for liberation, then theology emerges as a reflection on that praxis, which again propels more action.[39]

As in all theological methodologies, liberation theology relies on the Bible as its main source, but it places the passages about Moses, the prophets, and the ethical teachings of Jesus as normative. The hermeneutical lens of liberation theology avoids the mystical, supernatural passages in favor of an emphasis upon God's justice. For example, this story in chapter 3 of Exodus is a favorite: "Then the Lord said, 'I have observed the misery of my people who are in Egypt; I have heard their cry on account of their taskmasters. Indeed, I know their sufferings, and I have come down to deliver them from the Egyptians, and to bring them up out of that land to a good and broad land, a land flowing with milk and honey, to the country of the Canaanites, the Hittites, the Amorites, the Perizzites, the Hivites, and the Jebusites'" (Exod 3:7–8). The passages of liberation in the Bible are fairly easy to interpret as "signs of the times," and they parallel liberation from injustice and oppression in Latin America in modern times. As I described in the story about Fr. Genoel in Cuernavaca, members of BCCs were moved to action by reading about the stories of liberation in the Bible.

CELAM III: Puebla 1979

The work of base Christian communities was reaffirmed at the Third General Conference of CELAM (also known as CELAM III) in 1979, this time in Puebla, under the theme, "The Present and the Future of Evangelization in

38. Segundo, *La Liberación de la Teología*, 13.
39. Smith, *Emergence of Liberation Theology*, 28.

Latin America." In the final Puebla document, BCCs are lifted up as "centers of evangelization and motors of liberation and development."[40] Moreover, in the midst of their decreasing membership in Latin America, BCCs are celebrated for their commitment to the family, work, neighborhood, and the local community.[41] Finally, CELAM III noticed, in these small communities, the "interpersonal faith relationships . . . [and] a greater commitment to justice in the social reality environments where they live."[42] CELAM III celebrated and promoted BCCs as a model for evangelization in Latin America.

In March of 1979, a few months after the Puebla meeting, the Nicaraguan dictator Anastasio Somoza Debayle fled the country, and the Sandinista rebels rose to power with the support—and in some cases, direct support—of BCCs. This leftist revolution was magnified at the height of the Cold War, and greater Soviet influence was not welcome in the Western Hemisphere. US President Ronald Reagan drew upon this fear and lobbied for congressional funding for the Contra army stating that "the Sandinistas are just two days' drive from Harlingen, Texas."[43]

Concerned about the role of liberation theology and BCCs in Latin American leftist movements, a group of President Reagan's top advisors on Latin America met in Santa Fe, New Mexico to write "A New Inter-American Policy for the Eighties," which specifically named liberation theology as a front for communism. Much of the thinking was in the context of the Cold War, but very aware of the failings of the Vietnam War. The documents produced by this committee are popularly known as the Santa Fe Documents and set the policies of the National Security Council for Latin America during the Reagan administration. One of these policies was "low intensity conflict," which attempted to stop the spread of communism without American "boots on the ground."[44] The tactics were more ideological than military and involved discrediting Latin American liberation theology.

Liberation theology also faced opposition within the Roman Catholic Church from Pope John Paul II, who was from Poland and supported the Solidarity movement of resistance against communism in the 1980s. In 1983, the pope visited Nicaragua, just four years after a popular revolution with support from the base communities. The pope expressed his disagreement

---

40. CELAM, *Documento de Puebla*, 96.

41. CELAM, *Documento de Puebla*, 629.

42. CELAM, *Documento de Puebla*, 640.

43. Clift, "With Rebel Leaders at His Side, Reagan Presses for Contra Aid."

44. For more discussion of low-intensity conflict, see Nelson-Pallmeyer, *War Against the Poor.*

with liberation theology priests such as Ernesto Cardenal, who, at the time, was serving as the Minister of Culture in the Sandinista government. The pope waved his finger at Cardenal and ordered him to "straighten out the situation in your church."[45] In addition, Cardinal Joseph Ratzinger, who was in charge of doctrine under John Paul II and later became Pope Benedict XVI, called liberation theology "a fundamental danger for the faith of the church."[46] This internal ecclesial opposition eventually led to the silencing of noted Brazilian theologian Leonardo Boff and the removal of liberation theologian priests from parishes with heavy engagement in base communities.

In spite of the continued efforts of the base to continue the ministry of the BCCs, the removal of the priests and the active opposition from the church hierarchy has taken its toll, and participation in the BCCs has declined since the 1980s. Don Sergio Méndez Arceo was forced to retire as bishop, thus removing much institutional support for the BCCs. In fact, the CELAM IV meeting in Santo Domingo in 1992 cautioned that the BCCs should remain in communion with their parish and their bishop to avoid political and ideological manipulation.[47] Catholic priest Sebastian Mier wrote about the BCCs in 2001: "The communities do not develop anymore; rather they simply maintain themselves at the current level. . . . In several cases, previously, they were growing or prosperous, but the change of circumstances (principally the change of bishops and priests) made them shrink."[48]

Ethnographic Research in Cuernavaca

Several years ago, I conducted ethnographic fieldwork in a marginal neighborhood in both an ecclesial base community and a Pentecostal church. Given my earlier experiences with the BCCs in Nicaragua and my missionary work among charismatic Methodists in Cuba, I wanted to conduct research with both movements side-by-side. I was motivated by the question: Where are the poor? In other words, if the BCCs call themselves the church of the poor and yet many poor also are attracted to Pentecostal churches, where are the poor actually going? What is the socioeconomic constituency of each movement? In order to conduct this study, I needed to find the two movements working in close proximity to each other in order to keep

45. Kozloff, "Pope's Holy War Against Liberation Theology."
46. Goodman, "Church's Activist Clerics."
47. Pérez, "Base Communities," 71.
48. Mier, *Las Comunidades Eclesiales de Base*, 133–34.

constant as many variables as possible. Living in Cuernavaca at the time, I had a friend who had worked with the BCCs, and they gave me the initial contact to one of its members. I called her and asked permission to attend a Bible study; she agreed. I then explained that I would like to conduct some research. Once she asked the BCC members if this was acceptable to them, I began looking for a Pentecostal church. Driving up the main street through the neighborhood, I saw two large Pentecostal churches; I attended both of them on successive Sundays but did not really have a presence. One of the churches, however, caught my attention, because it was literally half a block from the Catholic Church. The simple proximity of the two churches was helpful for my methodology. I asked for an appointment with the pastor and permission to conduct the study. Subsequently, I learned that the Pentecostal church had cell groups throughout the neighborhood and beyond, which created helpful parallels to study two home Bible study movements in the same neighborhood, one Roman Catholic and one Pentecostal. In addition to attending worship services, Bible studies, and special services during Christmas and Holy Week, I also conducted surveys and interviews with key leaders. As I promised anonymity to my informers, I have therefore created pseudonyms for them.

This particular neighborhood was a working-class barrio on the outskirts of Cuernavaca. The capital of the state of Morelos, Cuernavaca enjoys a wonderful natural climate with an average yearly temperature oscillating between 70 and 90 degrees Fahrenheit. It has two main seasons, dry and rainy, with predictable rains coming in late May. It is about an hour from Mexico City on the southern slope of the altiplano heading toward the Pacific Ocean, and nearby are several volcanoes that produce thermal water and natural springs. The Aztec chief Moctezuma was known to come and bathe in nearby Oaxtepec, Morelos, in waters that were believed to have medicinal qualities. His rival, Hernán Cortés, created his plantation in Cuernavaca, the Palacio de Cortés, which still sits in downtown Cuernavaca. The city's climate and economic prosperity has attracted many migrants from nearby states as well as many of Mexico's elite, who have vacation homes here. After the devastating 1985 earthquake in Mexico City, many people lost their homes and moved to Cuernavaca permanently. As a result, Cuernavaca has grown tremendously without much city planning. Often, migrants will squat on a plot of land and build a shelter with tin, cardboard, or plastic tarps simply to have a place to live. Over time, they will build more permanent structures and, eventually, a home. The barrio that I studied began this way in the 1960s and is now a sprawling, working-class neighborhood that I have called Colonia de Alta Vista.

My Findings

As I began my research and got to know the people in the two movements, I discovered that most of the participants were migrants from the southern state of Guerrero and many were from the same village of Chichihualco. This was an example of chain migration, where one member of the village left, later writing or calling the family who followed. Through interviews and surveys, I actually discovered similarities between the two movements rather than the obvious differences. I observed that both the BCCs and the Pentecostals had small, home-based group Bible studies led by lay leaders, and I learned that this was very empowering for the individual lay leaders as well as the other participants who saw laity in this role. Also, I discovered that many of the leaders in the Pentecostal groups, and almost all in the BCC groups, were women. The studies in both groups were Bible-based, so both groups were learning the Bible. Reading was a challenge for the people in both groups as they came from humble backgrounds with limited formal schooling. There were a few illiterate people in both groups, although most had a least some schooling. So, the opportunity to read to oneself or to read out loud was a challenge, yet empowering. Reading develops other analytical and hermeneutical skills, one of which is to comprehend the reading and then interpret it in light of one's context. Speaking in public was another skill common to both groups. Individuals learned to find their voice and speak in front of others. At the same time, group members also had to wait their turn and listen to others' points of view, which developed empathy.

Often, these two groups were stereotyped as fitting into one category. For example, the BCCs were criticized as being political or a front for communism, while Pentecostals were considered apolitical or perhaps fundamentalist. However, in my observations, neither group fits neatly into one category. On the contrary, both empower laity, especially women, to develop reading and thinking skills, which are critical in a democracy. On this point, I can agree with the findings of Cecília Mariz, whose studies of BCCs and Pentecostals in northeastern Brazil found them both to help the poor cope with poverty.[49] My own research findings also support Douglas Peterson's claim that Pentecostalism encourages micro social change.[50] The Pentecostal church I studied was only involved with two social ministries: a food collection to assist families in need and a night school for adults to finish high school. The BCCs were more involved in broader political issues, such as supporting the Zapatistas in southern Mexico or encouraging

49. Mariz, *Coping with Poverty.*
50. Peterson, *Not by Power, Nor by Might,* 147.

parishioners to vote and inviting candidates from the political parties to share their political platforms. Yet both groups encouraged reading and em-powerment, the building blocks for the democratization of society.

While there were more similarities than I expected, I also found some differences. In my interviews and surveys, I discovered that, while both groups comprised primarily of migrants from the state of Guerrero, the members of the BCCs had come to Cuernavaca sooner (in the 1970s) and were much more established there. Starting off as squatters, they now had cinder-block houses in various stages of completion which were much sturdier than the those of the Pentecostal adherents, who tended to be much younger and more recent arrivals. Some of the Pentecostals rented their homes or were building their own as resources allowed. While neither group was wealthy by US standards, the BCC members were working poor with a higher income. The husbands had learned a trade, such as plumbing or masonry, or were taxi drivers who owned their own cars. Meanwhile, the Pentecostal men did not always have regular work or were just entering their trades.

The Pentecostal members also had more formal schooling; 42 percent had at least a ninth-grade education, as opposed to the BCC participants, of whom only 50 percent had reached the sixth grade. Most of the women BCC participants did not have a job outside the home (only 13 percent worked), although they did embroidery as a group to raise money and bring in some income. Thirty-nine percent of the Pentecostal women worked outside the home. The BCCs were almost entirely made up of women and had trouble attracting men. Even though most of the women were married, the husbands chose not to participate. They would sometimes come for the social occasions or the refreshments at the end, but they didn't participate in the Bible study. The BCCs were making a concerted effort to recruit younger people and had a separate Bible study led by one of the adults; this group had twelve youth, most of whom were children or grandchildren of the founders. The Pentecostal meetings, however, were more intergenera-tional, and sometimes there was a separate class in a different room for the children. The Pentecostals also had a Friday night youth service with loud, contemporary praise music and an average attendance of forty youth.

In sum, while there were differences, there were also similarities. Gen-erally speaking, the BCC meetings were more cerebral and had more open-ended questions that generally encouraged the participants to use critical thinking and analyze the scriptures in light of the current social and politi-cal reality. While also using scripture, the Pentecostal gatherings focused on converting new visitors as well as deepening the faith and biblical under-standing of existing participants. Political talk was discouraged as divisive, but participants did bring up personal issues or family difficulties, such as concerns with health, childrearing, and adapting to a modern lifestyle with working parents who were adapting to city life with the kids in school.

Closing Thoughts

Following up on David Stoll's prediction that certain countries would become majority Protestant by 2010, Rodney Stark and Buster G. Smith cite data from a 2007 Gallup Poll and determine that he was wrong. Not because Protestantism has not continued to grow; rather, Catholicism has responded to Protestant growth with a resurgence. Stark and Smith offer the hypothesis that where Protestantism has grown the most, Catholics have higher attendance and greater participation.[51] Therefore, rather than religion being a zero-sum game with limited pieces of pie that religious adherents must fight over, they believe that the dynamism of Protestants has made the Roman Catholic Church more active in meeting its people's spiritual needs. They point out the sixty million people in Latin America who are involved in the Charismatic movement as an example of the dynamism that has resulted from Protestantism's growth. They argue that any religion with the support of the state can resort to coercion. They believe that the religious pluralism has given the people more and different opportunities to express their faith and that the competition has been good for the Roman Catholic Church while also leading to the democratization of society.

Given all of the history that has gone before us and Stark and Smith's hypothesis, God is certainly ahead of us and working in a mysterious way. We may come from different traditions, with differing worship styles and theologies, but this pluralism may not be a bad thing. It may be forging a more democratic society in Latin America, and Mexico in particular. The diverse religious expressions may reach more people with different spiritual needs. What attracts and meets the needs of one person or family may not be fulfilling to another. In my ethnographic findings, the Pentecostals were appealing to newer migrants who were adjusting to the modern challenges of raising a family in the city. While not as overtly political or cerebral as the BCCs, the Pentecostal small groups were empowering lay people to read, interpret, speak in public, and learn new communication skills, all necessary to participate in a democratic society. While different people were attracted to one group or the other, I believe that the additional religious expression afforded more people a place to meet their spiritual and social

51. Stark and Smith, "Pluralism and the Churching of Latin America," 35–50.

needs in a way that will bring more people closer to God and Mexico closer to a democratic society.

Bibliography

Abbott, Walter. *The Documents of Vatican II*. New York: Guild, 1966.

Aponte, Edwin, and Miguel de la Torre, eds. *Handbook of Latino/a Theologies*. St. Louis: Chalice, 2006.

Arango, Obed. "The Evangelical (Protestant) Church in Mexico: A History of Its Involvement in Social Movements from 1870 to 2001." *American Baptist Quarterly* 22.2 (2003) 230.

Azevedo, Marcello de C. *Basic Ecclesial Communities in Brazil: The Challenge of a New Way of Being Church*. Washington, DC: Georgetown University Press, 1987.

Bastian, Jean-Pierre. *Protestantismo y Sociedad en México*. Mexico City: Casa Unida, 1983.

Bowen, Kurt. *Evangelicalism and Apostasy: The Evolution and Impact of Evangelicals in Modern Mexico*. Montreal: McGill-Queens, 1996.

Chavez, Leticia, and Giulio Girardi. *Don Sergio Méndez Arceo, Patriarca de la Solidaridad Libertadora: Testigo, Teólogo y Profeta de América Latina*. Mexico City: DABAR, 2000.

Cleary, Edward, and Hannah Stewart-Gambino. *Power, Politics, and Pentecostalism in Latin America*. Boulder, CO: Westview, 1998.

Clift, Eleanor. "With Rebel Leaders at His Side, Reagan Presses for Contra Aid." *Los Angeles Times*, March 4, 1986. Online. http://articles.latimes.com/1986-03-04/news/mn-15033_1_contra-aid.

Conferencia General del Episcopado Latinoamericano (CELAM). *Documento de Puebla: III Conference General del Episcopado Latinoamericano*. Santiago: Paulinas, 1979. Online. http://www.celam.org/doc_conferencias/Documento_Conclusivo_Puebla.pdf.

Diocese of Cuernavaca. *Don Sergio: Veinticinco Años de Obispo*. Cuernavaca, Mexico: Diócesis de Cuernavaca, 1976.

Emge, Donald Raymond. "Critical Thinking within a Religious Context: An Analysis of the History and Methodology of the Liberatory *Comunidades Eclesiales de Base*, Cuernavaca, Mexico, 1967 to 1990." PhD diss., Kansas State University, 1990.

Freire, Paulo. *Pedagogy of the Oppressed*. New York: Herder and Herder, 1970.

Gill, Kenneth D. *Toward a Contextualized Theology for the Third World: The Emergence and Development of Jesus' Name Pentecostalism in Mexico*. Berlin: Peter Lang, 1994.

Goodman, Walter. "Church's Activist Clerics: Rome Draws Line." *New York Times*, April 6, 1984. Online. http://www.nytimes.com/1984/09/06/world/church-s-activist-clerics-rome-draws-line.html?pagewanted=all.

Jayme, Luis. *Letter of Luis Jayme, OFM, San Diego, October 17, 1772*. Translated by Maynard Geiger. Los Angeles: Dawson's, 1970.

Kozloff, Nikolas. "Pope's Holy War Against Liberation Theology." *NACLA*, April 30, 2008. Online. http://nacla.org/news/popes-holy-war-against-liberation-theology.

"Libro Primero de los Bautismos." Microfilm Reel, MS-65. San Diego Mission Records, Diocese of San Diego, California.

López, Maclovio Gaxiola. *Historia de la Iglesia Apostólica de la Fe en Cristo Jesús de México*. Mexico: Libreria Latinoamericana, 1964.

Mariz, Cecilia. *Coping with Poverty: Pentecostals and Christian Base Communities in Brazil*. Philadelphia: Temple University Press, 1994.

Martin, David. *Pentecostalism: The World, Their Parish*. Oxford: Blackwell, 2002.

———. *Tongues of Fire: The Explosion of Protestantism in Latin America*. Oxford: Blackwell, 1990.

Mier, Sebastian. *Las Comunidades Eclesiales de Base: Los Pobres como Sujeto de Su Historia*, Mexico City: DABAR, 2001.

Miller, Daniel R. "Protestantism and Radicalism in Mexico from the 1860s to the 1930s." *Fides et Historia* 40.1 (2008) 43–66.

Nelson-Pallmeyer, Jack. *War Against the Poor: Low-Intensity Conflict and the Christian Faith*. Eugene, OR: Wipf & Stock, 2017.

Paul VI. *Lumen Gentium: Dogmatic Constitution of the Church*. Boston: St. Paul, 1964.

Pérez, Leopoldo. "Base Communities." In vol. 1 of *Hispanic American Religious Cultures*, edited by Miguel A. de la Torre, 67–71. Santa Barbara, CA: ABC-CLIO, 1999.

Peterson, Douglas. *Not by Power, Nor by Might: A Pentecostal Theology of Social Concern in Latin America*. Oxford: Regnum, 1996.

"Saint Junípero Serra: Spanish Franciscan Missionary." *Encyclopaedia Britannica*, July 20, 1998. Revised November 29, 2019. Online. https://www.britannica.com/biography/Saint-Junipero-Serra.

Segunda Conferencia General del Episcopado Latinoamericano. *Documentos de Finales de Medellín*. San Salvador: Universidad Centroamericana, 1968.

Segundo, Juan Luis. *La Liberación de la Teología*. Montevideo: Fundación de Cultural Universitaria, 1987.

———. *Teología de Liberación: Perspectivas*. Salamanca: Sígueme, 1971.

Silva, Ranulfo Peloso da, and Guillermina Hernández. "Personal Experiences." In *The Challenge of Basic Christian Communities: Papers from the International Ecumenical Congress of Theology, February 20–March 2, 1980, São Paulo, Brazil*, edited by Sergio Torres and John Eagleson, 214–15. Maryknoll, NY: Orbis, 1982.

Smith, Christian. *The Emergence of Liberation Theology: Radical Religion and Social Movement Theory*. Chicago: University of Chicago Press, 1991.

Stark, Rodney, and Buster Smith. "Pluralism and the Churching of Latin America." *Latin American Politics and Society* 54 (2012) 35–50.

Stoll, David. *Is Latin America Turning Protestant? The Politics of Evangelical Growth*. Berkeley: University of California Press, 1990.

Synan, Vinson. *The Holiness-Pentecostal Tradition: Charismatic Movements in the Twentieth Century*. Grand Rapids: Eerdmans, 1971.

———. "William Seymour." *Christian History* 19.1 (2000) 17–19.

Velasco, José Luis. *Mexico: Labyrinth of Faith*. New York: General Board of Global Ministries, 2002.

Wingeier-Rayo, Philip. "Hoover C. Willis." In *Historical Dictionary of Methodism*, edited by Charles Yrigoyen and Susan Warrick, 191–92. Lanham, MD: Scarecrow, 1996.

———. "Mission System." In vol. 1 of *Hispanic American Religious Cultures*, edited by Miguel A. de la Torre, 367–73. Santa Barbara, CA: ABC-CLIO, 1999.

———. "A Third Phase of Christianity: Reflections on One Hundred Years of Pentecostalism in Mexico." In *Latin America: Spirit Powered Movements Past, Present, and Future*, edited by Vinson Synan et al., 1–24. Vol. 2 of *Global Renewal Christianity*. Lake Mary, FL: Charisma, 2016.

PART TWO

Ecumenism of Blood

3

Ecumenical Cooperation in Contexts of Crisis: The Case of Chile under Military Dictatorship (1973–1990)

JUAN SEPÚLVEDA

AS IN ALL LATIN American countries, Catholicism was the only religion allowed in Chilean territory during the colonial period. After the achievement of national independence, Catholicism remained the official religion for more than a century, a period in which Protestantism, with the support of liberal political leaders, slowly gained the right to be "tolerated" as the private religious practices of foreign residents. Even so, non-Catholic immigrants were considered "dissidents," and they did not enjoy the fullness of civil rights until the so-called "lay [or secular] laws" (civil registry, civil marriage, and lay cemeteries) were approved between 1882 and 1884.[1]

In 1925, a new constitution established the separation between church and state, legalizing religious freedom. However, the Catholic Church retained a privileged legal status until 1999, when a common legal framework for the operation of all religious organizations was established.[2]

Despite the restrictions mentioned, the main denominations deriving from the reform were already beginning to enter the country by the mid-nineteenth century. While the first Protestant churches entered the country in connection with European immigration (Lutherans and Anglicans),

1. Sepúlveda, *De Peregrinos*, 28; see also Mecham, *Church and State*, 246–74.

2. Sepúlveda, *De Peregrinos*, 34.

others came later with a missionary purpose (Methodists, Presbyterians, Baptists, etc.). At the beginning of the twentieth century, a Pentecostal revival took place, mainly within the local Methodist Church, giving rise to a popular and dynamic indigenous Pentecostal movement. Later on in the twentieth century, other evangelical and Pentecostal denominations began their missionary work in Chile.[3] So emerged the current picture of Chilean Christianity, with 67.37 percent of the population identifying as Catholic and 16.62 percent belonging to the numerous Protestant or evangelical churches, mostly Pentecostals.[4] It is worth noting the presence of Orthodox churches which, although statistically less significant, are another actor within the Chilean ecumenical scene.

Until 1970, the impact of the ecumenical movement in Chile involved only the relations among the different Protestant and evangelical churches. In the context of the Roman Catholic Church's numerical, cultural, and political dominance, the evangelical and Protestant churches needed to work together to achieve some degree of influence on government authorities in order to move forward on the path toward a religiously-neutral state and a religiously-pluralistic society. In contrast, relations among Protestantism and Roman Catholicism continued to be marked by competition rather than by cooperation and mutual recognition.

The majority of Catholic clergy considered the missionary work of non-Catholic churches and religions to be a threat against the cultural and religious identity of the country, one that would inevitably lead to nonbelief (atheism or agnosticism). Such a view on the clergy's part generated conditions for discriminatory and intolerant behavior by the Catholic population against non-Catholic religious groups.

Meanwhile, the evangelical minority—which became mostly Pentecostal during the twentieth century—grew in resentment for what they perceived as discriminatory treatment ("We are treated as second-class citizens"). In addition, they interpreted such treatment as evidence that the country's Catholic majority was Christian in name only ("nominal Christians"). Thus, far from being seen as brothers and sisters in Christ, Catholic believers were considered non-believers and therefore targets of evangelization.[5]

Given the fact that some members of the Catholic Church's episcopate in Chile were quite active in the proceedings of Vatican Council II, the episcopate's plenary assembly made the decision as early as February

---

3. Sepúlveda, *De Peregrinos*, 47–115.

4. Instituto Nacional de Estadísticas, *Síntesis de Resultados*, 15.

5. Pape, "El Ecumenismo," 56.

1965 to promote ecumenism in Chile. A few months later, the Episcopal Commission on Ecumenism and the National Department on Faith and Ecumenism were created.[6] It was necessary, however, to wait until various political factors created the conditions for those emerging ecumenical relations to gain public visibility.

The first of these political factors that had an unexpected impact on the development of local ecumenism was the 1970 election of President Salvador Allende. A socialist politician who did not hide his atheism, Allende won the presidency on behalf of the "Popular Unity," a left-wing political coalition that included all secularist political sectors, among them the Communist Party. His election raised doubts as to whether he would respect the tradition of celebrating the presidential change of command with a Catholic *Te Deum* in the Roman Catholic cathedral of Santiago. Allende expressed his willingness to maintain that tradition but asked Cardinal Silva Henríquez to invite representatives of other Christian churches and religions to take part in the ceremony as well—a way to recognize the country's religious plurality.

Cardinal Silva Henríquez welcomed the request, and from that point forward, the Catholic *Te Deum*, which is held on two occasions—the presidential change of command and the commemoration of national independence—became an ecumenical event.[7] This new ecumenical character of the *Te Deum* meant that Protestant pastors and Orthodox priests participated in the Bible readings and prayers, while the homily remained a responsibility of the Catholic Archbishop of Santiago. It is worth noting that this change also had an interreligious dimension, as representatives of the Jewish and Muslim communities were also invited to pray. The beginning of these ecumenical liturgical practices generated the need for an official body of coordination among the churches. This initial communication between Catholic, Protestant, and Orthodox ministers is what eventually led to the creation of the Chilean Ecumenical Fraternity (*Fraternidad Ecuménica de Chile* [FRAECH]).

A second political factor was the growing division and polarization within Chilean society that generated the deep social and economic reforms promoted by Allende's government in an international context still profoundly marked by the Cold War. Relations between supporters and opponents of the government became increasingly violent, so much that, both in the press and in everyday conversation, the fear of civil war began to surface. The seriousness of this situation became a stimulus to strengthen

6. Muñoz, "El Ecumenismo," 181–82.

7. Lagos, *Crisis*, 63.

the emerging ecumenical relations established to coordinate the ecumenical *Te Deum*. Thus, on August 8, 1973, FRAECH was formally organized. One month later, at noon on September 9, 1973, an ecumenical public meeting to pray for peace was held in Constitution Square, in front of the Presidential Palace. The invitation came from the Catholic Church, various Protestant and Pentecostal churches, the Orthodox Church of Antioch, and the Jewish community. Given the deep political polarization of the time, convening this meeting seems to have created some concern on the part of President Allende about the risks of possible partisan use of the meeting. In response, Cardinal Silva Henríquez gave assurances of the meeting's religious nature, in support of the search for a nonviolent solution.[8]

This public ecumenical meeting, unprecedented in the religious history of Chile, was at the same time my first public ecumenical experience. I was then fifteen years old. Together with a small group of brothers and sisters, we left Sunday school at our church in a neighborhood on the south side of Santiago and accompanied our pastor to take part in this public prayer meeting.

A third and more determining political factor was the military coup, which took place just two days after this ecumenical public prayer meeting. In addition to the violent overthrow of the Allende government, the forced closure of Parliament, and the prohibition of political parties, the new military authorities imposed a series of measures which included: dismantling social and trade union organizations; eliminating benefits and social policies (many of which had been institutionalized even before the government of Allende); liberalizing the economy (including eliminating controls on the prices of food and other essential commodities); and brutally suppressing any attempt to resist or oppose this new state of affairs.

During the first days, the curfew and the eradication of the right to assemble affected the operation of churches. Soon, however, people understood that the new prohibitions did not eliminate the freedom to conduct religious services. This allowed churches to become a relatively protected space to meet and encounter others, not only for their regular members but also for neighbors shocked and frightened by the nation's prevailing circumstances.

On September 14, 1973, the same group of ecclesiastical authorities who had called for the day of prayer the previous Sunday made a public statement calling churches to pray "for all the fallen, for their families . . . and for a real respect for all human rights."[9] At the same time, they initiated

---

8. Lagos, *Crisis*, 97.
9. Lagos, *Crisis*, 124.

contact with the military authorities, asking them to allow the joint and organized action of churches in order to provide humanitarian assistance to those individuals and families most affected by the circumstances. The World Council of Churches (WCC) commissioned Mrs. Annie Went, director of the Dutch Interchurch Agency for Refugees, and Dr. Theo Tschuy, the Swiss former secretary of WCC's Latin American Desk, on a fact-finding mission. This delegation arrived in Santiago on September 25, 1973, lending international support to the efforts of the local ecclesiastical authorities.[10]

On October 3, 1973, the military junta authorized the National Committee of Refugees (CONAR) to operate for three months to assist refugees from other Latin American countries in leaving Chile under protection. A few days later, on October 9, 1973, these contacts led to the formation of the Committee of Cooperation for Peace in Chile (COPACHI), more commonly known as the Comité Pro Paz.[11] Even though, from a legal point of view, the latter operated under the cover of the Catholic Church of Santiago, both committees were ecumenical initiatives involving the Catholic, Orthodox, Protestant, and Pentecostal churches as well. These two committees also had the support of international ecumenical bodies coordinated by the World Council of Churches, which, by December 1973, had created the Chile Emergency Desk under Rev. Charles Harper's leadership. The Chile Emergency Desk soon became the Human Rights Resources Office for Latin America (HRROLA).[12]

In the context of the search for international support and legitimacy of the new military authorities, COPACHI's work was rapidly becoming a nuisance. Thus, the work during the first two years took place in a climate of constant pressure, not only on the part of the military regime but also on the part of sectors of the churches who backed the coup and the permanence of the military in power. Toward the end of 1975, these pressures were intolerable, with General Pinochet himself threatening to shut COPACHI down. The committee did indeed dissolve in December 1975, and on January 1, 1976, Cardinal Silva Henríquez signed the decree that created the Vicaría de la Solidaridad and gave continuity to the humanitarian work.[13]

The fact that the Vicaría de la Solidaridad was an internal pastoral structure of the Catholic Archdiocese of Santiago did not, however, mean the end of the work's ecumenical dimension. Although the formal

10. Harper, *O Acompanhamento*, 31; Bastías, *Sociedad Civil*, 61–66.

11. Bastías, *Sociedad Civil*, 75–88.

12. Bastías, *Sociedad Civil*, 73–74.

13. Valech, *Vicaría*, 54.

representation of other churches ended, the pluralistic character of its staff as well as the support of international ecumenical bodies remained.

While the military repression affected political activists and leaders of social and trade union organizations more selectively, the main impact of the military regime on the general public was the rise in prices and the accelerated increase of unemployment. Both of these resulted from the neoliberal economic measures imposed by the dictatorship. In the poorest urban sectors, this soon led to hunger and malnutrition. This was the challenge that motivated the first local ecumenical responses. Local church buildings, whether Catholic or Protestant, were used to house soup kitchens to ensure at least one meal a day, mainly for children and the elderly. Ecumenical groups of women volunteers were organized to carry out the work of collecting food donations, cooking meals, and serving tables.

The boys and girls being cared for in the soup kitchens were exposed to a variety of risks associated with impoverishment and the general climate of uncertainty and hopelessness (for example, an increase in drug addiction and youth crime). This situation raised the need to provide activities that would offer them emotional support, opportunities for play and recreation, and ways to strengthen their ethical formation. Responding to this need were young people who volunteered, forming ecumenical groups that organized informal play groups and, subsequently, "urban colonies," that is to say, recreational activity programs carried out in their own neighborhoods during the school holiday period.

Soon, this methodology of creating volunteer ecumenical groups was replicated in response to other problems the community was experiencing. Groups linked to local churches that were more active in a given territory—usually including Catholics, Protestants/evangelicals, and people without active membership in any church—were multiplying not only in the poor neighborhoods of Santiago but also in other cities around the country. These groups included workshops for women, housing committees, health committees, informal schools for parents, collective or group buying cooperatives, etc.

The development of these ecumenical practices of solidarity at the grassroots level was facilitated by the example and public impact of the ecumenical action carried out with the direct support of the ecclesiastical authorities. The mission of the institutions initially created to defend human rights was extended, and new entities were created to support the local ecumenical groups with training and funding, channeling resources provided by international ecumenical agencies of cooperation. So, in addition to the Vicaría de la Solidaridad, other ecumenical institutions were launched. Among them, the *Fundación de Ayuda Social de las Iglesias*

Cristianas (FASIC—Social Aid Foundation of Christian Churches), which, among other programs, gave continuity to the mandate of CONAR,[14] and the *Servicio Evangélico para el Desarrollo* (SEPADE—Evangelical Service for Ecumenical Development).[15]

Face-to-face contact and cooperation among Catholics and Evangelicals facilitated the overcoming of prejudices and stereotypes of the past and contributed, little by little, to their mutual recognition as brothers and sisters in Christ. Thus, there soon appeared a new dimension of this local ecumenism: praying, reading, and reflecting on the Word of God in ecumenical liturgies convened on special liturgical dates or in response to critical situations. During this period, the observance of the Week of Christian Unity, promoted and organized by FRAECH, had the highest level of participation ever, mainly in Santiago, with ecumenical prayer meetings held in various neighborhoods, whether in Protestant churches or Catholic parishes.

In 1983, when a movement of massive protests began demanding the return to democracy, political repression increased, and this time in a much less selective fashion; people were arrested for taking part in the demonstrations while many leaders were internally exiled to quite isolated places within Chile. Although the demonstrations were expected to be nonviolent, the repressive response generated clashes that often resulted in the death of some protesters and a greater number of injured people. In this context, the plight of those who were detained, internally exiled, or injured as well as the funerals for those who died became occasions for frequent ecumenical visits, liturgies, and vigils that involved grassroots Christians as well as ecclesiastical authorities. Some examples of these are the following:

> 9 August 1983—Thousands of people marched through the center of Santiago carrying a flower and a candle. They came from all kinds of backgrounds and had widely differing ideas: there were Catholics and Protestants, people of other religions and no religion at all . . . people from all sections of society—slum dwellers, workers, professional people, students, the upper classes—and all age groups. Yet different as they were, they were all singing the same songs: "Gracias a la vida" and "Escucha, hermano, la canción de la alegría." They were strangers, yet the sense of community was overwhelming; everyone joined hands; everyone was smiling; many could not contain tears of emotion. They had a common objective—the defense of life—and it left no room for argument. Even though many were not Christians,

14. Garcés and Nicholls, *Para una Historia.*
15. Sepúlveda, *Servicio Evangélico.*

they could identify with one sentence: "I came that you may have life and have it abundantly" (John 10:10, ESV).

4 September 1984—La Victoria shantytown. A priest, André Jarlan, was killed by a shot fired by a policeman. The news spread like wildfire, kindling emotions in the shantytown. Anything could have happened. But someone, perhaps a lot of people, had the idea of expressing their feelings by placing lighted candles in the trees and in the streets. And more and more candles appeared, lit by people who differed in many ways yet who lit these candles as a symbol of their shared longing for peace. . . . And for hours La Victoria, which is a violent district, became the island of peace its inhabitants longed for. People who walked in fear and trembling through its streets could walk there now in greater safety than ever before. There was a light to guide them. For many, this symbolized the light of Christ: "I have come into the world as light, so that whoever believes in me may not remain in darkness" (John 12:46, ESV).[16]

Early June [1986]—Gustavo Villalobos, a lawyer, and Dr. Ramiro Olivares, both employed at the Vicaría de la Solidaridad; Alvaro Reyes and Ramón Rojas, both doctors; and Claudio Muñoz, a medical auxiliary in a private clinic, completed a month in prison. The crime they were accused of is assisting a man suffering from gunshot wounds who came to the Vicaría de la Solidaridad for help. While they were in prison, there were many demonstrations of solidarity: symbolic gestures, statements, marches, fasting and—an unprecedented event—an ecumenical service in support of this Catholic agency attended by more than five hundred people and held at the invitation of a group of Protestant churches, perhaps the most significant ecumenical event in Chile's history. What is at stake here is the right to defend life itself.[17]

Also worth mentioning is the "Campaign of Prayer for Life, Peace, and Reconciliation," which culminated in an "Open Letter to General Pinochet" from the Christian Fellowship of Churches on August 29, 1986.[18] The Christian Fellowship of Churches (*Confraternidad Cristiana de Iglesias* [CCI]) was organized in 1981 by ten Protestant churches, including some

16. Sepúlveda, "Mission," 413–14.

17. Sepúlveda, "Mission," 412.

18. Harper, *O Acompanhamento*, 41–42; Atria, "Campaña," 23–27.

Pentecostal ones and the Orthodox Church of the Patriarchate of Antioch, all working in close cooperation with the Catholic Church.

What I have said so far demonstrates how under the exceptional conditions of Chilean society during the 1973–1990 dictatorship there arose a movement of intense cooperation and ecumenical fraternity among Catholic and Protestant Christians, both at the official and the grassroot levels, and this movement played a significant role in the process of rearticulating civil society. One permanent impact of the exceptional ecumenical practices under the dictatorship is that Catholic and Protestant-Evangelical churches in Chile have moved into a new relationship of mutual recognition and respect, overcoming the competitive and rather belligerent relationships that had previously existed.

During the first decade after the return to democracy, this atmosphere of improved interconfessional relations contributed to creating a dialogue with the government and the parliament which aimed to establish a common legal framework for all religious organizations. Such framework would eliminate the legal inequality between the Roman Catholic Church and other churches and religions active in the country. As mentioned in the introduction, this process culminated in 1999 with the promulgation of a new law on religious organizations. Enforcing this law implied a number of other administrative changes that resulted in the progressive deepening of the state's lay character and pluralism in relations among the state and the various churches and religious organizations working in Chile.

Also in 1999, on the eve of the celebration of the Great Jubilee of the Year 2000, an unprecedented ecumenical agreement was achieved. As a result of a process coordinated by FRAECH, a group of churches (including the Catholic Church and some Protestant and Pentecostal churches) signed a declaration of Mutual Recognition of Trinitarian Baptism based on the 1982 BEM (*Baptism, Eucharist, and Ministry*) Document.[19]

At the grassroots level, however, the significant ecumenical practices that evolved under the dictatorship did not last for long after the beginning of the democratic normalization process in 1990. With the rule of law restored, it was no longer necessary for churches to serve as "safe havens" as they had done under the dictatorship, greatly influencing the gradual disappearance of these practices. On the other hand, in order to ensure democratic governance and national reconciliation, the first democratic governments decided to downplay the role of an organized civil society despite the fact that it had been so decisive in ending the military regime.[20]

19. Errázuriz, "Documento de Santiago."
20. Bastías, *Sociedad Civil*, 281–312.

From the internal point of view of the churches, another important factor seems to have been the obvious difficulty the ecclesiastical leadership had in reassessing and reorganizing their role in an open society. For churches, this meant a loss of prominence within the public sphere and public deliberation. The resulting uncertainty and confusion on the part of the ecclesiastical leadership prevented them from taking a more active role in guiding their communities through rethinking the new ecumenical practices that were born under dictatorship in a now-democratic context.

Therefore, what happened was that churches entered their own process of "normalization," returning to their traditional pastoral strategies,[21] as if the rich experiences of ecumenical cooperation born under the dictatorship had been merely a parenthesis in their lives, justified only by the exceptional character of the political situation. Although cordial coexistence among Catholicism and Protestantism has become the norm, actual ecumenical cooperation on pastoral and social issues continues to be rather exceptional.

Bibliography

Atria, Cecilia. "Campaña de Oración por la Vida, la Paz y la Reconciliación." *Evangelio y Sociedad* 4 (1987) 23–27.

Bastías, Manuel. *Sociedad Civil en Dictadura: Relaciones Transnacionales, Organizaciones y Socialización Política en Chile.* Santiago: Universidad Alberto Hurtado, 2013.

Errázuriz, Francisco, et al. "Documento de Santiago: Acuerdo sobre el Bautismo." *Iglesia. cl—Conferencia Episcopal de Chile*, May 19, 1999. Online. http://documentos. iglesia.cl/documento.php?id=594.

Garcés, Mario, and Nancy Nicholls. *Para una Historia de los Derechos Humanos en Chile: Historia Institucional de la Fundación de Ayuda Social de las Iglesias Cristiana, FASIC, 1975–1991.* Santiago: LOM, 2005.

Harper, Charles. *O Acompanhamento: Ecumenical Action for Human Rights in Latin America 1970–1990.* Geneva: WCC, 2006.

Instituto Nacional de Estadísticas. *Síntesis de Resultados: Censo 2012.* Santiago: INE, 2012.

Lagos, Humberto. *Crisis de la Esperanza: Religión y Autoritarismo en Chile.* Santiago: Presor-Lar, 1988.

Mecham, J. Lloyd. *Church and State in Latin America: A History of Politico-Ecclesiastical Relations.* Chapel Hill: University of North Carolina Press, 1934.

Muñoz, Humberto. "El Ecumenismo en Chile." *Teología y Vida* 20 (1979) 179–99.

Ossa, Manuel. *Iglesias Evangélicas y Derechos Humanos en Tiempos de Dictadura: La Confraternidad Cristiana de Iglesias 1981–1989.* Santiago: Fundación Konrad Adenauer-Centro Ecuménico Diego de Medellín, 1999.

Pape, Carlos. "'El Ecumenismo en Chile': Informe Presentado en el Primer Encuentro Latinoamericano de Ecumenismo, CELAM, Bogotá, 19–23 de enero de 1970." *Teología y Vida* 9 (1970) 55–58.

21. Parker, "Religión," 35.

Parker, Cristian. "Religión, Cultura y Política en América Latina: Nuevos Enfoques." In *Religión, Política y Cultura en América Latina: Nuevas Miradas,* edited by Cristian Parker, 13–73. Santiago: Universidad de Santiago de Chile-Instituto de Estudios Avanzados, 2012.

Sepúlveda, Juan. *De Peregrinos a Ciudadanos: Breve Historia del Cristianismo Evangélico en Chile.* Santiago: Fundación Konrad Adenauer-Facultad Evangélica de Teología, 1999.

———. "La Defensa de los Derechos Humanos como Experiencia Ecuménica." *Persona y Sociedad* 3 (2003) 21–28.

———. "Mission in Christ's Way in Chile." *International Review of Mission* 300 (1986) 410–22.

Sepúlveda, Juan, ed. *Servicio Evangélico para el Desarrollo: Treinta Años Soñando con Porfía.* Concepción: SEPADE, 2005.

Valech, Sergio, ed. *Vicaría de la Solidaridad: Historia de su Trabajo Social.* Santiago: Paulinas, 1991.

4

Bishops Saving "Singers":
Ecumenism of Blood in Pinochet's Chile

MICHAEL L. COOPER-WHITE

The Horrific Events of Another September 11th

SINCE THE FALL OF 2001, for millions in the United States and around the
world, *September 11th* has conveyed a singular meaning. But twenty-eight
years earlier, there was another September 11th of equal magnitude in the
long, skinny South American nation of Chile. On *el once* ("the eleventh" in
Spanish), as it is still known there and elsewhere, Chilean Air Force Hawker
Hunter aircraft bombed the Moneda presidential palace in Santiago. On
September 11, 1973, tanks rolled throughout the capital and converged
on the Plaza de Armas as a military coup led by Army General Augusto
Pinochet toppled the democratically-elected government of socialist president Salvador Allende. Reported in official government press releases as
having been a suicide during the final moments before the Moneda fell into
military hands, Allende's death is believed by many Chileans to have been at
the hands of those perpetrating the *golpe del estado* (military coup).

Hailed initially by millions of *chilenos* as saviors providing relief from
the economic scarcity and social chaos resulting from Allende's three-year
presidency, the new military *junta* quickly revealed its true colors as it
unleashed an unprecedented reign of terror. Under the banner of "order"

and "liberty," the Pinochet regime launched wave after wave of repressive measures. A nighttime *toque de queda*, or curfew, was imposed and lasted for several years, under which anyone caught on the streets was subject to summary arrest or being shot without questioning. Thousands suspected of being leftist Allende-supporters were taken into custody and tortured and then they *disappeared*. Conservative estimates are that more than three thousand Chilean citizens and others were snatched up by the dreaded DINA[1] secret police and executed. For months after the coup, cadavers were routinely spotted floating down the Mapocho river in Santiago and other parts of the country.

Within days of the unleashing of Pinochet's reign of murderous mayhem, a handful of Christian leaders began to respond. Most prominent were the Roman Catholic cardinal Raúl Silva Henríquez, archbishop of Santiago, and the Reverend Helmut Frenz, bishop of the Evangelical Lutheran Church in Chile. Together with others, these two courageous Christian bishops formed the Committee for Peace (*Comité Pro Paz*), which began sheltering and offering succor to those fleeing for their lives. By the hundreds, former Allende government officials and others being persecuted by the junta's forces of terror were spirited into and granted political asylum by embassies of countries willing to receive them as refugees. The Committee's office soon was besieged also by relatives and friends of the "disappeared" (*desaparecidos*) who had been picked up and hauled away in dark-windowed vans and cars bearing the dreaded DINA investigators. One after another, those who had escaped with their lives came telling horrific stories of torture at the hands of the DINA and uniformed military or police officers. Their cases were carefully documented in order that the truth of what was occurring in Chile would be preserved, in hopes of someday bringing to justice in Chile or international courts the perpetrators of brutality that, while on a much smaller scale, mirrored the atrocities of Nazi Germany.

Case Study in Torture: A Tale of Terror

In his autobiography, *Mi Vida Chilena*, Frenz shares an extended, gripping account of the kind of torture that was being perpetrated upon thousands of Chileans from all walks of life and in all social strata. What was particularly surprising and somewhat unusual about the events recounted below is that, in this case, the victim was a foreigner from a European nation. In general, the DINA and Chilean armed forces tried to avoid harming those

---

1. DINA stands for *Dirección de Inteligencia Nacional* (National Intelligence Directorate).

who carried North American or European passports, lest the citizenry in nations deemed friendly to Chile demand that their governments intervene and perhaps reduce economic subsidies and military support. The reluctance of German diplomats, which Frenz amply documented, testifies to the widespread international hesitation to intervene and come to the aid of the thousands undergoing atrocities at the hands of the Pinochet regime.

In his autobiography, Frenz recounts:

> Soon, I begin to receive alarming news from my ministerial colleagues in the southern cities of Puerto Montt, Osorno, Valdivia, Temuco, and Concepción, and to the north from Valparaíso, regarding numerous criminal acts that are being perpetrated by soldiers against *Unidad Popular*[2] followers. They also have discovered the necessity of hiding persons in their homes and churches. Our minister to German seafarers in Valparaíso, Martin Posselt, informs me in early October 1973 about the dramatic situation in the Port of Valparaíso. The Chilean navy has come to be known in these days as especially adept at brutal torture. In the Valparaíso port, they are using old ships as prison camps. The conditions in these torture ships are out of control inasmuch as no civilians have access to them. Martin Posselt has become aware that, in one of the many ships, a German citizen named Werner Simon is being held prisoner. His relatives have informed us about his detention and subsequent transfer to the torture craft, Lebu. In the Committee for Peace, we have already become aware, from eyewitnesses, of the inhumane and cruel treatment aboard the Lebu. One simple method is to force male prisoners to lie naked on the deck in the blazing sun until their skin burns, cracks, and becomes infected. This torture persists for days on end, with increasing suffering, which also renders nighttime sleep impossible. Here, we are dealing with a method of torture that leaves no one with dirty hands. For systematic torture utilizing electricity, prisoners are taken from the ships to Valparaíso's Naval College, known as the place of education for Chile's elite. It can be said that now it is also a place of special, "elite" treatment. From this torture center, Werner Simon, in grave condition with broken bones, was transported back to the ship.
>
> The fact that Werner Simon is a German citizen gives me the opportunity to intervene by means of contacting the consul general in Valparaíso, beseeching him to appeal to the local

2. The *Unidad Popular* was the coalition of leftist parties that Allende's government represented.

military authorities for Simon's immediate release. I happen to know that this consul general is in sympathy with the military regime. He was very reserved in our first contact, informing me that Mr. Simon has not registered with the German consulate and therefore is not recognized as a German citizen residing in Chile. It takes a goodly measure of pressure to motivate the consul general to intervene with Chilean military officials on behalf of a suspected "German communist." Finally, together with our local Valparaíso pastor, Jochen Harder, I pay a visit to the consul general. It appears that he has investigated and learned more about Simon's situation, so that when we report what we have heard, he declares emphatically, "And that's only the half of it! They also burned his testicles a bit. As for the others, they are free to sit on the deck and sunbathe."

In order to fairly assess such conclusions by an official representative of the Federal Republic of Germany, one must read Mr. Simon's own official declaration, which he wrote at my request for Amnesty International shortly after his release. His testimony is both frightening and compelling. I was among the first to hear Simon's firsthand account of suffering on the Lebu and at the Naval College of Valparaíso. I will never forget how painful it was—it is, in fact, nearly impossible to express with words such suffering at the hands of torturers. Insofar as there are no words with which to adequately acknowledge such suffering, often we simply wept together while holding each other tightly.

Werner Simon's release after thirty-nine days of imprisonment accompanied by torture surely resulted from crucial interventions, albeit overdue, on the part of the German consul general. Simon was able to go home for only a few days, after which he is required to appear daily at a police station. He is constantly afraid of being detained again and is also scared for his two adult children who could be taken in his stead. Consequently, we decide that we will sequester both Simon and his children and seek their asylum in the German ambassador's residence in Santiago. This will be difficult inasmuch as Ambassador Lüdde-Neurath has refused to receive refugees. In a brief conversation, he dismissed my suggestion [that he grant political asylum] on the basis that, as a representative of the German public, he has received no authorization from Bonn for such action. Calmly and objectively, I respond that, in that case, we must concern ourselves with such instructions! "That I will leave to you," was his response, not counting that I would quickly turn my verbal proposal into action.

The German embassy is in the city center on the seventh floor of an office building. One can only ascend to it by elevator, and entrance thereto is easy to monitor. While it may be possible on occasion to ascend from the second or third floor, as the doors open on the seventh floor, one is faced immediately with an armed German guard who inquires regarding the visitor's intentions. Upon even hearing the word "asylum," the German guard pushes the "down" button, and the elevator goes back down. In other words, it is virtually impossible to get into the German embassy without official approval.

The same is true of the "international territory" of the ambassador's residence. This fabulous mansion is located on grounds resembling a park, encircled behind by a high wall with an iron grate fence in front. Its entrance area is guarded by two large white dogs with black spots. While these two dogs may have originally been symbols of social prestige, now their purpose clearly is to intimidate anyone who might consider gaining entrance to the ambassador's residence. I consider this a huge scandal.

Something similarly scandalous exists even at the embassy of the papal nuncio, the Vatican's official representative. It too sits on a side street behind a high wall. Its entrance is a tall and imposing gate. If one pushes the doorbell, the gate opens slightly, and clearly visible is a Chilean policeman armed with a submachine gun. Allowing an active Chilean police officer on its territory signifies in essence that the Nunciatura has given up its status as international territory.

On the other hand, we are able to verify that all the Latin American embassies, in accordance with longstanding tradition, remain open to refugees for whom diplomatic asylum is absolutely essential in order to escape political persecution. Likewise, nearly all the European embassies are offering diplomatic asylum to persecuted Chileans. Deserving special mention are the embassies of Eastern European countries, which in the immediate aftermath of the military coup, broke diplomatic relations with the Chilean military junta. Their buildings and international sites now are being administered at the hands of friendly states. Such is the case with the several buildings of the Cuban embassy over which the Swedish flag now flies. The Russian embassy is under Indian management, that of Poland under the Swiss. As expected, official representatives of the East German government have also been withdrawn, handing their properties over into Finnish hands. It is precisely these embassies under third-party jurisdiction that now play such an important role, inasmuch as the administering governments oppose the military dictatorship and extend compassion to the Chileans being persecuted. The Latin American embassies find themselves inundated with refugees in the immediate aftermath of the coup: the embassies of Mexico, Argentina, Venezuela, and the Central American countries are bursting at the seams with Chilean citizens seeking asylum. When the military command-ers discover this asylum-seeking rush, they immediately put in place permanent guards in front of all the embassy entrances. Within a few days after the coup, it is even more difficult for persecuted Chileans to avail themselves of the saving grace of diplomatic asylum, since all the embassies are now under heavy military guard. As a result, those being persecuted turn increas-ingly for help to the churches.

Word spreads quickly among persecuted Chileans in search of refuge which churches offer hope of assistance. Apparently, our Evangelical Lutheran churches are reputed to be places of asylum. During the weeks of October and November, so many refuge-seeking Chileans approach us, and it is absolutely essen-tial that we seek to protect them from the soldiers in pursuit. We soon find our sites unable to hide and attend to so many. Of course, all this must occur in secrecy, which understandably becomes very difficult given the fact that many of our church's members, including governing council members, are in sympa-thy with the perpetrators of the military coup. Time and again, we must also hide persecuted persons in our own homes. So it is that my family now must regularly hide persecuted Chileans in our parsonage on Lota Avenue, and of course, we must also feed and attend them. On one occasion, we were "offering hospital-ity" to nineteen persons. They live with constant fear of being found, tortured, and executed. I am in constant search of means by which to clandestinely gain their entrance into one embassy or another. I am indignant at the attitude of the West German ambassador, who continues to deny diplomatic asylum, giving me two reasons: (1) The GDR does not recognize "diplomatic asylum"—the concept is a purely Latin American fiction; and (2) he knows these "types" from his sojourn in Uruguay, and they are all *Tupamaros* [revolutionaries] who do not merit protection.[3]

Faced with the German ambassador's refusal to voluntarily grant dip-lomatic asylum to one of his nation's own citizens, Bishop Frenz and his

3. Frenz, *Mi Vida Chilena*, 167–71 (my translation).

associates remembered the scriptural admonition to be "wise as serpents and innocent as doves" (Matt 10:16, NRSV). Thanks to their serpentine wisdom, the Simons and a handful of other expatriates, together with hundreds of *chilenos*, were rescued from torture and saved from brutal deaths. In the Simons' specific case, Frenz took the risky measure of approaching the soldiers guarding the German embassy entrance in his Volkswagen van in order to distract them. As he did so by night, while the embassy gate was left unguarded momentarily by the unsuspecting and distracted soldiers, the Simons went sauntering down the sidewalk as if locals out for an evening stroll and slipped into the ambassador's residence! Once inside and thereby on the "official territory" of their homeland, the Simons could no longer be refused asylum.

Ecumenism of Martyrdom, or "Of the Blood"

In the same way that, a decade later, I would observe and play a small role in El Salvador at the height of its civil war, I was privileged as a young seminarian in Chile to have a front-row seat witnessing what this conference's planners referred to as "the ecumenism of martyrdom." Given the Chilean junta's frantic desire to court and continue in the favor of the US and European governments, those of us who carried American or European passports were in relatively minimal personal danger—though, of course, when bullets start flying from machine guns, there may not be prior request to see *carnets* (identity cards) or *pasaportes*. Indeed, few Americans or Europeans were actually martyred in Chile, though quite a few—including the US Lutheran intern who preceded me the year before—were spirited into their embassies or out of the country when accused of being communist sympathizers aiding those being persecuted. But many of those we sheltered and aided were martyred later themselves or had sisters, brothers, mothers, or fathers who disappeared. Many of those brave Chileans' bodies remain today undiscovered in unknown final resting places.

A German-born expatriate serving as a missionary in Chile for nearly a decade, Helmut Frenz held no pretensions of engaging in heroic efforts that some have compared to those of Dietrich Bonhoeffer, Martin Niemöller, and other towering figures of twentieth-century Christianity. Nor was Frenz a frontline ecumenist prior to the military coup and its aftermath. As other conference speakers here have acknowledged, the predominant Roman Catholic Church was the official national church. In its hegemonic influence, there was little need to reach out to Protestants. But neither is there much evidence that *los católicos* felt terribly threatened by other ecclesial communities, and I am aware of no evidence that Lutherans or other Protestants felt themselves persecuted or disparaged by the Catholic hierarchy in that era. There simply seemed little reason to have much interaction.

Eschewing any pretensions of being either a great champion for human rights or ecumenist, which history will surely ascribe to him, time and again Frenz said to his clergy colleagues and the broader public, "I am simply fulfilling my calling as a pastor."[4] Sheltering some of the most sought-after *MIRistas* (leaders of the far-left *Movimiento de Izquierda Revolucionaria,* or Leftist Revolutionary Movement) in his home and delivering vanloads of asylum-seekers to dozens of embassy doorways by night, Frenz knew he was constantly risking his own life and that of his large family. With fear and trembling—and I recall times that I literally watched the man tremble—he embraced the possibility of martyrdom. Boldly, he joined Cardinal Silva and other religious leaders in public statements decrying the outrages being perpetrated by Pinochet's police, paramilitary units, and armed forces. Frequently in receipt of death threats, Frenz persisted in unrelenting efforts to protect and pastor "the least of these" who found their way to his parsonage in Santiago's Providencia district. Indeed, he committed himself to what Pope Francis has called the "ecumenism of blood" in which Christians of many traditions, often alongside those of other faiths as well, confront evil, offer compassion and aid to those who suffer, and speak truth to power, come what may. On Christmas of 2013, when asked if Christian unity were a priority for him, our current pope said of martyred Christians in many lands: "Before they kill them, they do not ask them whether they are Anglican, Lutheran, Catholic, or Orthodox. Their blood is mixed. To those who kill, we are Christians. We are united in blood, even though we have not yet managed to take necessary steps toward unity between us, and perhaps the time has not yet come."[5]

In forming the Peace Committee in partnership with Bishops Silva and Ariztía, Helmut Frenz became a blood brother with his Catholic counterparts. As news stories and photos of the bishops standing shoulder to shoulder began appearing in Chile, despite the high levels of state control over the press, they gave powerful public witness in Chile and worldwide to what might be called "ecumenism of the streets."

4. From my own personal recollection of conversations that included Frenz.
5. Warner, "Pope Francis and the Ecumenism of Blood."

A Brutal President and Two Prelates

On November 13, 1974, Bishops Ariztía and Frenz had an appointment with the supreme army commander and head of the junta, General Augusto Pinochet. Once again, we hear in Frenz's own words a synopsis of that meeting's astounding conclusion:

> We conclude our presentation, and Pinochet continues leafing through the documents revealing torture. He has arrived at the section which establishes proof regarding those who are detained, transported, and disappeared. Among them appears the name of the Spanish priest Antonio Llidó. Bishop Ariztía prepares to expound further on the case of the disappeared Father Antonio, but Pinochet brusquely interrupts him, pointing his finger at the priest's picture and declaring, "This is no priest! This is a terrorist!"
>
> Giving us no further opportunity for discussion, Pinochet gets up to dispatch us with a brief soldier's declaration: "Look here, gentlemen, you are both priests who work within the church and can have the luxury of being merciful and generous. I am a soldier, and as the Chief of State, I am responsible for the entire Chilean people. The people have been attacked by the 'bacteria' of communism, which I must eradicate. The most dangerous communists are members of MIR [the Leftist Revolutionary Movement]. They must be tortured, for that is the only way to make them 'sing.' Torture is necessary to root out communism."
>
> With those words, Pinochet put an end to our audience.
>
> [In preparation for our meeting] we believed we had thought of everything—but not this discourse justifying torture. We had anticipated his denial of the possibility that torture was taking place within his government. Or I thought he might play down torture, as an occasional undesirable excess on the part of subordinates, for which he bore no direct responsibility. I had fully expected that, when presented with our ample documentation of torture, he would pretend surprise and say he had no knowledge of it whatsoever. But none of this! No pleading ignorance, no downplaying, certainly no pretended indignation! Instead, justification of torture, with full acknowledgement of the cruel, inhuman, and humiliating events taking place.[6]

6. Frenz, *Mi Vida Chilena*, 10–11.

Nansen Prize Awarded to Persona Non Grata

As Frenz's heroic Christian witness and human rights endeavors became recognized around the globe, the prestigious Nansen Refugee Award was conferred upon him in 1974 by the United Nations High Commissioner for Refugees. First granted to Eleanor Roosevelt twenty years previously, this award ranks in global prestige second only to the Nobel Peace Prize, for which Frenz was also later nominated. Upon receiving the Nansen medallion in Oslo, Bishop Frenz gave powerful public witness, declaring: "I try to identify myself with those who are suffering in our world, for I find that in giving myself to them, I encounter Christ, the Lord."[7] Finally, in October 1975, while traveling in Europe in search of funds and political pressure that might help halt the reign of terror in Chile, Helmut Frenz was declared *persona non grata* by the Pinochet government and refused reentry into his beloved Chile on the grounds that he posed "a threat to the interior security of the State."[8] In justifying its actions, the junta could also point to the fact that several hundred right-wing members of Frenz's own church had, in a full-page ad in Santiago's *El Mercurio* daily newspaper, called for his resignation as bishop and repatriation to Germany.[9] The junta's action was immediately challenged by leaders around the world, among them US Senator Edward Kennedy, with whom Frenz had worked closely for some time in advocating asylum for those being persecuted.

Following this gut-wrenching uprooting from his ministry and expulsion from his beloved Chile, Frenz lived out the remainder of his active ministry in Europe, continuing his service to refugees and the earth's "tired and poor." Once back in Germany, Frenz and his wife Barbara were divorced, their marriage perhaps a victim of the intensity experienced in Chile. Upon his retirement as executive director of Amnesty International in Germany, Frenz returned to Chile, where he remained until his death in 2012. He remarried a young *chilena* and fathered two more children. When Helmut, his successor, my vicar-father Esteban Schaller, and I reunited in the Frenz home a decade ago, it was an absolute delight watching Helmut bounce his beloved baby girl on his lap!

In 2007, Chile's democratically-elected president, Michelle Bachelet, invited Bishop Frenz to the restored Moneda Palace for a formal ceremony in which she awarded him full Chilean citizenship following an overwhelming

7. From my own personal notes and papers.

8. Frenz, *Mi Vida Chilena*, 267. In response, Frenz quipped: "To this day, I can live very well with this accusation; I have always simply threatened humanity [on the perils of] giving way to inhuman states!"

9. "Nuevas Adhesiones se Suman a la Solicitud de Renuncia."

vote by the Chilean Senate. In conferring this high honor upon the one formerly declared an "unfavorable person," President Bachelet declared, "With this law, the Republic of Chile recognizes Pastor Frenz's great commitment to our community and his courageous dedication in defense of human rights during the most painful and darkest hours of our history." She commented further upon Frenz's "permanent identification with the most vulnerable among us, to whom he has dedicated and continues giving maximum efforts."[10] Many Chileans today believe that no other action has fostered a greater measure of national reconciliation, beginning to close at last the most frightful chapter in Chile's long history.

Can "Ecumenism of Blood" Be Sustained in "Ordinary Time"?

As I have observed in my travels, particularly through leading student study groups to Central America over the past fifteen years, the "ecumenism of blood" tends to wane when bloodshed is diminished. Fervor for "ecumenism of the streets" appears to be reduced rather rapidly when the streets grow quieter. From conversations with contemporary Chilean Lutheran leaders, it appears that in recent decades, by and large, ecumenical endeavors—particularly Protestant-Catholic relations—have been moved to and remain on the back burner.

Over the course of a half-dozen years in the first decade of this century, I was privileged to serve as a consultant with the Evangelical Lutheran Church in Argentina. In my several sojourns in that South American nation, whence comes our current bishop of Rome, I heard little about Protestant–Catholic relations, though the spirit of Francis we have experienced during his papacy offers hope that his ecumenical leadership on the world scene will surpass that achieved in his native land.

Since the inauguration of a US president whose very demeanor (particularly facial scowl) reminds me in some ways of Pinochet, we have seen encouraging signs of a resurgence of ecumenism of the streets. In our profoundly pluralistic religious contexts, in some places, like right here in Chicago, when the blood begins to flow in the streets, when threats persist of widespread tightening of the noose by US Immigration and Customs Enforcement (ICE) agents, perhaps there will be a revival of the ecumenism of blood. We can hope for such new impulses to embody that vision of which our Lord spoke and for which he prayed so fervently when he yearned, "that they may all be one" (John 17:21, NRSV).

---

10. "Nacionalidad Chilena para Pastor Helmut Frenz."

Amidst Lessons Unlearned, Hope Is Not Lost

As we gather in this ecumenical and international conference, may we pray for the courage to be bold and faithful people of God for just such a time as this. So many lessons the world's leaders might have embraced from the events that occurred in Chile over four decades ago remain unlearned. Wisdom from prophets of the past—like Frenz, Ariztía, and Silva Henríquez—goes unheeded. People who are oppressed by the sheer brutality of poverty and violence are not ignorant animals who threaten us and must be kept at bay by building walls; rather, they are sisters and brothers who deserve compassion and a warm welcome to contribute and become neighbors. Shoving aside or ignoring orderly democratic processes and imposing strong-arm despotic measures inevitably build widespread resentment and result in prolonged societal strife and disunity. Rebuilding institutions devastated by the removal—and imprisonment or assassination—of key leaders takes decades, during which opportunities are missed and a nation's reputation tarnished. In nations around the world where right-wing hyper-nationalism seems on the rise, so many lessons that could have been gleaned from Chile's darkest hours in the 1970s have gone unlearned.

Lest we North Americans dismiss the events of the 1970s in Chile and other places in Latin America and elsewhere as other nations' problems of brutality, our complicity with the Pinochet regime's gross human rights abuses has come to light more fully in the twenty-first century. Journalist Marc Cooper worked with the Allende government, and in the aftermath of the coup was himself the target of Chile's armed forces roundup of "communist sympathizers." In his brief account of personal experiences and events since 1973, Cooper reports that, beginning in early 2000, "Thousands of formerly classified documents being released by the US government revealed ever more details about the inner workings of Operation Condor—the continent-wide murder consortium set up by Chile and neighboring dictatorships in the 1970s."[11] Cooper notes, "In late September of 2000, the CIA released a report that morally excoriated not only the dictator's regime but the American spy agency itself. . . . The new report, *CIA Activities in Chile*, finally confirmed what we have all assumed but could never prove. 'CIA actively supported the military Junta after the overthrow of Allende,' said the report. 'Many of Pinochet's officers were involved in systematic and widespread human rights abuses. . . . Some of these were contacts or agents of the CIA or US military.'"[12]

11. Cooper, *Pinochet and Me*, 133.
12. Cooper, *Pinochet and Me*, 135.

Despite widespread inclinations to dismiss the lessons from Chile and a general decline in ecumenical fervor forged under duress, I conclude with a word of personal hope; better said, it goes beyond hope to deep yearning. This past Friday evening, the Gettysburg Seminary community, which I have served the past seventeen years as president, gathered in a lavish banquet setting for my retirement celebration. One always wonders a bit about the meaning of having her/his retirement "celebrated"! After more than four decades in active ordained ministry, I have come to the end of an amazing journey. Much I imagined when I was ordained has been experienced in full measure. There is satisfaction in some tasks accomplished. But so much remains to be done and must now be accomplished by others. And some of those deep yearnings that seemed so within our grasp—and here I speak of the ecumenical fervor I experienced as a seminarian and young pastor in the 1970s—now seem beyond our grasp. One must adjust one's hopes and dreams and, with many things, embrace the sad realization: "Not in my lifetime. Others' eyes may see it someday, but mine will forever close before it transpires."

And so I ask at this later stage in my career, has that time of sad acceptance arrived in terms of our ecumenism? Even if I follow in my father's footsteps and live to the age of one hundred, at this stage of the game, where I'm probably at least on third base, is it too much to hope that before I move along to the great banquet hall of eternity, we shall sit at table and share the holy food of the Eucharist? Can "ecumenism of blood" give its fullest and boldest witness to our fragmented and polarized world if we do not share the body and blood of the Savior? On those days when I become discouraged and accept that it may not occur in my lifetime, I do not despair. When I left Santiago and returned to North America in mid-1975, had you told me that three decades later in Chile a democratically elected female president would confer citizenship and pay the highest tribute to the humble German bishop who had been declared a non-person, I would have suggested you rush to find the first therapist who could help relieve you of your delusions. Similarly, had I been told just two or three years before those world-changing events that the Berlin Wall would be torn down and the Soviet Union dismantled, the prediction would have been met with disbelief. Sometimes God's Spirit really does blow unimpeded where it wills, and the rush of that mighty wind can come upon us unexpectedly and unannounced.

Bibliography

Aguilera, Pilar, and Ricardo Fredes, eds. *Chile: El Otro 11 de Septiembre*. New York: Ocean, 2006.

Cooper, Marc. *Pinochet and Me: A Chilean Anti-Memoir*. New York: Verso, 2001.

Dinges, John, and Saul Landau. *Assassination on Embassy Row*. New York: Random House, 1980.

Frenz, Helmut. *Mi Vida Chilena: Solidaridad con los Oprimidos*. Santiago: LOM, 2006.

Gómez, Medardo Ernesto. *Fire Against Fire: Christian Ministry Face-to-Face with Persecution*. Minneapolis: Augsburg, 1990.

———. *Latinoamerica: Testimonio de Vida y Esperanza*. San Salvador: Iglesia Luterana Salvadoreña, 1993.

Magariño, Aurelio. *Justicia Social en un Mundo Injusto: La Iglesia como Agente de Cambio*. Saint Louis: Editorial Concordia, 2009.

"Nacionalidad Chilena para Pastor Helmut Frenz." *El Mercurio*, July 30, 2007.

"Nuevas Adhesiones se Suman a la Solicitud de Renuncia del Obispo Luterano Señor Helmut Frenz." *El Mercurio*, September 14, 1974.

Romero, Óscar Arnulfo. *La Voz de los Sin Voz*. San Salvador: UCA, 1980.

Warner, Christopher. "Pope Francis and the 'Ecumenism of Blood.'" *Catholic World Report*, December 18, 2013. Online. http://www.catholicworldreport.com/2013/12/18/pope-francis-and-the-ecumenism-of-blood.

5

Anglicans, the Ecumenism of Blood, and Postcolonial Problems

MARK CHAPMAN

MARTYRDOM HAS BECOME A defining narrative of African Christianity from the beginnings of the modern missionary period: this was most clearly expressed in Pope Paul VI's canonization in 1964 of the twenty-two Roman Catholic martyrs who died in Uganda between the years 1885 and 1887.[1] They are commemorated on June 3, the day in 1886 when the best-known Carlo Lwanga was burned alive in Namugongo along with another twelve Catholics by Mwanga II, *Kabaka* (or ruler) of the African nation of Buganda. The day has since become a national holiday in Uganda. The Catholic Church of Uganda built a shrine to the martyrs in Namugongo, which was completed in 1968, and in 1993 the Catholic Uganda Martyrs University was opened in Nkozi. When he visited the shrine in 1969, Pope Paul re-emphasized the importance of martyrdom, or what he called the "greatest and most beautiful of all actions." The Ugandan Martyrs became great examples to those who followed them in the faith:

> They have . . . laid down their lives for their Faith, that is, for their
> religion and for the freedom of their conscience. Therefore, they
> are our champions, our heroes, our teachers. . . . Your Martyrs

1. See Faupel, *African Holocaust*, which builds upon Thoonen's earlier works and the unpublished collections of René Lefèbre. See also Rowe, "Purge of Christians at Mwanga's Court"; Marion, *New African Saints*, a children's book produced to coincide with the canonization.

teach us just how true Christians should be, especially young Christians, African Christians. For Christians must be courageous, they must be strong, they must, as Saint Peter wrote, "be firm in the faith" (1 Pet 5:9). Your Martyrs teach us how much the Faith is worth![2]

In his homily at the canonization on October 18, 1964, Pope Paul identified the martyrs of the modern Church, including Lwanga and Mattia Mulumba Kalemba, with the great African martyrs and confessors of the early Church, including Cyprian, Felicity and Perpetua, and the great Augustine.

It is noteworthy, however, that even in 1964, Pope Paul was able to recognize the inherent ecumenism of martyrdom. In addition to the Catholic martyrs, he noted that another ten or eleven Christians from other denominations, principally Anglicanism, died on the same day: we do not "wish to forget the others who, belonging to the Anglican confession, confronted death in the name of Christ." Indeed, he went on to mention the Anglican martyrs four times in the homily.[3] The Anglican Church of Uganda counts twenty-three martyrs compared with twenty-two Catholics.[4] Altogether, it would appear that there were fifty-seven Christians who were put to death. The vast majority of the rest were expelled, and some later went on to become prominent church leaders.[5]

The two most influential white missionaries in Buganda at the time— Alexander Murdoch Mackay (1849–1890) of the Evangelical Anglican Church Missionary Society and Père Siméon Lourdel (1853–1890) of the White Fathers—were forced to look on as their converts were arrested and taken to be executed. Mackay sought permission to leave the country. He wrote home: "Nearly all our best friends [were] arrested suddenly, almost before our very eyes."[6] Lourdel watched as the pages (mes chers enfants, "my dear children," he said) were led to their deaths.[7] Martyrdom did not respect denominational differences. As Adrian Ddungu commented in a commemoration sermon:

2. Paul VI, "Visit to the Shrine of Namugongo." See also Kavulu, Uganda Martyrs, a booklet published to coincide with the papal visit.

3. Faupel, African Holocaust, 224–26. Translation from Spanish of selected parts of Paul VI's homily at the canonization of the Uganda Martyrs.

4. On the Protestant martyrs, see Faupel, African Holocaust, 207–17.

5. Faupel, African Holocaust, 217. See Rowe, "Purge of Christians at Mwanga's Court," 58–59.

6. Harrison, A. M. Mackay, 276–77.

7. Nicq, Le Père Siméon Lourdel, 340.

In dying together for Christ, as children of God in the faith, both the members of the Anglican Church and of the Catholic Church offer us a shining example of joint ecumenical Christian witness.[8]

After the martyrdom, the churches quickly grew in Uganda. Indeed, as David Kavulu writes, "Seldom in the history of Christianity has this maxim ['the blood of the martyrs is the seed of the Church'] been so dramatically demonstrated as in the case of the Uganda Martyrs."[9] Similarly, John V. Taylor claimed in his history of the Church in Buganda:

As a result of the persecutions the Church had become a well-organized underground movement, with a system of secret communications and escape routes, and any underground movement is an incipient political party.[10]

Yet martyrdom became more than simply a witness to future generations of the persistence of faith. It also provided one of the key defining narratives for the progress towards Christian civilization that was later expressed in the modern process of liberation and independence from the colonial powers. Pope Paul noted:

These African martyrs open a new epoch; oh! we don't wish to think of persecutions and religious quarrel but of Christian and civil regeneration. Africa, bathed with the blood of these martyrs, the first of the new era . . . rises again free and redeemed. The tragedy which devoured them is so unheard of and expressive as to offer representative elements sufficient for the moral formation of a new people, for the foundation of a new spiritual tradition, to symbolize and to promote the passage from a primitive civilization, not lacking in magnificent human values, but infected and weak and almost a slave of itself, to a civilization open to the superior expressions of the spirit and to superior forms of social life.[11]

The connection in the rhetoric between martyrdom and the development of Christian civilization is important: martyrdom was a sign of what Paul claimed was the superiority of Christian social life against a so-called "primitive" civilization, and it was also associated with the freedom of the

8. Ddungu, "Uganda Martyrs," 244.

9. Kavulu, *Uganda Martyrs*, 38.

10. Taylor, *Growth of the Church in Buganda*, 57.

11. Faupel, *African Holocaust*, 224–26. Translation from Spanish of selected parts of Paul VI's homily at the canonization of the Uganda Martyrs.

new, independent "redeemed" African nations. Similarly, it is also interesting to note that, in his 1969 address, it was "freedom of conscience" that he praised (something that had not been regarded as a virtue at earlier stages in Catholic history). It is clear that the events that occurred at Namugongo have been central in defining an ecumenical Christian identity for Ugandans, for East Africans, and even for sub-Saharan Africans, more generally.[12]

During his visit to Namugongo in 1993, Pope John Paul II continued to emphasize the importance of the martyrs in establishing African Christian identity. He spoke of Christ's bright light shining "in the great fire which consumed Saint Charles Lwanga and his companions. All that is truly African," he went on,

> all that is true and good and noble in Africa's traditions and cultures, is meant to find its fulfilment in Christ. . . . Here at Namugongo, it is right that we give thanks to God for all those who have worked and prayed and shed their blood for the rebirth of the Church on this Continent. We give thanks for all who have carried on the work of the Martyrs by striving to build a Church that is truly Catholic and truly African.

Emphasizing the importance of Christian unity, he urged the congregation to take heed of the martyrs who "showed their love for God by keeping his commandments."[13]

In November 2015, Pope Francis visited the shrine for the fiftieth anniversary of the canonization. The ecumenical theme had become increasingly important. Along with the twenty-two Catholic martyrs, he also remembered in his homily

> the Anglican martyrs whose deaths for Christ testify to the ecumenism of blood. All these witnesses nurtured the gift of the Holy Spirit in their lives and freely gave testimony of their faith in Jesus Christ, even at the cost of their lives, many at such a young age. . . . The gift of the Holy Spirit is a gift which is meant to be shared. It unites us to one another as believers and living members of Christ's mystical Body. We do not receive the gift of the Spirit for ourselves alone, but to build up one another in faith, hope, and love.[14]

During his visit to Namugongo, Francis was taken on a private tour of the new Uganda Martyrs' Museum at the Anglican Shrine by Stanley

---

12. See Blevins, "When Sodomy Leads to Martyrdom."
13. John Paul II, "Eucharistic Celebration."
14. Francis, "Holy Mass for the Martyrs of Uganda."

Ntagali, archbishop of the Anglican Church of Uganda. As they meditated at the fire pit where the martyrs were burned on June 3, 1886, Francis said: "This is ecumenism." The archbishop responded: "The Roman Catholic martyrs died for the same Jesus Christ as the Anglican martyrs. Together, they suffered; together, they sacrificed; together, they sang. Together, their blood has been the seed of the church in Uganda."[15]

Francis and the Ecumenism of Blood

Francis had anticipated this theme at a July 2015 meeting of charismatics in St. Peter's Square where he stated: "The blood of the martyrs makes us one. We know that those who kill Christians in hatred of Jesus Christ, before killing, do not ask: 'Are you an Evangelical, or [Anglican], or Orthodox?' They say: 'You are Christian,' and behead them."[16] Later that year, Fr. Raniero Cantalamessa, preacher to the Papal Household, spoke on this same theme to the Church of England's General Synod at its inaugural service in the presence of the Queen: "In many parts of the world, people are killed and churches burned not because they are Catholic, or Anglican, or Pentecostals but because they are Christians. In their eyes, we are already one! Let us be one also in our eyes and in the eyes of God."[17]

In February 2017, Pope Francis visited the Church of England's Church of All Saints in Rome. Responding to a question from an Anglican seminarian from Nigeria about the vitality of churches in the global South, Francis told an anecdote about Paul VI to make the point that "ecumenism is often easier in young churches":

> When Blessed Paul VI beatified the Ugandan martyrs—a young Church—among the martyrs were catechists, all were young, while some were Catholics and others Anglican, and all were martyred by the same king in hate for the faith, because they refused to follow the obscene proposals of the king. And Paul VI was embarrassed, saying: "I should beatify both groups; they are both martyrs." But in that moment of the Catholic Church, such a thing was not possible. The Council had just taken place. . . . But that young Church now celebrates all of them together; Paul VI, too, in his homily for the Mass for beatification wished to name the Anglican catechists as martyrs for the faith at the same level as the Catholic catechists. This was done by a

15. Church of Uganda, "Pope to Anglicans."
16. Roberts, "Church Leaders Must Resign."
17. Cantalamessa, "Rebuild My House."

young Church. Young Churches have courage, because they are young.[18]

Answering a subsequent question about ecumenism in Africa, Francis commented:

> The young Churches have a different vitality, because they are young. And they seek a way of expressing themselves differently. . . . The young Churches have more creativity, and at the beginning here in Europe it was the same. When you read, for instance, in the Didaché, of how the Eucharist was celebrated, the encounter between Christians, there was a great creativity. As she grew, the Church became more consolidated and matured to an adult age. But the young Churches have more vitality and also have a need to collaborate.[19]

In the same conversation, Francis spoke about his experience of ecumenism in Argentina, citing the example of joint Catholic and Anglican work among aboriginal people in the northern part of the country. The "aborigine in the north of Argentina says to you, 'I am Anglican.' But there isn't a bishop, there isn't a pastor. . . . 'I want to praise God on a Sunday, and so I go to the Catholic cathedral,' and vice versa. These are the riches of the young Church." Francis concluded: "I think this is a wealth that our young churches can bring to Europe and to the churches with a long tradition. . . . Ecumenism is easier there . . . which does not mean that it is more superficial. . . . They do not negotiate faith and identity."[20] While it would be wrong to read too much into these unscripted remarks, it is important to note the continuity with Pope Paul's remarks of fifty years earlier. The metaphor of youth is still being used for the African churches, as is that of maturity and adulthood for the European churches. These metaphors were frequently used in the early missionary period itself.

The language of martyrdom has also been adopted by Justin Welby, Archbishop of Canterbury and leader of the world's approximately seventy million Anglicans. For instance, in a visit to the Ecumenical Patriarch in 2014, he spoke of the Orthodox Church's witness to martyrdom, the cost of which "is seen in so many places today, especially in Syria."[21] In an address to Pope Francis that same year, he noted that "we also know that from the start,

18. Holy See Press Office, "Pope's Historic Visit." See also Holy See Press Office, "Pope Repeats that Ecumenism Is a Journey."

19. Holy See Press Office, "Pope's Historic Visit."

20. Holy See Press Office, "Pope's Historic Visit."

21. Lambeth Palace Staff, "Archbishop of Canterbury Meets Ecumenical Patriarch Bartholomew."

as for so many at this time, [missionary activity] has been a witness unto death. I was moved to be in Santa Bartolomeo where, amongst many recent martyrs, the seven members of the Anglican religious order the Melanesian brotherhood are commemorated."[22] At a recent meeting, the pope and archbishop announced the possibility of a shared journey to South Sudan, which has become one of the most troubled parts of the Christian world.[23] The Anglican Communion has also addressed the issue of martyrdom and persecution in a lengthy report published in 2016.[24]

The phrase "ecumenism of martyrdom," or "ecumenism of blood," however, has not been reserved solely for the new churches of Africa. In an interview with the Vatican journalist, Andrea Tornielli, published in the Turin daily, *La Stampa,* in December 2013, Francis commented that, for him, "ecumenism is a priority." He explained:

> Today, there is an ecumenism of blood. In some countries, they kill Christians for wearing a cross or having a Bible, and before they kill them, they do not ask them whether they are Anglican, Lutheran, Catholic, or Orthodox. Their blood is mixed. To those who kill, we are Christians. We are united in blood, even though we have not yet managed to take necessary steps towards unity between us, and perhaps the time has not yet come. Unity is a gift that we need to ask for. I knew a parish priest in Hamburg who was dealing with the beatification cause of a Catholic priest guillotined by the Nazis for teaching children the catechism. After him, in the list of condemned individuals, was a Lutheran pastor who was killed for the same reason. Their blood was mixed. The parish priest told me he had gone to the bishop and said to him: "I will continue to deal with the cause, but both of their causes, not just the Catholic priest's." This is what ecumenism of blood is. It still exists today; you just need to read the newspapers. Those who kill Christians don't ask for your identity card to see which Church you were baptized in. We need to take these facts into consideration.[25]

Similarly, on May 8, 2014, Francis held an audience with Karekin II, patriarch of the Armenian Apostolic Church, in which he observed that "the sufferings endured by Christians in these last decades have made a unique and invaluable contribution to the unity of Christ's disciples." He went on:

22. Welby, "Address of His Grace Justin Welby."
23. "Pope Francis 'Studying Possibility' of South Sudan Visit."
24. Anglican Inter Faith Network, *Out of the Depths.*
25. Tornielli, "Never Be Afraid of Tenderness."

So, too, in our time, the blood of innumerable Christians has become a seed of unity. The ecumenism of suffering and of the martyrdom of blood are a powerful summons to walk the long path of reconciliation between the Churches, by courageously and decisively abandoning ourselves to the working of the Holy Spirit. We feel the duty to follow this fraternal path also out of the debt of gratitude we owe to the suffering so many of our brothers and sisters, which is salvific because it is united to the Passion of Christ.[26]

The following year, speaking at an ecumenical gathering shortly after the February 2015 murder of twenty-one Coptic Christians by ISIS militants in Libya, Francis noted that those killed only said, "Jesus, help me." He continued:

They were killed simply for the fact that they were Christians. ... The blood of our Christian brothers and sisters is a testimony which cries out to be heard. It makes no difference whether they be Catholics, Orthodox, Copts, or Protestants. They are Christians! Their blood is one and the same. Their blood confesses Christ. As we recall these brothers who died only because they confessed Christ, I ask that we encourage each another to go forward with this ecumenism which is giving us strength, the ecumenism of blood. The martyrs belong to all Christians.[27]

In an ecumenical address in October 2016, Francis also noted that Christians who suffer persecution are brought together by an "ecumenism of blood":

They do not ask: "Are you Lutheran? Are you Orthodox? Are you Catholic? Are you a Reformed Christian? Are you Pentecostal?" No. "You are Christian." They recognize this alone: the Christian. The enemy does not err; he knows well how to recognize where Jesus is.[28]

Similarly, in a message addressed to the Coptic Pope Tawadros II, Francis again argued that "today more than ever we are united by the ecumenism of blood."[29] This message was repeated in their joint statement of April 28, 2017, issued during Francis's brief visit to Egypt:

26. Francis, "To His Holiness Karekin II."
27. Francis, "To the Moderator and Representatives."
28. Francis, "To Participants in the Conference."
29. "Pope Francis to Pope Tawadros."

The mystery of Jesus who died and rose out of love lies at the heart of our journey towards full unity. Once again, the martyrs are our guides. In the early Church, the blood of the martyrs was the seed of new Christians. So too in our own day, may the blood of so many martyrs be the seed of unity among all Christ's disciples, a sign and instrument of communion and peace for the world.[30]

What this reveals is that the ecumenical language of martyrdom which might have begun with Paul VI and his references to the Ugandan martyrs has taken on a new dimension in the context of the Middle East and in other places of religious persecution.

Questions

There are several questions raised by this renewed emphasis on an ecumenism of blood, questions which point back to the original context of the Ugandan Martyrs. First, in the African context, the importance of the foundation narrative of the Namugongo martyrs has taken on a variety of sometimes contested and frequently complex meanings.[31] These have been particularly apparent in the Anglican Communion. Because of its highly decentralized polity and its division into thirty-eight independent member churches, each with its own canons and structures, the Anglican Communion frequently reveals divisions which might remain implicit in the Roman Catholic Church. Paul VI's homily at the canonization emphasized the "primitive" culture which the missionaries and early converts had faced and how important the example of martyrdom had become for the spread of civilization. At the time, it led to the British annexation of Uganda, which was all but complete by 1888, and Christianity quickly became the dominant religion.

Early on, homosexuality was linked with the Kabaka's behavior and was considered part of this "primitive" world. One contemporary diary of 1882 noted:

We have no doubt about the motive which brings the Baganda to be taught our Holy Religion. It was perhaps to do wrong with our children. And to achieve their aim more easily and surely, they have to win and ensnare our children by giving them trifles while practicing sodomy with them. The king not being satisfied

---

30. Francis and Tawadros II, "Joint Statement."

31. See the colorful account in Hoad, *African Intimacies*, 1–20.

with his wives and with his favorite pages with whom he has sodomy wants each Muganda to practice sodomy. And also that vice seems to be prevalent in the villages.[32]

Similarly, the authoritative account of the martyrdom by J. P. Thoonen from the 1940s reveals some of the reasons behind the martyrdom. It was noted that the *majordomo* reproached the king when he sent for the pages under "suspicious circumstances."[33] The *Processus Apostolicus* reported that he implored the Kabaka: "Oh my master, I ask and implore you, do not act like that, for Katonda detests uncleanness. Leave my Christians alone, and rather leave to the Moslems the vileness with which Satan inspires them." "Fortunately," Thoonen comments, "the king was restrained by public opinion which still abominated the practice of unnatural vice." Andrew Kiwá-nuka reported to the *Processus*:

> At that time, the king practiced the works of Sodom. Moslems and pagans were prepared to do those things with the king, but the Catholics absolutely refused. For that reason, the king began to detest us and deliberated with the pagans and Moslems about putting us to death, us the Catholics. With my own ears, I heard the king utter words of anger, because the young Catholics refused to sin. I, for one, was often importuned by him, but refused.[34]

Another witness spoke of "lewd practices at court," in which the Christian young men refused to participate: "The Moslem or pagan pages who committed those sins were afraid of even speaking of them in the presence of Christians. . . . Lust and pride were therefore the two motives which made [the King] hate religion."[35]

In his brief and dispassionate discussion of homosexuality at the Kabaka's court, Kavulu reports that although all the Ganda and mission sources claim that homosexual practices were introduced by the Arabs, "it is still difficult to establish the origin of the practices. Mwanga must have acquired the habits while still a young prince, because the practice of sodomy appears to have been known during the days of Muteesa," He went on: "Under the puritan leadership of men like Mukasa Balikuddembe and Charles Lwanga,

32. Rubaga Diary, July 30, 1882, and October 25, 1882, cited in Gale, "Muteesa I," 18.

33. A brief overview of the *Processus* was published at the time of the beatification on June 6, 1920. See Streicher, *Martyrs of Uganda*.

34. Thoonen, *Black Martyrs*, 105. See also Faupel, *African Holocaust*, 133.

35. Thoonen, *Black Martyrs*, 106. See also Streicher, *Martyrs of Uganda*, 4–5, where he speaks of the "infamy of [the King's] private life."

the Christian converts stubbornly refused to co-operate in these practices much to the annoyance of the monarch."[36] Similarly, according to Rowe, although homosexuality was undoubtedly an issue, it was certainly not the most important:

> When the explosion finally came, Mwanga's angry and violent reaction was probably due to the discovery that the Christian boys were attempting to convert one of his few cooperative pages. In any case, Mwanga's personal rebuff only provided the spark to ignite those highly explosive larger issues—issues of priority of allegiance—which had long been in confrontation, unresolved.[37]

It is interesting to note that the explicit linking of homosexuality was not made in the process of canonization, and in Catholic discourse in general, it has been played down (even if Francis alluded to it during his visit to All Saints' Church in Rome).[38] For instance, in the 1984 pastoral letter of the Ugandan Roman Catholic Bishops, "Celebrating our Ancestors," there was an explicit effort to reinterpret African cultures and move away from the narratives of the "primitive": "In our devotion to the Martyrs," the letter noted, "we see this traditional belief of ours taken up and purified, so that we can truly say that it is from their blood that we have been born anew in the faith."[39] Similarly, in the 1960s among the first generation of postcolonial historians, there were frequent efforts to praise Mwanga II because of his resistance to colonialism (and it would also appear that he was rather less violent than his predecessor).[40] The English Anglican missionary historian Kevin Ward, who taught for many years in Uganda, quotes from a letter sent to the president during that time:

> It surprises me to see that our intelligent historians have not written any books praising Mwanga . . . for trying to resist any foreign domination. . . . It is so annoying to see intelligent citizens spending their precious time canonizing a group of disloyal servants; these disloyal servants refused to obey the orders of the king and sided with a foreign master who had promised them thrones in heaven. The canonization of these disloyal pages and

36. Kavulu, *Uganda Martyrs*, 18; Faupel, *African Holocaust*, 137–38.
37. Rowe, "Purge of Christians at Mwanga's Court," 64, on the political background and idea of rebellion, see 70. Most Christians, it seems, kept their heads below the parapet. Mwanga was also happy to make allies with Christians when it suited his purposes.
38. Ward, "Same-Sex Relations in Africa," 89.
39. Catholic Bishops of Uganda, *Celebrating Our Ancestors*, 8.
40. Rowe, "Purge of Christians at Mwanga's Court," 68.

the condemnation of both Mwanga and Kabalega[41] is a manifestation of the colonial mentality still rampant in our nation.[42]

Similarly, at the commemoration of the centenary of the martyrdom
in 1986, some interpreters emphasized the geopolitical aspects of the martyrdom. In the newspaper *The Daily Nation,* Ronnie Mutebi (a descendant
of the Kabaka) wrote:

> The young Mwanga was besieged and in fear of losing the sov-
> ereignty of his country. Moreover, at this time of national crisis,
> the young men who formed the body of Buganda's emergent
> establishment—the people who would make up the nation's
> administrative, political, and military elite—were showing that
> their allegiance lay elsewhere than with the Kabaka. The pages
> took the king's secrets and passed them on to the missionaries—
> as was the case with the death in Busoga of Bishop Hannington.
> Their actions were nothing short of treason, although they did
> not see it that way. No leader worth his salt could ignore that
> threat. It would be easy to get engrossed in the moving and very
> powerful, tragic, heroic story of the martyrs and overlook the
> fact that geopolitical considerations were paramount. Faupel
> plays down the geopolitical aspect and gives greater weight to
> the evangelical dimension.[43]

While the complexities of this interpretation are beyond the scope of
this chapter and raise issues in social organization in precolonial societies,
there is an evident tension in assessments of the role of the martyrs.[44]

In recent years, something very different has been propagated by other
interpreters of the martyrs who, building on the occasional references in
earlier historians such as Thoonen, have stressed the importance of a stand
against homosexuality as the chief cause of the martyrdom.[45] The martyrs'
feast day was gradually transformed into an occasion where homosexuality

41. Chwa II Kabalega (1853–1923) was ruler, or *Omukama*, of Bunyoro in Uganda
from 1870 to 1899.

42. Ward, "Same-Sex Relations in Africa," 90.

43. Mutebi, "Boys Who Smiled on the Way to Death," cited in Maloney, "Religion,
Politics, and the Uganda Martyrs," 8. The first British Church of England missionaries
who reached Buganda in 1877 carried with them credentials from the Church Missionary Society as well as the Foreign Office. The political aspects certainly played a strong
part in the death of Bishop James Hannington in 1885. Ward, "James Hannington," 278.

44. See Maloney, "Religion, Politics, and the Uganda Martyrs," 10–13. On social
organization in Buganda, see Rowe, "Purge of Christians at Mwanga's Court," 57.

45. See Blevins, "When Sodomy Leads to Martyrdom," 60–62.

was denounced.[46] One Ugandan gay activist wrote in 2009 of his experiences in churches:

> [The martyrs] have been used to justify the genocidal tendencies of Ugandans against gay Ugandans. . . . I know for a fact that the reality of this history was not widespread until recently, when the dear religious leaders saw fit to use it to justify their anger and desire to kill gay Ugandans. . . . Shame upon you, Ugandan Christians.[47]

Ward dates the beginning of opposition to homosexuality to a number of meetings organized by conservative members of the Episcopal Church in the run-up to the 1998 Lambeth Conference, and these continued through very close links with dissident groups into the 2000s. Particularly prominent was Canon Alison Barfoot, an American priest who had become international officer for the Church of Uganda.[48]

In 2006, immediately after the election of Katherine Jefferts Schori as presiding bishop of the Episcopal Church, Henry Orombi, archbishop of Uganda, wrote in his pastoral letter about the Episcopal Church's failure to repent of its actions in consecrating a bishop (Gene Robinson of New Hampshire) in a homosexual relationship:

> Our problem with the new Presiding Bishop of ECUSA is that she has publicly denied what the Bible teaches about faith and morality. . . . Since ECUSA officially approved of homosexual relationships in 2003, we have earnestly prayed they would repent and return to the Word of God. But their General Convention in June 2006 made it clear that they are not intent on repentance. In fact, they seem even more committed to their erring ways and the revision of the Biblical and historic faith that brought life to us and that we gratefully proclaim.
>
> Therefore, and in light of all these developments, the House of Bishops and the Provincial Assembly in its meeting in August reaffirmed our position of broken communion with ECUSA and our decision to support in practical ways those churches, dioceses, and leaders in America who uphold and promote the

---

46. See also Ward, "Role of the Anglican and Catholic Churches." Ward seeks to show that homophobia is relatively recent in Uganda and relatively shallow.

47. Cited in Ward, "Role of the Anglican and Catholic Churches," 140.

48. Ward, "Role of the Anglican and Catholic Churches," 136. On the influence of Barfoot, see Hoad, *African Intimacies*, 55. For a profile of Barfoot, see Political Research Associates, "Globalizing the Culture Wars."

Biblical and historic faith of Anglicanism for which our own Ugandan martyrs died.[49]

The alliance between conservative church leaders and the state was strong, especially in the run-up to the discussions about increased penalties for homosexuality. Speaking in Namugongo in 2010, President Yoweri Museveni claimed,

> The African Church is the only one that is still standing against homosexuality. The Europeans are finished. If we follow them, we shall end up in Sodom and Gomorrah. . . . I hear there was homosexuality in Mwanga's palace. This was not part of our culture. I hear he learnt it from the Arabs. But the martyrs refused these falsehoods and went for the truth, which is why we are honoring them today.[50]

Similarly, while addressing the Uganda Martyrs Conference in October 2013, Museveni noted that "the significance of the Uganda Martyrs transcends even our borders, as is manifest by all the pilgrims from other countries" who attended the annual pilgrimage to Namugongo. He went on to praise the clergy for defending morality against Western liberalism:

> It is in this era that Africa is faced with immoral invasions which are not originally African but are proclaimed as human rights universal to all humanity. Such influences like homosexuality [and] drug abuse . . . are not only threats to the church and state but the future of humanity in general. I wish to take this opportunity to thank religious leaders in Uganda who have stood firm in line with [the] Uganda Martyrs and vehemently rejected such foreign deviations.[51]

Although the Anglican Church of Uganda helped in changing the penalty for homosexuality from death to life imprisonment, there was nonetheless widespread support for the bill that was passed. Archbishop Stanley Ntagali told a rally: "The Lord has the power to help us Ugandans to overcome the battle against homosexuality."[52]

Without wishing to rehearse the long and highly contested disputes in the Anglican Communion over the legitimacy of homosexuality,[53] I simply wish to note that the emphasis of the Ugandan martyrs as an example

49. Church of Uganda, "Re: Pastoral Letter."
50. Kagolo, "Museveni Warns on Dangers of Sodomy."
51. Museveni cited in Ford, "'Who Am I to Judge?'"
52. Ntagali cited in Ford, "'Who Am I to Judge?'"
53. For a concise account, see Hall, *Thorn in the Flesh*.

of resistance to what is regarded by some as the "un-African" practice of homosexuality has become an important part of Anglican rhetoric and has frequently led to alliances between Africans and Western conservatives.[54] Indeed, opposition to homosexuality has become a key aspect of Anglican identity: it is what Murray Edelman calls a "condensation symbol,"[55] which brings together a set of wider issues that have emerged between the different provinces. In a manner that is not always easy to explain, approaches to homosexuality and same-sex relationships have taken on a powerful symbolic meaning and have come to be the single most important marker of identity and belonging in some parts of the Anglican Communion. The earlier disputes over rituals or doctrine have been supplanted by a new cultural symbol: a conservative stance on homosexual practice has come to be seen by many Anglicans as a badge of orthodox Christian belief and opposition to Western neocolonialism. In this, the rhetoric of martyrdom has been key in reaffirming this identity.[56]

As some of the earlier interpreters of the Ugandan martyrs noted, there was also a linking of the Kabaka's behavior with Arab traders, which points to an important point: a martyrdom founded on persecution can easily slide into a projection of Islam as inherently hostile to Christianity, even if, for the most part, this has been avoided in the recent discussion of ecumenism of blood, at least among the mainline denominations.[57] In parts of Africa, Christians face serious persecution from militant Islam. For instance, in Nigeria, home to the largest Anglican Church in the Communion, there have been numerous acts of violence as well as infringements of civil rights, especially in the northern part of the country. Kidnappings of bishops have been common.[58] The rhetoric of martyrdom has been important in ensuring Christian solidarity worldwide and also in promoting cooperation among the mainline denominations in Nigeria (as well as in other places, such as South Sudan).[59] At the same time, the common ecumenical front against militant Islam can sometimes mean that the internal threats to mainline churches from other forms of Christianity are downplayed. In Nigeria, for example, neo-Pentecostalism is seriously challenging the hegemony of

54. See Hassett, *Anglican Communion in Crisis.*

55. See Edelman, *Constructing the Political Spectacle.*

56. Anglican Inter Faith Network, *Out of the Depths*, 104.

57. Interestingly, Kavulu's 1969 booklet devotes a section to the Muslim Martyrs. See Kavulu, *Uganda Martyrs*, 10–13.

58. See Idowu-Fearon, "Anglicans and Islam in Nigeria"; Zink, *Backpacking through the Anglican Communion.*

59. See, for instance, the website of the Open Doors charity for persecuted Christians (http://www.opendoorsuk.org).

the missionary churches, which is having an effect on those churches. In the Anglican Church in Nigeria, this has led to the development of what Jesse Zink calls "Anglocostalism," which is reshaping Anglican identity and worship.[60]

Conclusion

What this brief discussion reveals is that an "ecumenism of martyrdom," or "ecumenism of blood," carries with it a range of meanings and needs some serious analysis. The rhetoric of modern martyrdom can carry with it the complex cultural baggage of the colonial churches' missionary enterprise, and, as with so much else in mission history, is never quite as simple as it might appear at first sight. Furthermore, the absoluteness of the language of martyrdom, used by religious militants from across the spectrum, means that it is a high-risk strategy and could potentially lead to a demonization of Islam. That said, it is important not to downplay the bravery of those who bear witness to their faith and who stand against the corruptions of power or the evils of unbridled violence. Archbishop Janani Luwum, a later Ugandan Anglican martyr, was killed on the orders of Idi Amin on February 16, 1977, which was being kept as the centenary year of the Anglican Church in Uganda.[61] As somebody who spoke out against the regime, he is commemorated as one of the statues of twentieth-century martyrs, unveiled on the western front of Westminster Abbey in 1998. His grave[62] has inspired further political resistance: "Instead of being something that discourages us, the empty grave spoke to us of the victory that we have over death; that whatever happens to a person's body, there is an everlasting life that is quite indestructible."[63]

Bibliography

Anglican Inter Faith Network. *Out of the Depths: Hope in Times of Suffering: Theological Resources in Times of Persecution: An Anglican Contribution to Ecumenical Engagement*. London: Anglican Consultative Council, 2016. Online. http://nifcon.anglicancommunion.org/media/217261/out-of-the-depths.pdf.

---

60. See Zink, "Anglocostalism."

61. Otunnu, *Archbishop Janani Luwum*.

62. His body was placed in an unmarked grave at the Primary School in Wii Gweng.

63. Wooding and Barnett, *Uganda Holocaust*, 103.

Blevins, John. "When Sodomy Leads to Martyrdom: Sex, Religion, and Politics in Historical and Contemporary Contexts in Uganda and East Africa." *Theology and Sexuality* 17 (2011) 51–74.

Cantalamessa, Raniero. "Rebuild My House: Sermon to the General Synod of the Church of England by Father Raniero Cantalamessa." *Anglican Communion News Service*, November 25, 2015. Online. http://www.anglicannews.org/news/2015/11/rebuild-my-house-sermon-to-the-general-synod-of-the-church-of-england-by-father-raniero-cantalamessa.aspx.

Catholic Bishops of Uganda. *Celebrating Our Ancestors in the Faith: The Martyrs, Models of Christian Commitment: Pastoral Letter of the Catholic Bishops of Uganda in Preparation for the Centenary of the Death of the Uganda Martyrs.* Kampala: St. Paul, 1984.

Church of Uganda. "Pope to Anglicans: This is Ecumenism." November 30, 2015. Online. http://churchofuganda.org/info/pope-to-anglicans-this-is-ecumenism.

———. "RE: Pastoral Letter from His Grace, the Archbishop of the Church of Uganda." November 9, 2016. Online. http://churchofuganda.org/news/press-releases/pastoral-letter-from-archbishop-henry-orombi-to-ugandan-christians.

Ddungu, Adrian K. "The Uganda Martyrs Challenge Our Level and Conviction of Faith." *African Ecclesiastical Review* 31 (1989) 239–46.

Edelman, Murray. *Constructing the Political Spectacle.* Chicago: University of Chicago Press, 1988.

Faupel, J. F. *African Holocaust: The Story of the Uganda Martyrs.* London: Geoffrey Chapman, 1961.

Ford, Matt. "'Who Am I to Judge': Will the Pope Condemn Homophobia in Uganda?" *Atlantic*, April 3, 2014. Online. https://www.theatlantic.com/international/archive/2014/04/who-am-i-to-judge-will-the-pope-condemn-homophobia-in-uganda/284216.

Francis. "Address of His Holiness Pope Francis to Participants in the Conference of Secretaries of Christian World Communions." October 12, 2016. Online. https://w2.vatican.va/content/francesco/en/speeches/2016/october/documents/papa-francesco_20161012_christian-world-communions.pdf.

———. "Address of His Holiness Pope Francis to the Moderator and Representatives of the Church of Scotland." February 16, 2015. Online. https://w2.vatican.va/content/francesco/en/speeches/2015/february/documents/papa-francesco_20150216_moderatore-chiesa-scozia.html.

———. "Address of Pope Francis to His Holiness Karekin II, Supreme Patriarch and Catholicos of All Armenians with His Entourage." May 8, 2014. Online. https://w2.vatican.va/content/francesco/en/speeches/2014/may/documents/papa-francesco_20140508_patriarca-armeni.html.

———. "Holy Mass for the Martyrs of Uganda: Homily of His Holiness Pope Francis." Catholic Shrine of the Martyrs of Namugongo, Uganda, November 28, 2015. Online. https://w2.vatican.va/content/francesco/en/homilies/2015/documents/papa-francesco_20151128_uganda-omelia-martiri.html.

Francis, and Tawadros II. "Joint Statement by Pope Francis and Tawadros II." *Catholic News Agency*, April 28, 2017. Online. http://www.catholicnewsagency.com/news/full-text-of-joint-statement-by-pope-francis-and-tawadros-ii-89877.

Gale, H. P. "Muteesa I—Was He a God?" *Uganda Journal* 20 (1956) 72–87.

Hall, Caroline J. Addington. *A Thorn in the Flesh: How Gay Sexuality Is Changing the Episcopal Church.* Lanham, MD: Rowman and Littlefield, 2013.

Harrison, Alexina Mackay. *A. M. Mackay: Pioneer Missionary of the Church Missionary Society to Uganda by His Sister.* London: Hodder and Stoughton, 1890.

Hassett, Miranda K. *Anglican Communion in Crisis: How Episcopal Dissidents and Their African Allies Are Reshaping Anglicanism.* Princeton: Princeton University Press, 2007.

Hoad, Neville Wallace. *African Intimacies: Race, Homosexuality, and Globalization.* Minneapolis: University of Minnesota Press, 2007.

Holy See Press Office. "Pope's Historic Visit to 'All Saints' Anglican Church." *Summary of Bulletin*, February 26, 2017. Online. https://press.vatican.va/content/salastampa/en/bollettino/pubblico/2017/02/26/170226c.html.

———. "The Pope Repeats that Ecumenism is a Journey and Praises the Vitality of the Young Churches." *Summary of Bulletin*, February 26, 2017. Online. https://press.vatican.va/content/salastampa/en/bollettino/pubblico/2017/02/26/170226d.html.

Idowu-Fearon, Josiah. "Anglicans and Islam in Nigeria: Anglicans Encountering Difference." *Journal of Anglican Studies* 2 (2004) 40–51.

John Paul II. "Eucharistic Celebration at the Shrine of the Holy Uganda Martyrs of Namugongo." Homily given in Kampala, Uganda, February 7, 1993. Online. https://w2.vatican.va/content/john-paul-ii/en/homilies/1993/documents/hf_jp-ii_hom_19930207_kampala.html.

Kagolo, Francis. "Museveni Warns on Dangers of Sodomy." *New Vision*, June 3, 2010. Online. http://www.newvision.co.ug/new_vision/news/1289061/museveni-warns-dangers-sodomy.

Kavulu, David. *The Uganda Martyrs.* Kampala: Longmans of Uganda, 1969.

Lambeth Palace Staff. "Archbishop of Canterbury Meets Ecumenical Patriarch Bartholomew." *Episcopal News Service*, January 14, 2014. Online. https://www.episcopalnewsservice.org/2014/01/14/archbishop-of-canterbury-meets-ecumenical-patriarch-bartholomew.

Maloney, Raymond. "Religion, Politics, and the Uganda Martyrs." *African Ecclesiastical Review* 29 (1987) 7–15.

Marion, Francis. *New African Saints: The Twenty-Two Martyrs of Uganda.* Milan: Ancora, 1964.

Mutebi, Ronnie. "The Boys Who Smiled on the Way to Death." *Daily Nation*, June 4, 1986.

Nicq, Abbé Augustin. *Le Père Siméon Lourdel de la Société des Pères Blancs et les Premières Années de la Mission de l'Ouganda (Afrique Équatoriale).* Algiers: Maison-Carree, 1932.

Otunnu, Olara. *Archbishop Janani Luwum: The Life and Witness of a Twentieth-Century Martyr.* Kampala: Fountain, 2015.

Paul VI. "Visit to the Shrine of Namugongo." Homily given at the Shrine of Namugongo, Kampala, Uganda, August 2, 1969. Online. https://w2.vatican.va/content/paul-vi/en/homilies/1969/documents/hf_p-vi_hom_19690802.html.

Political Research Associates. "Globalizing the Culture Wars: US Conservatives, African Churches, and Homophobia." *Political Research Associates*, December 1, 2009. Online. https://www.politicalresearch.org/2009/12/01/globalizing-culture-wars#27.

"Pope Francis 'Studying Possibility' of South Sudan Visit." *Catholic Insider,* February 27, 2017. Online. https://insider.catholic.sg/pope-francis-studying-possibility-of-south-sudan-visit.

"Pope Francis to Pope Tawadros: Ecumenism of Blood Unites Us." *Vatican Radio,* May 10, 2015. Online. http://www.archivioradiovaticana.va/storico/2015/05/10/pope_francis_to_pope_tawadros_ecumenism_of_blood_unites_us/en-1143066.

Roberts, James. "Church Leaders Must Resign, Francis Tells Charismatics." *The Tablet,* July 9, 2015. Online. http://www.thetablet.co.uk/news/2225/0/church-leaders-must-resign-francis-tells-charismatics.

Rowe, J. A. "The Purge of Christians at Mwanga's Court: A Reassessment of this Episode in Buganda History." *Journal of African History* 5 (1964) 55–72.

Streicher, Henry. *The Martyrs of Uganda.* London: Catholic Truth Society, 1920.

Taylor, J. V. *The Growth of the Church in Buganda: An Attempt at Understanding.* London: SCM, 1958.

Thoonen, J. P. *Black Martyrs.* London: Sheed and Ward, 1941.

Tornielli, Andrea. "Never Be Afraid of Tenderness." *Vatican Insider,* December 16, 2013. Online. http://www.lastampa.it/2013/12/16/vaticaninsider/eng/the-vatican/never-be-afraid-of-tenderness-3sMZy95oJWmaNvfq4m1sTN/pagina.html.

Ward, Kevin. "James Hannington." In *Biographical Dictionary of Christian Missions,* edited by Gerald H. Anderson, 278. Grand Rapids: Eerdmans, 1998.

———. "The Role of the Anglican and Catholic Churches in Uganda in Public Discourse on Homosexuality and Ethics." *Journal of Eastern African Studies* 9 (2014) 127–44.

———. "Same-Sex Relations in Africa and the Debate on Homosexuality in East African Anglicanism." *Anglican Theological Review* 84 (2002) 81–111.

Welby, Justin. "Address of His Grace Justin Welby, Archbishop of Canterbury to Pope Francis." *Ecumenism in Canada,* June 16, 2014. Online. https://ecumenism.net/2014/06/the-addresses-of-archbishop-welby-pope-francis.htm.

Wooding, Dan, and Ray Barnett. *Uganda Holocaust: They Faced Amin's Terror Machine Undaunted.* Grand Rapids: Zondervan, 1980.

Zink, Jesse. "'Anglocostalism': In Nigeria: Neo-Pentecostalism and Obstacles to Anglican Unity." *Journal of Anglican Studies* 10 (2012) 231–50.

———. *Backpacking through the Anglican Communion.* Harrisburg, PA: Morehouse, 2014.

PART THREE

Ecumenical Engagement with Social Issues

6

One Family, Many Systems? Ecumenical Alliances and the Defense of the Domestic in Post-Handover Hong Kong

JUSTIN K. H. TSE

Introduction: Hong Kong Ecumenism and the Family in the Shadow of China

AMIDST PREPARATIONS FOR POPE Francis's 2015 Synod on the Family, the Catholic bishop of Hong Kong at the time, John Cardinal Tong Hon, commented about divisions within the domestic spheres of the faithful in his 2014 Christmas pastoral letter. "Christmas celebrations will bring joy and peace, not only to our families," he said, "but also to our relatives and friends living abroad and those who have left home and are working in Hong Kong, as well as those families that are separated, living both in Hong Kong and mainland China." Here, Tong touched on a central nerve of contemporary Chinese societies, especially in recent times—and most especially in that particular year of 2014. "Catholic families, like others, in mainland China," he said, "see their young members move from the countryside to work, study, or do business in cities. They usually go home only once or twice a year, weakening their relationship with both the family and the Church." He went on to say that many Chinese "Catholic couples have not received any formation for the Sacrament of Marriage, premarital, or after-marriage care." However, he was pleased to see, nonetheless, the uptick in "awareness of family values." He concluded with a reference to the series of pro-democracy occupy protests known as the Umbrella Movement that had blocked main streets in Hong Kong for seventy-nine days that year: "Recently, some members of families in Hong Kong have become hostile towards one another because of differences in opinion regarding public issues. I sincerely hope that they can reconcile with those among whom they are not at peace."[1] The Anglican archbishop Paul Kwong had similar things to say about the Umbrella Movement in his Christmas letter that year. He was "anxious indeed to bid farewell to 2014, a most unsettling year in this city's recent history," noting "the foundations of basic human social relations— mutual trust, acceptance, respect, and tolerance—have been gutted." Citing a recent survey, he noted how "close to 19 percent" of Hong Kong residents had had relationships "deteriorate due to the political differences" over that year, of which "almost 59 percent reported terrible loss among friends, and 27 percent among family members. . . . That breakdown in relationships and human connection," he said, "has cascaded down to colleagues, classmates, and relatives."[2]

It might be tempting to position these two Christmas pastoral letters, one from the cardinal-bishop of the Catholic Diocese of Hong Kong at the time and the other from the current archbishop of Hong Kong Sheng Kung Hui (the Anglican Province of Hong Kong), as the basis for ecumenism in that city. After all, they do outline some of the central ecumenical issues in Hong Kong after its 1997 handover from British colonial rule to the sovereignty of the People's Republic of China (PRC). Within this national structure, the city is a Special Administrative Region (SAR) of the PRC, existing in a constitutional framework enshrined in the Basic Law as "one country, two systems." This arrangement is a bit of a purposeful contradiction: there are provisions for Hong Kong's political, economic, and social autonomy, but there are also avenues for integrating the society into the PRC in terms of national consciousness and political economy. Writing in 2014, the bishops criticize what they see as the radicalization of democracy activists in the Umbrella Movement, in which protesters emphasized the autonomy of Hong Kong over against the sovereignty of the PRC. This independence streak, the bishops suggest, has exacerbated unrest in post-handover Hong Kong. Familial domestic life has especially been socially taxed by such radical activities because coming down on the one country or the two systems

1. Tong, "Christmas Pastoral Letter."
2. Kwong, "Archbishop's Christmas Message 2014."

is a matter of ideology, a way of imagining what political sovereignty has to do with everyday life and personal consciousness in Hong Kong. The bishops thus encourage ideological opinions to be set aside in order to heal Hong Kong at the level of the family, the most intimate space of quotidian social relations. Here, the seductive move is to categorize these episcopal pronouncements as the real work of ecumenism, the healing of schism not only at the ecclesial level but also in social relations—in the *oikoumenē* as it is inhabited by people living their lives regardless of religious affiliation.

It is especially easy, then, to fall into the trap of seeing these two bishops, Tong and Kwong, as spokespersons for Hong Kong ecumenism. After all, they oversee the two churches that have often been seen in ecumenical relationship to each other, especially in the relations between the Catholic Diocese founded in 1946 and the Hong Kong Christian Council (HKCC) established in 1954, the Anglican-Roman Catholic International Commission (ARCIC) that met in Hong Kong in 2012, and the Ecclesiological Investigations conference hosted by the Anglican Church in 2016. But this view from above, as it were, is incomplete at best. Since the 1997 handover, there has been a temptation for these ecclesial edifices, especially the HKCC and the Catholic Diocese, to align with the city's new secular political masters. As a number of scholars (including Archbishop Kwong himself in his published doctoral thesis) have brilliantly shown, the SAR government has made consistent efforts to court these religious establishments for their political influence in helping their people to develop a stronger identification with the PRC.[3] The result has not been social stability. In 1996, controversy ensued when the HKCC responded positively to the official PRC newspaper, *Xinhua News Daily*, when it called for religious organizations to host an interfaith celebration of National Day on October 1 to commemorate the founding of the PRC.[4] Another point of contention has been the state's identification of official religious organizations to participate in its "Election Committee" for Chief Executive, a group of twelve hundred business elites and civil society representatives who vote on behalf of the people of Hong Kong, effectively denying suffrage to ordinary residents.[5] More recently, Cardinal Tong defended former Chief Executive Donald Tsang, also a devout Catholic, from corruption charges, stating, "Let the one who is without sin cast the first stone." So, too, one of the first events that occurred after the election of current Chief Executive Carrie Lam Cheng Yuet-ngor,

3. Leung and Chan, *Changing Church-State Relations in Hong Kong*; Kwong, *Identity in Community*; Ko, *Sacred Citizens and the Secular City*; Tse and Tan, *Theological Reflections*.

4. Chan, "Nationalism and Religious Protest."

5. Chan, "Nominating Protestant Representatives."

who is also Catholic, was an interreligious ceremony offering prayers for the stability of Hong Kong within a PRC framework. Archbishop Kwong himself is a member of the Chinese People's Political Consultative Conference (CPPCC), a gathering of advisors in the PRC drawn from throughout greater China and the diaspora as apologists for the PRC. The newly appointed successor to Cardinal Tong as bishop of Hong Kong, Michael Yeung Ming-cheung, has voiced his desire for full reconciliation between Hong Kong and PRC Catholics, relativizing the PRC's acts of repression of Chinese Christianity in taking down crosses and bulldozing buildings as merely enforcing construction codes. That each of these events has been marked by dissent should evoke some suspicion. Are official ecclesial establishments—like the Catholic Diocese, the Anglican Province, and the HKCC—the only voices of ecumenism in Hong Kong? Do they really speak for families in Hong Kong?

What I hope to describe is a more complex picture of ecumenism in Hong Kong and its relationship to family values advocacy. I argue that post-handover collaborations between Protestants and Catholics advocating for the integrity of the family have actually tended to frame the domestic sphere as needing to be defended from incursions by the PRC as the "one country" has systematically eroded Hong Kong's "two systems" autonomy since the handover. There may be some surprises here. Usually taken to be a socially conservative issue, advocacy for family values might be easily cast as reinforcing the power of the ecumenical establishment. However, the evangelical organizations that invoked Catholic teaching on sexuality to lobby against the Sexual Orientation Discrimination Ordinance (SODO) in the early 2000s framed their actions as democratic activism that opposed the government's imposition of liberal sexual norms onto their understanding of the family. They even compared their activities to that of the Catholic and Protestant alliance known as the Civil Human Rights Front (CHRF), which organized a demonstration of about half a million people in 2003 against an anti-sedition bill. The bill, based on Basic Law's Article 23, would have restricted freedoms of speech and religion, including the freedom to criticize the PRC. Similarly, since 1999, the Catholic Diocese of Hong Kong has been organizing a coalition with other members of civil society, including Protestants, to fight for the "right of abode" as outlined in Basic Law's Article 24, the promise of permanent residency after seven years of working in Hong Kong for migrant workers and children living in the PRC but born to Hong Kong parents. Here, too, the activism is situated in solidarity with Hong Kong autonomy, as it is pressure from the PRC's central government that is preventing these residency rights for migrants and splintering their families. In other words, religious institutions are not all aligned with the state all the time. Sometimes, evangelical organizations, members of ecumenical institutions, and even the Catholic Diocese may side with a democratic movement resisting the state, often in defense of the family.

The surprising argument reached from this analysis of these religious activist alliances, each centered on the family, is that ecumenical work defending the domestic sphere's integrity in Hong Kong is usually aligned with the demand for some kind of autonomy from the PRC. This contention runs contrary to the bishops' social analysis of the Umbrella Movement. During the occupations, student protesters, democracy activists, and their allies demanded "genuine universal suffrage," the right for each Hong Kong resident to vote without Beijing determining who their candidates were to be. The origins of this formulation of political autonomy lay in the 2013–2014 civic education movement called Occupy Central with Love and Peace (OCLP). In deliberation forums which OCLP conducted, what became popularized was the notion of "civil nomination," the possibility for Hong Kong people to write in their own candidates for election. Civil nomination became the *mot du jour* in a referendum in June 2014 in which nearly eight hundred thousand people—more than 10 percent of the population—participated. But that same month, the PRC's National People's Congress's Standing Committee slammed the idea with a "White Paper" clarifying that the practice of "one country, two systems" emphasized the sovereignty of the one country that is integrating Hong Kong into its fold. What then followed in August was a "Green Paper" mandating that political candidates in Hong Kong should "love Hong Kong and love China," effectively nixing the notion of autonomy inherent in civil nomination because this would guarantee vetting of candidates by Beijing. When Hong Kong residents took to the streets in protest in September, the police brutality they experienced stimulated an occupation of the streets that became the Umbrella Movement. Out of those protests came the novel idea that Hong Kong might even be conceptualized as independent of the PRC, though the politics of Hong Kong independence have proven controversial because of their occasional recourse to street violence and ethnic slurs uttered at PRC citizens.

In order to see this ecumenical dynamic from below, relating geopolitics and the family in Hong Kong, my strategy in this paper is to move backward in time. There are several stages in this chapter, then. First, I offer a methodological statement. I then examine family values politics in the wake of Article 23, through which I show that even social conservatives in Hong Kong defending the heteronormative family over against sexual liberalization position themselves as defenders of democracy and even of the autonomy of Hong Kong. Next, I examine the ecumenical network led by the Catholic Church to advocate for the right of abode for migrant families as also centered on the question of Hong Kong's judicial independence from the PRC. I conclude with some thoughts about ecumenism and the family in Hong Kong in the wake of the Umbrella Movement.

Methodology

This chapter is based on research trips I conducted in Hong Kong in 2010 and 2012 as well as the archiving of print and online sources that has continued into the present. In 2010, I took a five-week research trip to Hong Kong, informally having conversations about how Protestant and Catholic Christians engage civil society there. In 2012, my research was more formal but focused on the same question. I conducted forty-three semi-structured interviews with persons I identified as "key informants," people who could speak knowledgeably about the Hong Kong situation based on their positions of leadership in churches, parachurch organizations, theological schools, or the democracy movement. This was part of a larger project on Cantonese-speaking Protestants engaging civil society on the Pacific Rim. My comparative sites were Vancouver (where I conducted fifty interviews) and San Francisco (where I conducted forty-five). These interviews were then transcribed and analyzed. Most of the interviewees agreed to go on record by name and signed consent forms to that effect; those who did not want their names used have been pseudonymised. Triangulating these interviews were five focus groups that I conducted in churches that were self-selected and not randomized. The objective of the focus groups was not to gather any new information but to check whether the themes generated in the key informant interviews were part of the consciousness of those who were not in leadership positions. Based on this data, I also began gathering an audiovisual archive, which continues to this day. Unlike my other two sites, I found it very difficult to research Protestantism without Catholicism in Hong Kong because of the strong ecumenical ties across ideological strains.

When it comes to my positionality, I write as an outsider to Hong Kong. I grew up in the San Francisco Bay Area and did all of my higher education in Vancouver. Until recently, I was a Protestant Christian, mostly attending churches where the dominant language was Cantonese. However, having grown up in North America, my preferred language is English, though I speak Cantonese because my family taught it to me; I can read and write with the help of a dictionary and phonetic tools because of Chinese schools I attended as a child. Strictly speaking, I am not a "Hong Kong person," although my political sympathies lie with the Umbrella Movement due to its alignment with the poor and excluded in Hong Kong society. I saw this move also as a connection with Catholic social teaching, which I had learned about in high school and has inspired my personal faith commitment. Because a Byzantine Jesuit led the solidarity movements with the Umbrella Movement in Vancouver, my participation in them slowly moved me to be received by chrismation in an Eastern Catholic Church in a Vancouver suburb. In this way, I am a sympathetic outsider to some of the ecumenical movements about which I write in Hong Kong, but in no way do the movements that I either support or oppose mirror me. Society is not a mirror. My task is only to describe the people in it in the best way I can.

The "Sex-Culture" Version of Article 23: A Contrast of Democratic Ecumenisms

In 2004, the Society for Truth and Light (STL), the Hong Kong Sex-Culture Society, and the Hong Kong Alliance for Family Values issued a statement in *Ming Pao*, a mainstream newspaper in Hong Kong, that featured some nine thousand eight hundred signatures and two hundred Christian organizations. They opposed the Sexual Orientation Discrimination Ordinance (SODO), a hate crime bill that would severely penalize crimes and discriminatory actions committed against sexual minorities. When I asked Matthew Mak, the project director at the Hong Kong Sex-Culture Society, what he thought of SODO, he had an interesting response:

> It's supposedly to protect a group of homosexuals not to be discriminated against, but when we observed cases in North America and Europe, we found out that it doesn't only target Christianity—especially in Asia where Christianity is not the mainstream religion, it's also a minority—but it's targeting groups who disagree with homosexuality, using policy and law to take them apart. When a group or a band of people very much agree with homosexuality, the law has no relation to them. But once you use your faith, your very traditional values, your Chinese traditional values, your religion, even Buddhism, all feel that they don't accept homosexuality, then the law becomes—like we always say here—like a knife above your head. It's like a few years ago in Hong Kong, we all opposed Article 23, the national security and anti-sedition law to protect national security, but it's really just to protect the political regime. I feel that this is just like the homosexual version of Article 23. It is stripping away the freedoms of those who oppose homosexuality—their social freedoms and their freedoms to assembly. So, so-called

Hong Kong is a diverse and pluralistic society, we should be free to have our rights, and Basic Law also protects our freedoms, but you see that as gay activists promote this law, they package it as very beautiful, saying that this law really has no executive power, this law actually doesn't affect basic freedoms very much, but when we see in North America and Europe, the countries that do have this law, do have this policy, they have many rights that will be impinged upon.[6]

Mak's reference to the National Security Bill is fascinating, because it has putatively nothing to do with SODO—or even sexual minorities for that matter. Strangely enough, it is a reference to yet another ecumenical story. Having come into effect on the day of the July 1, 1997, handover of Hong Kong to Chinese sovereignty, Basic Law serves as a mini-constitution that enshrines "one country, two systems" in law. Its twenty-third article—commonly referred to as "Article 23"—reads that the SAR "shall enact laws on its own to prohibit any act of treason, secession, and subversion against the Central People's Government." In other words, Hong Kong's mini-constitution has it that the SAR government is supposed to pass laws—it *shall* pass them, in fact—preventing sedition against the PRC, prohibiting the "theft of state secrets," the operation of "foreign political organizations or bodies from conducting political activities in the Region," and the establishment of "ties with foreign political organizations or bodies."

In 2002, Hong Kong's Legislative Council indeed started to work on an anti-sedition bill based on Article 23. Some of the most controversial portions included its vague definitions of "treason" as attempts to "overthrow," "intimidate," or "compel" the "Central People's Government."[7] Another section banned "proscribed societies" blacklisted by Beijing, a veiled jab at the Buddhist sect called the Falun Gong that had been banned in the PRC since 1999.[8] Critics of the bill alleged that such veiled threats and bans on a religious group would lead to the widespread persecution of churches and the democracy movement with the PRC using the SAR government as a proxy. Accordingly, an ecumenical combination of forces fronted by the Hong Kong Catholic Diocese's Justice and Peace Commission and the Hong Kong Christian Institute (a progressive Protestant think tank) assembled the Civil Human Rights Front (CHRF) to organize a series of marches against Article 23. On July 1, 2003, there was a manifestation of the fullest force of opposition to the Article 23 bill: CHRF managed to turn

---

6. Interview with Matthew Mak, March 22, 2012.

7. Legislative Council of Hong Kong, *National Security Bill* 4.2.1.

8. Legislative Council of Hong Kong, *National Security Bill* 16.6.

an estimated half a million people onto the streets in protest. To Beijing's chagrin, the SAR government shelved the measure. Every year since, the CHRF protest has been repeated with similarly sizable numbers. With more of these protests—including in the aftermath of the Umbrella Movement— pressure from Beijing has been felt in Hong Kong to revisit the bill, ironically in an effort to police the demonstrations.

Mak's linkage of SODO to Article 23 offers a unique grounding of such ecumenism in the family. Managing projects at the Hong Kong Sex-Culture Society, Mak emphasized that it was an organization dedicated to research on pro-life, pro-family, and pro-democratic issues. In other words, it was also opposed to Article 23, but it also saw threats to democracy coming at the level of the family *from the state,* the SAR government. This Sex-Culture Society's backstory is also intriguing: it had become autonomous the Society for Truth and Light (STL). In the late 1990s, STL had been started as an activist organization to highlight the misreporting of stories on the media, especially tabloids. By the early 2000s, their sense was that this misinformation was beginning to bias the public sphere toward narratives favoring the liberalization of sexual morality in Hong Kong. One of the board members of that organization, Professor Kai-man Kwan, is a philosopher of religion at the Hong Kong Baptist University. He told me in an interview that he was not trying to incite an "irrational moral panic" or to have "imposed our Christian morality on the society." Instead, he named a number of "sexual crimes" he had recorded in his archives from 2000 to 2004 throughout Hong Kong, Taiwan, and the PRC that included serial rape, incest, reports of indecent thoughts, father-and-son gang rapes, teachers playing games with their students with sexual connotations, pimping, the usage of peeping video cameras, and young boys engaging in oral sex rape. As he went through this list in our interview, he said repeatedly, "I think this is horrifying."[9] Starting the Sex-Culture Society in 2001, Kwan decided with STL that it would be more strategic for the two institutions to become autonomous from each other. While STL continued its broader project of contesting media biases toward liberalism in Hong Kong, the Sex-Culture Society focused more on researching how sexual liberalization in the SAR's law might lead to what they portrayed as the undemocratic domination of a singular discourse on sexuality and the family in society. In pushing back against what it saw as the government's allowances for sexual crimes, the Sex-Culture Society imagined itself to be promoting democracy by maintaining the family as a sexually safe space.

9. Interviews with Kai-man Kwan, March 21, 2012; April 2, 2012.

Not only was 2003 the year of opposing the Article 23 bill, but it was also around the time for evangelicals to protest SODO, which the Legislative Council was also preparing. Kwan noted that he had originally supported SODO; the reduction of discrimination in a society is, after all, always healthy. But as he looked into a fund that had been started in the 1990s in the government's Equal Opportunity Commission (EOC) to reduce discrimination for sexual minorities, he found that "the fund was not used to educate people not to discriminate homosexuals, but it seemed to positively encourage a homosexual lifestyle. And we think that has crossed the line; that is not the original purpose of the education fund to reduce discrimination." In reaction to this fund and the government's proposed next step to pass SODO, Kwan wrote a book titled *"Right or Wrong?" "Crooked or Straight?" Reflections on the Ethics of Human Rights and Homosexuality*,[10] which included a lengthy chapter in which he tried using "academic reason, public reason; I do not base it on the Scriptures; I query whether this law is a just law or really a feasible law. That was really my first endeavor."[11]

Evangelicals, especially those working in the Sex-Culture Society, saw this activism as an ecumenical move to protect the freedom of religious groups to speak about the family in the same vein as opposition to Article 23. In fact, they saw themselves as sympathetic to the Catholic Church. After all, on August 17, 2003, eight lesbian and gay activists from Rainbow Action as well as another advocacy group for sexual minorities had interrupted a Mass at the Cathedral of the Immaculate Conception and staged a same-sex kiss in the nave. They were protesting an article published in *Kung Kao Po*, the local Hong Kong Catholic newspaper, on August 10.[12] The piece had clarified that the Vatican's position was that same-sex marriage was not permissible in Catholic teaching. Matthew Mak found that this incident resonated with him as an evangelical Protestant:

> So that year, in August 2003, there were some gay activists that rushed into a Catholic Mass to protest, saying that the Catholic Church was attacking gay and lesbian people and that Cardinal Zen at the time had no conscience and was discriminating against gay and lesbian people. But in the hearts of Hong Kong people, Cardinal Zen is a symbol of justice because he will lead people to oppose Article 23, to protect the rights of citizens, human rights, and even will oppose the Beijing government. So,

10. My translation.

11. Kwan, 「是非」、「曲直──對人權、同性戀的倫理反思．As a collection of articles, the whole book was published in 2004, then extensively revised and republished as a second edition in 2005.

12. "Catholic Church Alarmed."

> Cardinal Zen is an icon of democracy and human rights. But I think *Kung Kao Po*'s position made a lot of ordinary people shocked because they didn't think about the Catholic Church's position, the curia's position, but they do not understand how the Catholics' participation in society is very coherent—like they preserve the justice in the society and also preserve the integrity of marriage, so I think to evangelicals, we can accept this. We can accept this. On the one hand, we need to fight for democracy and human rights; on the other, we need to preserve the integrity of marriage.[13]

In other words, Mak framed the Catholic Church as modeling an integral social ethic for evangelical Protestants, one that did not divide democracy and human rights from traditional marriage. The only reason this is shocking, Mak suggests, is because outsiders to Catholicism (and evangelicalism, for that matter) might not be familiar with this kind of coherence, operating as they might from a framework that merges social justice with support for the legalization of same-sex marriage. Here, then, it should be noted that this claim of ecumenism was tenuous. While the Catholic Church's Marriage Office has since come out against SODO and same-sex marriage explicitly (especially in the lead-up to the Synod on the Family in 2015), Cardinal Zen in fact took a line of pacification with the gay and lesbian activists at the time. Following their protest, he held a meeting with them. "We have our doctrine, but whatever we could do to help you, we did," he told them, citing how the Catholic Church had advocated for the decriminalization of homosexuality since 1982, nine years before it was decriminalized in 1991, and had also supported their struggle for equality in employment and housing in the 1990s.[14]

Yet the fact remains that the evangelicals were able to assemble a critical mass. By 2003 and 2004, STL and the Sex-Culture Society, along with the Alliance for Family Values, had gathered almost ten thousand people to oppose SODO, including with street protests and the advertisement in *Ming Pao*. As Matthew Mak emphasized to me, "It was the largest showing of pro-democracy action since the June 4 incident in 1989," the Tiananmen Incident that had sent over one million Hongkongers into the streets to protest state-sponsored atrocities committed against students demanding democratic reform in Beijing. This reference to yet another Chinese protest suggests that the Sex-Culture Society is very much a part of the democracy

13. Interview with Matthew Mak, March 22, 2012.
14. Interview with Joseph Zen, March 29, 2003.

movement: they oppose the SAR government because they ultimately do not want to be under the authoritarian rule of the PRC.

In the anti-SODO campaign, then, the various evangelical organizations imagined themselves to be the voice of the people challenging the misrepresentation of sexual liberalization in the law. In part, this was because they imagined themselves to speak for the rights of all Christians, an ecumenical gesture that may not have been totally reciprocated but certainly mirrored the ecumenical opposition to Article 23. But there is also a backdrop here: their activism is against what they see as the SAR government's attempt to impose onto the people of Hong Kong a set of policies that would police their speech and silence their religious institutions. Ecumenical coalition-building is meant to gather the critical mass to oppose such state impositions, and what the Sex-Culture Society implies is that their success is due to the locus of the state's attack: the intimate sphere of the family.

The Right of Abode:
Ecumenism and the Question of Family Reunification

But is this the only way that the family is positioned against the state through ecumenical networks? From here, we might move from the right to the left via the Catholic Diocese of Hong Kong. As I said earlier, the Diocese's Marriage Office has also opposed SODO. However, the Catholic agenda on the family has also taken into consideration the question of migrant rights. Much of this has to do with the episcopal tenure of Joseph Cardinal Zen Ze-kiun as Hong Kong's bishop from 2002 to 2009. He was also one of the organizers of the original July 1, 2003, demonstration against Article 23, working alongside the CHRF.

In our interview, Zen offered an alternative way of politicizing the family, although he also cast the Catholic Church on the side of democracy. Zen said to me that the foremost social issue in Hong Kong was the "right to abode" for migrant workers and family reunification for those with relatives in the PRC. The backstory here has to do with yet another section of Basic Law: Article 24. This outlines what it calls the "right of abode," the constitutional guarantee of official residency for anyone who has lived and worked in Hong Kong for seven years. The problem was that the SAR government tends to deny permanent residence to temporary foreign workers from the Philippines and Indonesia as well as pregnant women from the mainland giving birth in Hong Kong hospitals and children of parents born in Hong Kong but living on the mainland. What makes this even more complicated is the role of Beijing. In *Ng Ka Ling v Director of Immigration* (1999), Hong

Kong's highest court, the Court of Final Appeal, ruled that children born
to Hong Kong parents on the mainland had the right of abode due to the
human right of family reunification. The Hong Kong Government did not
like this decision, alleging that it would bring an influx of migrants into a
city that was crowded enough already. The SAR then forwarded the decision to Beijing's National People's Congress's Standing Committee. Beijing
vacated the judgment. This act challenged the autonomy of Hong Kong's
courts, the discourse of migrant family reunion, and the right of abode in
one fell swoop.

For Zen, this incident set a bad legal precedent for family values.
Quoting his predecessor, John Baptist Cardinal Wu, Zen emphasized the
familial implications here in a pastoral letter titled "God Is Love," which he
had helped to draft as a coadjutor bishop:

> Now that was still the time of Cardinal Wu, and so the three of
> us [bishops, ordinary, and coadjutors] decided we should say
> something . . . the title [of our pastoral letter] is "God is love."
> It starts from talking about charity to be concerned of other
> people, to say that we must be open, it's the teaching of the Old
> Testament, New Testament, to welcome people into our com-
> munity because family union is very important; it's also guaran-
> teed by international covenant. So, the Cardinal reminded the
> people of Hong Kong, "No, you, you, you are all immigrants,
> descended of new immigrants, so why do you now refuse people
> to come?"[15]

The text of the pastoral letter is even more radical. "Based on the belief
that 'blood is thicker than water,' that 'all within the four seas are one family,'" the bishops write, "the Chinese people have always shown kindness to
others and taken delight in sharing. Faced then today with the question of
children born to Hong Kong parents in the Motherland, how can we harden
our hearts, look on with indifference and a lack of humanity, and use 'interpretation' to deny them hope?"[16] Here, the bishops straddle an interesting
tension. They point out that the Basic Law guarantees the SAR an independent judiciary, but they also say that Hong Kong and mainland Chinese
persons are *one people*. Family takes on a special meaning here: scaling out
from the intimate sphere, the bishops make the case that Chinese people
between Hong Kong and the PRC are also a family linked by blood and
bound by their common humanity. What is intriguing, then, is that it is the
autonomy of the SAR government to make judicial decisions that ensures

15. Interview with Joseph Zen, March 30, 2012.
16. Wu, "God Is Love."

this common consciousness. Ironically, the erosion of judicial autonomy by the PRC destabilizes these families—and the Chinese family, on a larger scale. Integration, in other words, is disintegration.

The ecumenical dimensions of this Catholic familial framework can be seen by scaling out to the coalition formed around the "right of abode" issue. Even within the Catholic diocese, there is a diversity of ideological viewpoints. For example, the Diocese's Justice and Peace Commission (HKJP) is headed by Jackie Hung Yu-Ling, a graduate of the Chinese University of Hong Kong's Centre for Catholic Studies. For Hung, the right of abode issue should be vigorously promoted within a human rights framework:

> Many of these rights issues need to be hard-sell. If I keep on selling these people as "so pitiful," I don't think that's the right approach. So, it's very hard . . . not to victimize them, we don't want to do that. . . . I am just saying that we are all the same. Like foreign domestic workers, the issue is very simple. In the Basic Law, it says that everyone who comes here to work for seven years has the right of abode. But why would the law exclude the foreign domestic workers? They do thirty years of work, they still have no right of abode![17]

Placing the HKJP in solidarity with migrant workers, Hung argues that everyone should be equal in the eyes of Hong Kong's law. This is a similar view to the bishops, but Hung makes the point that the appeal to pathos is overrated. Instead, she invokes legal fairness in a "hard-sell" way, a term in Hong Kong that refers to a pressure tactic in salesmanship in a way that is almost imposing. Here, there are already intimations of ecumenism: in her capacity of heading the HKJP, Hung was a founding member of the CHRF who protested the Article 23 bill, another use of the "hard-sell" tactic to oppose yet another iteration of the SAR government following the PRC's lead to subvert human rights in Hong Kong.

There was a broader Christian dimension, too. Italian liberation theologian Fr. Franco Mella, a longtime activist among workers in Hong Kong, condemned the SAR government for reinterpreting Basic Law to keep migrant workers and mothers from China out. By the time I interviewed him in 2012, Mella had made the issue of migrant residency a central part of his activism, even founding a "Right of Abode University" to educate migrant workers in subjects as diverse as English, Italian, German, history, political science, and economics. For Mella, the issue was theological: "The first sinner is the Hong Kong government, who haven't done their jobs. I feel that our church or principled people would say that humans are the most

17. Interview with Jackie Hung, March 26, 2012.

important—migrant workers or China mothers—and we must call on the courts." When we spoke, the chief executive elections were looming in 2012, and during the candidate debates, one of the favored candidates, Henry Tang Ying-yen, insisted that he would not allow pregnant women from the PRC to enter Hong Kong to give birth. Tang was also a self-advertised evangelical Protestant. The scandal of those elections, though, was that Tang quickly fell out of favor with both the public and the SAR's political masters in Beijing. The media discovered that he had built a structure at his house for which he did not have a city permit, and after he blamed his wife, it was discovered that he had had an affair with another woman and, to boot, had thrown his own spouse under the proverbial bus. Mella couched his comments in this context:

> So, when Henry Tang says he will not give China mothers a bed, and then we discover he has children out of wedlock and an illegal structure, we can forgive you for that, but we can't forgive you unless you give beds to China mothers. . . . *That's* the sin! Henry Tang, he is a Christian, yes, but if you reinterpret Basic Law and manipulate the Court of Final Appeal, *that's* the crime![18]

Mella's commentary introduces yet another reason to advocate for the right of abode: the politicians who claimed to be Christian were not acting in a theologically consistent way and needed to be held accountable at a theological level. Here, then, is a broad Catholic consensus among three parties: the appeal to the Chinese people as a nation, a human rights framework, and a Christian theological critique. As differently as these three Catholic groups might come at the issue, they held that part of advocating for family values in Hong Kong was to work for the right of abode for migrant workers, mothers from China, and children born to Hong Kong parents on the mainland.

Scaling even further out, the Catholic Church was joined by an alliance of younger Protestant activists, who have also made the right of abode one of their central political agendas. The base of this network was the progressive Hong Kong Christian Institute (HKCI)—incidentally the place where CHRF, including HKJP's Jackie Hung, had first convened to plan out the activism against the Article 23 bill. The HKCI director from 2000 to 2007, feminist theologian Rose Wu Lo-sai, framed HKCI as a "minority dissenting voice" teaming up with the HKJP on a number of issues related to the CHRF, including the right of abode. When I asked her to speak explicitly

18. Interview with Franco Mella, March 15, 2012.

about the nature of this ecumenism, Wu admitted that there was a bit of difficulty on questions of familial constitution:

> With Catholics, there are a lot of positions that we have coop-
> erated with them, like on these right of abode issues, migrant
> worker issues, human rights issues. But on the sexual minorities
> issues, then it's harder, maybe. Like they might have some pro-
> gressive groups, but under the structure, it's harder. The bishop
> is now different, but in the past when it was Cardinal Joseph
> Zen, we had frequent collaboration.[19]

Here, what is frustrating Wu as a Protestant is that the Catholic Church does not separate right from left in terms of family values. Although Cardinal Zen was a moderating voice when it came to the question of sexual minorities, Wu points out that, because the structure of the Catholic Church is still conservative, all it took was the accession of a new bishop, Cardinal Tong in this case, to undo the moderation. Nevertheless, there are no obstacles for ecumenical collaboration when it comes to the right of abode issue, not to mention the issues of democracy and human rights. As Wu noted in another part of the interview, these are "basic" issues. However primal sexuality might be, the right of abode speaks to something elementary, too: the rights of families to be together. As far as ecumenism between the HKJP and HKCI went, then, the focus was, therefore, not on sexual minorities but much more on what they could confidently share in common: the plight of migrants and the right of abode.

An even more radical group associated with HKCI was Narrow Church. Comprised of a group of young divinity graduates from the Chung Chi Divinity School at the Chinese University of Hong Kong (CUHK), its *modus operandi* was to accuse social conservatives like STL and the Sex-Culture Society for being part of a "religious right." Indeed, progressive seminary faculty had laid the intellectual groundwork for this accusation with the 2010 publication by Dirty Press of a book titled *Religious Right*. The text incensed the targeted conservatives so much that, the next year, a volume arguing that social conservatives saw themselves as part of the democracy movement was compiled in response—precisely the argument that I presented in the previous section.

Like HKCI, Narrow Church also operates ecumenically. When I interviewed its members, they spoke of tensions over their direct way of vulgar speaking between themselves, the HKJP, and another evangelical group called Christians for Hong Kong Society—a tenseness that bespoke frequent collaboration. Publicly protesting an anti-SODO rally on January

---

19. Interview with Rose Wu, March 22, 2012.

13, 2013, one of their spokespersons, Tak Chi "Fastbeat" Tam, accuses the "religious right" of being apolitical on anything but sex:

> Why suddenly, when it's homosexuality, do they tell you to go protest and go to Government House? Why is the pastor so contradictory? Now if he answers you that it is a black-and-white moral issue forbidden by the Bible—God doesn't like homosexuality—then, you should ask him a second question: the Bible also says that you must be good to the poor, not to promote poverty, to not have the officials abuse their power. . . . Why, pastor, don't you support these?[20]

At this farthest end of the spectrum, members of Narrow Church have publicly demanded answers as to why socially conservative evangelicals had such strict views on sexuality while seldom taking seriously the scriptural injunctions to love the stranger and to enact economic justice. Opposing the "religious right," the issue of the right of abode and its family values had managed to pull together what might be called an *ecumenical left*. Contesting the "religious right's" focus on the heteronormativity of the family, this version of family values observes that when a government's migration policy is exclusionary, it breaks up families across borders, especially those families that are economically disadvantaged. Fastbeat suggests in turn that what this activism does is shed light on what is really going on within the social conservatives' narrow view of family values politics. Hinting that clergy tend to be drawn to issues of sexuality while forgetting that the Bible also speaks about poverty and the abuse of government power, he suggests that they must take a broader view on the family. Granted, he is also not exactly fair in his portrayal of the social conservatives, who understand themselves also to be opposing the government, highlighting abuses of power, and advocating for democracy; this is, in fact, the overall criticism that has been launched at the book *Religious Right*. Yet, what this showdown also emphasizes is the centrality of the family in ecumenical debate. For the so-called "religious right," ecumenical action centers on the family that is presumably under attack by a government seeking to be liberal in its treatment of sexual minorities. For Fastbeat and his allies, the family is materially attacked by that same government, only with the backdrop of the PRC being much less metaphorical than the Article 23 analogy invoked by the conservatives.

What is striking, then, about this mode of ecumenical activism is that the family has to be defended against an SAR government that is backed by Beijing. Just like the socially conservative invocation of Article 23, the central case framing the right to abode is the Hong Kong-Beijing debacle

20. SOCREC, "快必問[恐同教會]牧師2個問題."

regarding the *Ng Ka Ling* decision. What this suggests yet again is that the political backdrop to these family values politics has, since the handover, revolved around the geopolitics of Hong Kong-Beijing relations. Ecumenical groups mediate between affected families and the ideological state apparatus. The only difference is in their views of how the family is being mistreated by this political structure.

Conclusion:
Ecumenism and the Family after the Umbrella Movement

In light of this analysis, perhaps the episcopal claims that the Umbrella Movement divided families over political ideology are a bit of an exaggeration. Instead, it can be said, since the 1997 handover, ecumenical alliances in Hong Kong have been focused, in large part, on defending the family from the incursion of the PRC. I outlined several cases to this effect: the so-called "religious right's" activism against SODO, the "right of abode" politics of what I call the "ecumenical left," and even the division in the intimate sphere unleashed by the Umbrella Movement. In each case, the institutional edifice that is being defended seems to be the post-handover SAR government and their political masters in Beijing. For the "right of abode" activists, the PRC's erosion of judicial autonomy in Hong Kong results in the splitting of families, some between Hong Kong and China and others between their workplaces in Hong Kong and the countries from which they migrated. This is the same problem that the CHRF—the alliance of HKJP and HKCI, along with other civil society groups—protested in the July 1 Demonstration in 2003 against Article 23, which would have opened the door for a PRC-controlled security state in Hong Kong. In turn, the Hong Kong Sex-Culture Society compared its activities to the Article 23 demonstrations, framing them as also opposing the government for the sake of establishing a truly democratic society. Each of these groups is ecumenical in the sense of including both Catholics and Protestants in their activities, but they are divided from each other based on how to oppose the PRC's erosion of "one country, two systems" in Hong Kong. These political structures matter to them, in turn, because of their effect on the constitution of the family, whether on the question of sexual minorities, the right of abode, or the freedom of domestic life without the shadow of a police state.

What these grounded ecumenisms highlight is how Christian politics actually play out on the ground in Hong Kong. Certainly, there are formal ecclesial edifices with bishops who make pronouncements on society that might be taken to be the ecumenical word on social and political matters, including on the Umbrella Movement. But reception by civil society is key. In Cardinal Zen's actions on the right of abode, Article 23, and dealing amicably with sexual minorities, alliances for social justice became easily formed. So too, when evangelical Protestants framed the issue of sexual liberalization as eroding a democratic society, they were able to muster wide support. In each of these cases, a family structure of some sort is being defended against incursion by the PRC through the SAR government. In this way, the presumptions of Cardinal Tong and Archbishop Kwong to diagnose the Umbrella Movement as dividing families might, in fact, be seen themselves as a division from these grounded ecumenical activities. For them, the democratic protesters themselves are to blame for the social fragmentation. The shadow is still China, but the ecumenical ideology surrounding the family is shifting toward conciliation with the Chinese state as a stabilizing force, at least at the official levels.

What this perhaps means is that the issue of ecumenical concerns about the family in Hong Kong will be one to watch. Given the Umbrella Movement's own production of newly grounded ecumenisms, could it be that there will be an increasing rift between the ecumenism of the official churches and the ecumenical work of building a democratic and autonomous society in Hong Kong at the ground level? And might this new polarization, which still sits in the shadow of the PRC, engender a new proliferation of ideologies of the Hong Kong family, dividing families even more?

Bibliography

"Catholic Church Alarmed as Gay Activists Desecrate Sunday Mass." *UCANews*, August 18, 2003. Online. https://www.ucanews.com/story-archive/?post_name=/2003/08/18/catholic-church-alarmed-as-gay-activists-desecrate-sunday-mass&post_id=22958.

Chan, Shun-Hing. "Nationalism and Religious Protest: The Case of the National Day Celebration Service Controversy of the Hong Kong Protestant Churches." *Religion, State, and Society* 28.4 (2000) 359–83.

———. "Nominating Protestant Representatives for the Election Committee: Church-State Relations in Hong Kong after 1997." *Hong Kong Journal of Sociology* 4 (2003) 155–83.

Ko, Tinming. *The Sacred Citizens and the Secular City: Political Participation of Protestant Ministers in Hong Kong During a Time of Change*. Farnham, UK: Ashgate, 2000.

Kwan, Kai Man.「是非」、「曲直——對人權、同性戀的倫理反思 [*"Right or Wrong," "Crooked or Straight": Reflections on the Ethics of Human Rights and Homosexuality*]. 2nd ed. Hong Kong: China Alliance, 2005.

Kwong, Paul. "Archbishop's Christmas Message 2014." *Echo*, December 21, 2014. Online. http://echo.hkskh.org/news_article_details.aspx?lang=1&nid=106.

———. *Identity in Community: Toward a Theological Agenda for the Hong Kong SAR.* Zürich: LIT Verlag Münster, 2011.

Legislative Council of Hong Kong. *National Security Bill to Amend the Crimes Ordinance, the Official Secrets Ordinance, and the Societies Ordinance Pursuant to the Obligation Imposed by Article 23 of the Basic Law of the Hong Kong Special Administrative Region of the People's Republic of China and to Provide for Related, Incidental, and Consequential Amendments.* October 7, 2003. DMA72814v.5.

Leung, Beatrice, and Shun-Hing Chan. *Changing Church-State Relations in Hong Kong, 1950–2000.* Hong Kong: Hong Kong University Press, 2003.

Ng Ka Ling v. Director of Immigration, 1 HKLRD 315 (1999).

SOCREC. "快必問[恐同教會]牧師2個問題 [Fastbeat Asks 'Homophobic Church' Pastors Two Questions]." YouTube video. No longer available online.

Tong, John Hon. "A Christmas Pastoral Letter from John Cardinal Tong: Blessings to All Families and People in Need." *Catholic Diocese of Hong Kong*, December 8, 2014. Online. https://catholic.org.hk/en/2014%E5%B9%B4%E8%81%96%E8%AA%95%E7%AF%80%E7%89%A7%E5%87%BD.

Tse, Justin K. H. "Under the Umbrella: Grounded Christian Theologies and Democratic Working Alliances in Hong Kong." *Review of Religion in Chinese Society* 2.1 (2015) 109–42.

Tse, Justin K. H., and Jonathan Y. Tan, eds. *Theological Reflections on the Hong Kong Umbrella Movement.* New York: Palgrave, 2016.

Wu, John Baptist. "God Is Love." *Catholic Diocese of Hong Kong*, June 6, 1999. Online. https://catholic.org.hk/v2/en/message_jw/y1999_4_god.html.

7

Ecumenism and Immigration: The "New Christians" in Italy

CHUKWUMAMKPAM VINCENT IFEME

IN THE EARLY YEARS following the Second Vatican Council, the Italian Catholic bishops established an episcopal commission for ecumenism and dialogue at the national level: Ufficio Nazionale per l'Ecumenismo e Dialogo Interreligoso (UNEDI). At the regional level, initiatives were taken to establish regional ecumenical councils or boards that could unite various Christian churches and denominations. The Catholic Church in Italy also established some specialized institutes and research centers to study and promote ecumenism. But the great vital and dynamic force and fruits of the ecumenical movement released by Vatican II are also greatly felt at the grassroots level. With the recent phenomenon of immigration in Italy, a new pathway and opportunity for ecumenism is envisaged. This is especially true when considering the "new Christian" immigrants of non-Roman Catholic traditions—for example, the rising number of immigrants of evangelical and Protestant traditions from the global South as well as immigrants from the Eastern Orthodox Churches, now on the decline as some of their Eastern European home countries now offer more job opportunities having entered the European Union.

Official Ecumenical Dialogue of the Roman Catholic Church in Italy Following Vatican II

There were so many circumstances and so many personalities, known and unknown—laity, priests, religious, theologians, prelates, etc.—that prepared the way for the Second Vatican Ecumenical Council which Pope Saint John XXIII inaugurated and Pope Saint Paul VI continued and concluded. Through their dedication, tenacity, and sometimes silent but constructive dialogue, these numerous men and women struggled amongst themselves to weaken and dismantle the age-old barriers and hostilities that had been erected and fortified for centuries within, around, and outside the Church.

Among the people that I would highlight are the following:

- Antonio Fogazzaro (1842–1911), an Italian liberal Catholic lay person, who authored works such as *Piccolo Mondo Moderno* and *Il Santo*, concentrating on social and human analysis against the religious fundamentalism and clericalism of the time.

- Augustin Bea (1881–1968), first president of the Secretariat for the Promotion of Christian Unity, created in 1960, and the main architect of the Vatican II documents, *Unitatis Redintegratio* (on ecumenism) and *Nostra Aetate* (on interreligious dialogue). He helped convince his colleagues in the Roman curia to turn from their prejudice to a positive attitude in dialogue.

- Yves Congar (1904–1995)

- Karl Rahner (1904–1984)

- Hans Urs von Balthasar (1905–1988) whose milestone works included *Razing the Bastions*

- Cardinal Johannes Willebrands (1909–2006), president of the Secretariat for the Promotion of Christian Unity, whose numerous initiatives intensified the dialogue between the Roman Catholic Church and other Christian Churches. He was a member of the mixed working groups of the Roman Catholic Church and the Anglican Church, the Lutheran World Federation of Churches, and the World Council of Churches; he also had various contacts within the Orthodox Churches.

Also worthy of mentioning are some important milestone documents, declarations, decrees, and encyclicals on ecumenism that followed Vatican II:

- *Unitatis Redintegratio* (November 21, 1964): This decree on the restoration of Christian unity could be called the Roman Catholic Church's most official document on ecumenism under the authority of Vatican II. It affirms that attainment of unity among the Christian Churches "is the concern of the whole Church, faithful and shepherds alike" (5).[1]

- *Ecclesiam Suam* (August 6, 1964): This was the first encyclical of Pope Saint Paul VI who brought Vatican II to a close and assured its implementations. With a very special emphasis on ecumenism, the encyclical dwelt on the urgency of dialogue among different Churches and ecclesial communities with the world and other religions.

- *Redemptoris Missio* (December 7, 1990): In this encyclical, Pope Saint John Paul II insisted that each member of the faithful and all Christian communities are called to practice dialogue.

- *Ut Unum Sint* (May 25, 1995): This encyclical of Pope Saint John Paul II states that "the entire life of Christians is marked by a concern for ecumenism; and they are called to let themselves be shaped, as it were, by that concern. . . . Thus, it is absolutely clear that ecumenism, the movement promoting Christian unity, *is not just some sort of 'appendix'* which is added to the Church's traditional activity. Rather, ecumenism is an organic part of her life and work, and consequently must pervade all that she is and does; it must be like the fruit borne by a healthy and flourishing tree which grows to its full stature" (15, 20).

- *Joint Declaration on the Doctrine of Justification* (October 31, 1999): Without concealing the divergences that continue to exist, this was a fundamental agreement between the Catholic Church and the Lutheran World Federation on the doctrine of justification.[2] The churches

---

1. Denzinger and Hünermann, *Enchiridion Symbolorum*, 4191.

2. Lutheran World Federation and the Catholic Church, *Joint Declaration on the Doctrine of Justification*. The agreement on the doctrine of justification is, of course, not without criticism from members of both faiths, and it has some basic problems and difficulties. There seems to be a reaction on both sides against a certain compromise declared in the document but not actually in the exact teaching or language of the members. For instance, some Catholics demand further clarification on certain issues raised in the agreement, especially regarding the following paragraphs: "The Justified as Sinner" (28–30); on the importance for Catholics and Lutherans of the doctrine as a criterion for the life and practice of the Church (18); on the Catholic understanding of "cooperation" and the Lutheran understanding of "mere passivity" (20–21); on the sacrament of penance as "the sacrament that justifies anew" and different from Baptism (30); on understanding the differences between Catholics and Protestants to consist simply in questions of emphasis or language (whereas, it may concern some aspects of substance) (40); and the different character of the two signatories (that is, the real authority of Lutheran synodal consensus in the life and doctrine of the Lutheran community). For all these lacking clarifications, the Catholic Church's official response to the *Joint Declaration*, given by the Pontifical Council for Promoting Christian Unity, made

signed this common declaration after long years of ecumenical meetings and theological discussions.

With this background established, I would like now to return to the Italian context and discuss UNEDI, the episcopal commission for ecumenism and dialogue. Its specific functions are to encourage the prayer for Christian unity (such as the one in January during the Week of Prayer for Christian Unity) and provide guidance to local communities through formative programs and meetings in order to bring them to maturity regarding issues of Christian unity. The topics addressed have included: "Problemi e prospettive dell'ecumenismo nelle Chiese locali e nelle comunioni regionali di Chiese d'Italia"—the problems and prospects of ecumenism in the local churches and the regional Communion of Churches in Italy (1979); "La ripresa del dialogo ecumenico in Italia dopo il giubileo del 2000 alla luce della Novo Millennio ineunte e della Charta Oecumenica"—continuing ecumenical dialogue in Italy after the Jubilee Year 2000 in light of the Novo Millennio Inuente (At the Beginning of the New Millennium) and the charter for ecumenism (2001); "In Unitate Spiritus"[3] and some interconfessional national conferences (2008), such as the "Our Father" (1999), the Beatitudes (2003), and the Ecumenical Charter (2006).

The National Office for Ecumenism and Interreligious Dialogue (UNEDI) under the Italian Episcopal Conference (CEI) also organizes annual conventions for diocesan directors and UNEDI representatives. In Bari in 2015, for example, its theme was "Unico è la sposa di Cristo" (One is the Spouse of Christ); the seventeenth edition in Trento in 2016 addressed the topic, "Cattolici e protestanti a 500 anni dalla Riforma: Uno sguardo comune sull'oggi e sul domani" (Catholics and Protestants Five Hundred Years after the Reformation: The Present and the Future).

The Catholic Church in Italy has also established some specialized institutes and research centers for ecumenism. Very prominent ones include the Istituto di Studi Ecumenici San Bernardino in Venice, which grew out of the experience of various ecumenism courses that began in 1975 in Verona's theological institute of the Friars Minor of San Bernardino, affiliated with the theological faculty of Rome's Pontificio Ateneo "Antonianum." There

---

it clear that "we cannot yet speak of a consensus such as would eliminate every difference between Catholics and Lutherans in the understanding of justification" (Pontifical Council for Promoting Christian Unity, "Response of the Catholic Church," para. 2.)

3. "In the Unity of the Spirit"—the title of UNEDI's November 2008 national convention in Rome that brought together delegates from all of Italy's diocesan ecumenical offices. For more information, see https://ecumenismo.chiesacattolica.it/2009/01/22/in-unitate-spiritus-2.

is also the Centro per l'Ecumenismo in Italia[4] (Center for Ecumenism in Italy) founded in Venice in 2008 to encourage the collection, preservation, and study of ecumenical historical artifacts in Italy by sustaining historical-theological research projects so as to promote the reconstruction of the people and events related to the ecumenical movement and dialogue. The center produces a monthly online bulletin, *Veritas in Caritate,* that is mainly a collection of information on ecumenism in Italy. It is also very pertinent to mention the Centro di Documentazione del Movimento Ecumenico in Italia established in Livorno in 2000. The initiative of Msgr. Alberto Abbondi (†2010) and other convinced supporters of ecumenical movements—for example, Bishops Pietro Giachetti (†2006), Clemente Riva (†1999), and Vincenzo Savio (†2004)—the center's main objectives are to keep ecumenism alive, especially in the diocese of Livorno, and promote interconfessional dialogue at the national level. Another prominent center is the Istituto Ecumenico-Patristico Greco-Bizantino San Nicola, Bari, managed by the Dominicans as part of the Pontifical University of St. Thomas Aquinas—the Angelicum—in Rome.

Italy also has regional ecumenical councils, or boards, that unite various Christian communities. They meet several times a year to share ideas, pray together, and propose and promote common initiatives and activities. For instance, in the Marche region where I work, the Consiglio delle Chiese Cristiane delle Marche (CCCM) comprises members who are Baptist, Methodist, Anglican, and Seventh-Day Adventists as well as Orthodox of the Patriarchates of Bucharest, Constantinople, etc., and, of course, Roman Catholics. In April 2016, for instance, the CCCM organized a day of prayer for the care of creation at the national park of Fiastra Abbey (*Camminiamo insieme per il Creato*); the second edition was held in 2017 at the *Monastero san Silvestro Abate Fabriano, AN.* All of these churches participated with numerous representatives; the day consisted of silent walks in the woods while listening to the Word of God as well as intermittent prayers and reflections from representatives of these ecclesial communities.

It is also at the grassroots level[5] that we experience the great and vital, dynamic force and fruits of ecumenical movements set in motion by the Second Vatican Council. For example, we have the remarkable testimony of the Segretariato Attività Ecumeniche (SAE)[6]—Secretariat for Ecumenical Activities—an interconfessional lay association devoted to the promotion

---

4. Learn more on its website, http://www.centroecumenismo.it.

5. On the importance of simultaneous official and grassroots dialogues, see Daneo, *Impensate Vie,* 133–41.

6. See the SAE website, http://www.saenotizie.it.

of ecumenism and dialogue that originated with formal Jewish–Christian dialogue. The SAE organizes local groups and annual programs for ecumenical formation that are open to all, and the program proceedings are published regularly. The SAE traces its roots to Venice, around 1947, and the efforts of Maria Vingiani, who later became its president and tireless enthusiast thanks to her friendship and collaboration with Jules Isaac (1877–1963). When the Second Vatican Council was announced in 1959, she transferred to Rome under the tutelage and encouragement of Pope Saint John XXIII. SAE's members include Roman Catholic laity, Evangelicals, Orthodox, and Jews. It is important to note that priests, pastors, and religious can be part of the association but simply as friends. There is a permanent committee of biblical experts and theologians from various ecclesial confessions that assists in formation and theological research. Some SAE representatives who are worthy of note for their ecumenical efforts include the Waldensian Evangelical Church pastors Renzo Bertlot, Giorgio Giradet (†2011), and Paolo Ricca. From the Catholic side, we have Fr. Carlo Molari, Fr. Germano Pattaro (†1999), Msgr. Luigi Sartori (†2007), and Fr. Giovanni Cereti. At the grassroots level, there are also some ecumenical and interreligious movements overlapping at various points. Two examples are the "People and Religions" meeting promoted by the Community of Sant'Egidio and the Focolare Movement's annual Centro Uno event which hosts face-to-face dialogue among different faith groups in Rocci di Papa, Italy.[7]

Ecumenism and Immigration: The "New Christians" in Italy

Why "New Christians"?

When you say the "Christian Church," the only thing that comes to mind for the average Italian is the Roman Catholic Church. The religious situation in Italy could be described as "complete monopoly" or, at best, an "imperfect pluralism." Italian public opinion considers every other religion or ecclesial community apart from the Roman Catholic Church as little known or of lesser value. And in some cases, these other faith communities are even despised and often much more disadvantaged than the majority or the mainstream Roman Catholic Church.[8]

7. See Salvarini, "Le Esperienze del Pluralismo," 142.

8. See Trombetta, "Aspetti Conflittuali del Dialogo Ecumenico." Franco Garelli, in his book *L'Italia Cattolica nell'Epoca del Pluralism*, shows that 86 percent of Italians identify themselves as Roman Catholics, less than 5 percent as members of other religions, and 9 percent as unaffiliated with any religion.

Regarding Christianity in particular, the peculiarity of the Italian Roman Catholic Church is that, until recent times, it had almost no contact with or experience coexisting with other Christian communities (unlike its northern European counterparts in Germany, Great Britain, etc). Aside from the minority Waldensian Evangelical Church born in a very small part of northern Italy before the Reformation, Italy could historically be described, in very general terms, as being religiously "monolithic."

This is also evident at the juridical level. Aside from the Roman Catholic Church, which enjoys the *Concordato* with the Italian government (the Lateran Treaty of 1929 and its successive modifications), the minority Methodist-Waldensian community, and the Assemblies of God in Italy (recognized in 1960 and given juridical status in 1988), no other religious community has true juridical status in Italy. Thus, all the other Churches are handicapped because their ritual, religious, devotional, and economic needs are not specifically legally protected or guaranteed.

Statistics and the Situation

Fifty years ago, the original Europeans represented 20 percent of the world's population. Today, they account for more or less 10 percent. In the next fifty years, this number could drop to around 5 percent of the total world population. Thus, in this sense, Europe is becoming smaller and smaller. Italy is one of the countries at major risk of a decreasing population; since 1993, its native Italian population has been continuously declining. But this fact is not widely considered because of the continual increase of immigrants arriving in the *Bel Paese*. Since 1990, thanks to immigrants, the number of births and number of deaths of Italy's residents seem to be in equilibrium.[9]

In 2010, immigrants represented 7 percent of the total population of Italian residents, up from 3.4 percent in 2003.[10] The official numbers from Italy's National Statistics Institute, ISTAT, show a continual increase of immigrants in recent years. Romanians comprise 23 percent of the total immigrant population, followed by Albanians and then Moroccans.[11] But as Eastern European countries like Poland have begun to enter the European Union, the number of Italy's immigrants from this region is declining, while the number of those from the global South is on the rise.

9. Paglia, "Immigrazione e Opportunità Ecumeniche," para. 10. See also "Istat"; Istituto Nazionale di Statistica, "Indicatori Demografici"; "L'Italia Cresce Solo Grazie agli Immigrati."

10. Buonasorte, "I Cristiani Immigrati."

11. Istituto Nazionale di Statistica, "Anno 2016," 11.

In 2016, there were around five million legal, regular immigrants in Italy and over half a million irregular immigrants (those who overstayed their visas).[12] Over fifty thousand children are born from mixed marriages between Italians and immigrants, and from 1992 to 2005, around 150,000 immigrants acquired Italian citizenship, especially through marriage with Italians who are not classified as foreigners.[13]

In 2009, over 50 percent of immigrants were Christians,[14] and in 2013, it was 53.8 percent (2.7 million), debunking the popular belief that Muslims were "invading" Italy (or Europe in general). In 2013, Muslims were 32.2 percent of the resident immigrant population in Italy (around 1.6 million people), and those affiliated with Eastern religions—Hindus, Buddhists, Sikhs, etc.—were 6.7 percent (about 330,000 people). Those who practice Judaism numbered about 7,000.[15]

Presently, the most numerous of the Christian immigrants are of the Orthodox tradition. And the majority of these Orthodox Church members—about 1.2 million in 2009 and 1.6 million in 2016[16]—are from Eastern European countries, especially Romania. The majority of Catholics (about 775,000 in 2007 and one million in 2016) are from Latin American countries, the Philippines, and Poland, while the majority of Protestants and Evangelicals (about 121,000) hail from Africa and South America. There is a much smaller number of immigrants—around 19,000—who come from the Middle East, Egypt, Eritrea, and Ethiopia and belong to the ancient Eastern Christian Churches of the non-Chalcedonian tradition, especially the Coptic Church.[17]

The few mainstream Protestant and Evangelical Churches originally present in Italy try to gather under the umbrella of the FCEI, the Federation of Evangelical Churches in Italy. Composed of immigrants mainly from the global South (Africa and South America), these Protestant churches are primarily autonomous faith communities in terms of juridical status and do not always identify with the FCEI. There are a few, however, of these immigrant Protestant churches—mostly those with Pentecostal roots and tendencies—that try to connect with the traditional Protestant churches already present in Italy. And they are usually accepted, included, and allowed to reflect their ethnic and cultural origins.

12. Istituto Nazionale di Statistica, "Anno 2016," 1.

13. Paglia, "Immigrazione e Opportunità Ecumeniche," para. 2.

14. Caritas/Migrantes, *Immigrazione*, 37.

15. "Migranti e Religioni."

16. See Cerquerti, "Immigrati, I Cristiani Ortodossi Superano I Musulmani."

17. See Cerquerti, "Immigrati, I Cristiani Ortodossi Superano I Musulmani."

It is important to note that most of these immigrant Pentecostal churches spring up spontaneously and are sometimes manifest as energetic religious enterprises, especially in places where these immigrants, especially Ghanaians and Nigerians, feel marginalized or threatened. Because of this spontaneity and independence, little is officially known about them. Some belong to the Federation of Pentecostal Churches without any rigid imposition on their jurisdiction and organization. This liberty of religious, theological, and liturgical expression enables these immigrant Pentecostal churches to integrate some cultic elements such as animism, spirit possession, exorcism, blessings, anointing with oil, deliverance, miraculous prayer sessions, and above all, the "prosperity gospel" message promising members that such an interpretation of the Gospel is a sure way to achieve the success and opulence which is typical of the practices in their native countries.

Immigration as an Opportunity for Ecumenism[18]

Already in 2010, in the materials presented for the Week of Prayer for Christian Unity,[19] attention was called to a phenomenon requiring the concern and generosity of all Christians, especially Roman Catholics, in Italy:

> The immigration of Christians in this country [Italy]. We are talking about hundreds of thousands of our brothers and sisters, not only Roman Catholics but also from the Protestant and Orthodox traditions, who are coming into our country in search of a better future. Their presence in our midst is like a prayer that demands from us a response of love. In the same way, ecumenism in Italy must lend an ear to their cry; we must open the ears of our hearts, expand our minds, and unite our hands to welcome these brethren and help them also to grow in their faith.[20]

This is also true, because for us as Christians, immigration is an authentic *kairos*, a time of grace, a situation through which God wants to tell us something and to reveal Himself somehow to us. Immigration today is a parable

---

18. Bishop Vincenzo Paglia, former president of the Italian Episcopal Conference's Commission on Ecumenism and Dialogue, made this observation and call in his article, "Immigrazione e Opportunità Ecumeniche," lines 3–8.

19. These were signed by Bishop Vincenzo Paglia (bishop of Terni-Narni-Amelia), then president of the Italian Episcopal Conference's Commission for Ecumenism and Dialogue, together with Prof. Domenico Maselli, president of the Federation of Evangelical Churches in Italy, and Archbishop Gennadios Zervos, metropolitan of the Italian-Malta Orthodox Churches and exarch of southern Europe.

20. Catholic Church et al., "Voi Sarete Testimoni di Tutto Ciò" (my translation).

in action written on the secular lines of mundane social and economic processes underlined by structural injustice.[21] This means that immigration offers a new pathway and opportunity for ecumenism in Italy today. It is an opportunity to dismantle the condemned myth of the Tower of Babel so as to reconstruct a common home: *oikoumene*.[22]

Pastorally, the Roman Catholic Church had already begun to focus on this phenomenon of immigration before 2010. In November 2004, the Italian Episcopal Conference issued "All the People Will Come to You: Letter to the Christian Communities on Migration and a Pastoral Approach of Mutuality," reminding Italy's Christians that immigration is a concrete opportunity to practice ecumenism. It solicits concrete gestures of fraternal acceptance. The common faith and experience shared with immigrants makes it possible and easy to share common cultural roots and to recognize the essential elements of sanctification and truth in our lives. We must allow dialogue and fraternity to grow, helping the immigrant communities to exercise their faith while deepening our own knowledge of their faith and seeking moments of common sharing and glorification of Christ.[23]

Previously, in May of 2004, the Pontifical Council for the Pastoral Care of Migrants and Itinerant People issued the instruction, *Erga Migrantes Caritas Christi* (The Love of Christ Towards Migrants). In particular, I would like to note section 56 of this document:

> The growing number of Christian immigrants not in full communion with the Catholic Church offers particular Churches new possibilities of living ecumenical fraternity in practical day-to-day life and of achieving greater reciprocal understanding between Churches and ecclesial communities, something far from facile irenicism or proselytism. What is called for is a spirit of apostolic charity that, on the one hand respects other people's consciences and recognizes the good inherent in them, but which can also wait for the moment to become an instrument for a deeper encounter between Christ and a brother. The Catholic faithful must not in fact forget that it is also a service and a sign

21. "Per noi credenti cristiani, l'immigrazione si presenta come un autentico kairos, un tempo di grazia, una situazione a partire dalla quale Dio vuole dirci qualcosa, ci sta chiedendo qualcosa, ci si sta rivelando in qualche modo. L'immigra-zione è oggi una parabola in atto scritta sulle righe secolari dei processi sociali ed economici mondiali attraversati da un'ingiustizia strutturale" (Tabares, "Il Senso Biblico dell'Immigrazione," lines 1–4).

22. "È un'opportunità per disfare il mito*condanna della torre di Babele e ricostruire la casa comune, la oikoumene*" (Tabares, "Il Senso Biblico dell'Immigrazione," lines 17–18).

23. Italian Episcopal Conference, "Tutte le Gente verranno a te," para. 3.

of great love to welcome our brothers into full communion with the Church. In any case, however, "If priests, ministers, or communities not in full communion with the Catholic Church do not have a place or the liturgical objects needed for celebrating worthily their religious ceremonies, the diocesan Bishop may allow them to use a church or a Catholic building and also lend them whatever may be necessary for their services. In similar circumstances, permission may be given them for interment or for celebration of services at Catholic cemeteries."[24]

In this document, it is important to note the phrases "ecumenical fraternity" and "existential experiences" expressed in the "concrete fraternal gestures" of "practical day-to-day life." Today in Italy, these attitudes are expressed generously in various ways as an evangelical testimony; I would like to mention five examples:

1. Caritas consultation and welcome centers: There are over three thousand such centers available in Italy, and the majority of people who visit these centers are immigrants. People can receive assistance here regardless of their faith tradition or community. Similar to this Caritas apostolate are other parish, diocesan, and religious centers, like the Sisters of Mother Teresa; St. Vincent de Paul Society; the Community of Sant'Egidio; l'Api-Colf, l'Acli-Colf, a professional association in Italy for family collaborators and home assistants; as well as Centers for Life, centers for family consultation, and other organizations of Christian inspiration. Most of the staff in these organizations are volunteers, and in practicing the morals of the Good Samaritan parable, they are practical witnesses of the gospel and part of authentic, existential ecumenical outreach and dialogue.

2. Catholic Churches in use by Orthodox Churches: The document, "Erga Migrantes Caritas Christi," cited paragraph 137 of the Pontifical Council for the Promotion of Christian Unity's "Directory for the Application of Principles and Norms on Ecumenism": "If priests, ministers or communities not in full communion with the Catholic Church do not have a place or the liturgical objects needed for celebrating worthily their religious ceremonies, the diocesan Bishop may allow them to use a church or a Catholic building and also lend them whatever may be necessary for their services." This is already in practice in many parts of Italy today. Our ecumenical UNEDI office, for example, has negotiated and obtained places of worship for some

24. Pontifical Council for the Pastoral Care of Migrants and Itinerant People, *Erga Migrantes Caritas Christi*, 56. See also Pontifical Council for Promoting Christian Unity, "Directory for the Application of Principles and Norms on Ecumenism," 1090.

of our sister Orthodox Churches (Romanian, Serbian, Ukrainian, Russian, Coptic, etc.). UNEDI has also collaborated with the Italian Episcopal Conference's National Office for Juridical Issues to provide pastoral guidelines called *Vadaemecum*,[25] outlining how Catholic parishes can pastorally assist members of the non-Catholic Eastern Churches.

Since 2008, Bishop Siluan Șpan, the bishop of the Diocese of Romanian Orthodox in Italy, has had an official presence in Italy. On several occasions, he has been officially invited to the Synod of Bishops in the Vatican, gestures greatly appreciated by the Orthodox Patriarchate of Bucharest to which Bishop Siluan belongs. In the same way, there are also some local faith communities of Protestant traditions who welcome and accommodate new immigrant Evangelical and Pentecostal churches.

3. *Corridoi umanitari* (humanitarian corridors): *Corridoi umanitari* are the fruit of an agreement between the Italian government (also now effective in France) and the Federation of Evangelical Churches in Italy, the Waldensian Evangelical Churches, and the Roman Catholic Church's Community of Sant'Egidio. These "corridors" are founded on what could be called an "ecumenism of charity." Their purpose is to assist people in emergency situations, beginning with the most vulnerable (especially those from war-torn territories like Syria and Iraq), helping them to be transferred to Italian territory with refugee status. In two years' time, around one thousand people are expected to receive "corridor" assistance. Here, I would like to recall that, on April 6, 2016, when Pope Francis visited the Greek island of Lesbos, he brought sixteen Syrian, Muslim refugees back to Italy with him on his own flight, a Christian testimony of charity.

4. Hospital and prison apostolates: Prison and hospital chaplains, often primarily Catholic priests, serve the spiritual and temporal needs of Christians of different denominations without discrimination. In our area, in collaboration with Religions for Peace, the ecumenical offices of the Catholic Church, and the Focolare Movement, a plan is on course to negotiate a common space where the spiritual needs of hospital patients of various faiths can be addressed.

5. Ecumenical celebrations: In the week of Prayer for Christian Unity and the week of Pentecost especially, there is active participation and sharing by various Christian communities with special attention given in particular to incorporating ecclesial communities of immigrants.

25. See UNEDI and Ufficio Nazionale per i Problemi Giuridici della CEI, *Vademecum.*

By offering moments of relaxation, we try to foster personal friendships as well as try to cement individual trust and confidence. Sometimes, we meet for an ecumenical dinner and personal sharing, in the spirit of openness with one another, all in hopes of promoting ecumenical collaborations.

Conclusion

Considering the situation prior to Vatican II, it is clear that many gaps have been bridged, in both theological approach and praxis, between the Roman Catholic Church and other ecclesial communities and even within these ecclesial communities themselves. There is an obvious desire to move from hostility to fraternity and communion. Christians of one denomination no longer consider other Christians as enemies or strangers but rather see them as brothers and sisters with whom they can engage in practical Christian cooperation. There are gaps yet to be bridged, however; for instance, some Christian communities still find it difficult to be part of the ecumenical body of our regional Council of Christian Churches in Italy or to participate at organized ecumenical prayers and initiatives.

Nonetheless, the expression "separated brethren" tends to be replaced today by expressions which more readily evoke the deep communion—linked to the baptismal character—which the Spirit fosters in spite of historical and canonical divisions. Today, we speak instead of "other Christians," "others who have received Baptism," and "Christians of other communities."[26] Currently, and especially under the leadership of Pope Francis, we could say that the ecumenical movement is gradually shifting from the era of ecclesial communities merely signing common declarations to an era of a more pragmatic approach, where there is cooperation on concrete, existential issues that enhance ecumenism from the base. This is quite evident in the pope's characteristic simplicity, prioritizing to *encounter* and *possible common collaboration* rather than dwelling simply on theological disputes. As expressed in the title of sections 231–33 of Pope Francis's *Evangelii Gaudium*, "realities are more important than ideas."

Therefore, today in Italy, we must see and seize the current phenomenon of immigration as an opportunity for Christian testimony and concrete grounds for ecumenical collaboration. We cannot limit ecumenical dialogue only to doctrinal issues or leave it to the theoretical theologians, or the Lord Jesus may come back for the second time to meet us before we can even agree together on any one issue.

26. Cf. John Paul II, *Ut Unum Sint*, 42.

Bibliography

Buonasorte, Nicla. "I Cristiani Immigrati: Fratelli Stranieri." *Treccani*, 2011. Online.   http://www.treccani.it/enciclopedia/i-cristiani-immigrati-fratelli-stranieri_%28Cristiani-d%27Italia%29.

Caritas/Migrantes. *Immigrazione: Dossier Statistico 2009—XIX Rapporto sull'Immigrazione*. Rome: IDOS Centro Studi e Ricerche, 2009. Online. http://www.ristretti.it/commenti/2009/ottobre/pdf16/dossier_caritas.pdf.

Catholic Church, et al. "Voi Sarete Testimoni di Tutto Ciò." *Settimana di Preghiera per l'Unita dei Cristiani* 2010. Online. http://www.pro.urbe.it/att-act/i_sett-preg_2010a.html.

Cerquerti, Giulia. "Immigrati, I Cristiani Ortodossi Superano I Musulmani." *Famiglia Cristiana*, July 20, 2016. Online. http://www.famigliacristiana.it/articolo/religioni-immigrati.aspx.

Daneo, Silvio. *Impensate Vie: Evoluzione del Dialogo Ecumenico e Interreligioso nella Chiesa Cattolica, da Augustin Bea, SJ, a Jorge M. Bergoglio, SJ*. Turin: Hevier, 2014.

Denzinger, Heinrich, and Peter Hünerman. *Enchiridion Symbolorum, Definitionum et Declarationum de Rebus Fidei et Morum*. Bologna: EDB, 2000.

Francis. *Evangelli Gaudium*. Vatican: Libreria Editrice, 2013.

Garelli, Franco. *L'Italia Cattolica nell'Epoca del Pluralismo*. Bologna: Mulino, 2006.

"Istat: La Popolazione Italiana Diminuisce e Invecchia: Nel 2015 Meno Nascite." *Toscana Oggi*, May 20, 2016. Online. https://www.toscanaoggi.it/Italia/Istat-la-popolazione-italiana-diminuisce-e-invecchia.-Nel-2015-meno-nascite.

Istituto Nazionale di Statistica (ISTAT). "Anno 2016: Bilancio Demografico Nazionale." June 13, 2017. Online. https://www.istat.it/it/files/2017/06/bilanciodemografico-2016_13giugno2017.pdf?title=Bilancio+demografico+nazionale+-+13%2Fgiu%2F2017+-+Testo+integrale.pdf.

———. "Indicatori Demografici: Stime per l'Anno 2016." March 6, 2017. Online. https://www.istat.it/it/files/2017/03/Statistica-report-Indicatori-demografici_2016.pdf.

Italian Episcopal Conference (Conferenza Episcopale Italiana). "Tutte le Gente verranno a te: Lettera del Consiglio Episcopale Permanente alle comunità cristiane su migrazioni e pastorale d'insieme." November 21, 2004. Online. http://www.siti.chiesacattolica.it/siti/allegati/890/Lettera%20alle%20comunit%E0%20cristiane%20-%20su%20migrazioni%20e%20pastorale%20d%27insieme.pdf.

John Paul II. *Ut Unum Sint*. Vatican: Libreria Editrice, 1995.

"L'Italia Cresce Solo Grazie agli Immigrati: 59.6 Mmilioni di Cittadini, Ma Nascite in Calo." *La Repubblica*, June 25, 2013. https://www.repubblica.it/cronaca/2013/06/25/news/istat_in_italia_oltre_59_6_milioni_di_residenti-61819160.

Lutheran World Federation, and the Catholic Church. *Joint Declaration on the Doctrine of Justification*. Grand Rapids: Eerdmans, 2000.

"Migranti e Religioni: In Italia 2.6 Milioni di Cristiani e 1.6 Milioni di Musulmani." *Redattore Sociale*, March 2, 2016. Online. http://www.redattoresociale.it/Notiziario/Articolo/502296/Migranti-e-religioni-in-Italia-2-6-milioni-di-cristiani-e-1-6-milioni-di-musulmani.

Paglia, Vincenzo. "Immigrazione e Opportunità Ecumeniche." *Fondazione Migrantes: Servizio Migranti 6/09*. Online. http://www.chiesacattolica.it/documenti/2010/02/00014985_immigrazione_e_opportunita_ecumeniche_v_p.html.

Pontifical Council for Promoting Christian Unity. "Directory for the Application of Principles and Norms on Ecumenism." *Acta Apostolicae Sedis* 85 (1993) 1039–1119.

————. "Response of the Catholic Church to the Joint Declaration of the Catholic Church and the Lutheran World Federation on the Doctrine of Justification." November 1, 1999. Online. http://www.vatican.va/roman_curia/pontifical_councils/chrstuni/documents/rc_pc_chrstuni_doc_01081998_off-answer-catholic_en.html.

Pontifical Council for the Pastoral Care of Migrants and Itinerant People. *Erga Migrantes Caritas Christi* [*The Love of Christ Towards Migrants*]. London: Catholic Truth Society, 2004. Online. http://www.vatican.va/roman_curia/pontifical_councils/migrants/documents/rc_pc_migrants_doc_20040514_erga-migrantes-caritas-christi_en.html.

Salvarini, Brunetto. "Le Esperienze del Pluralismo." In *La Scuola e il Dialogo Interculturale*, edited by Mara Clementi, 141–48. Milan: Quaderni ISMU 2, 2008.

Tabares, Estéban. "Il Senso Biblico dell'Immigrazione: Ecumenismo Umano." *Adista*, September 14, 2009. Online. http://www.adista.it/articolo/45913.

Trombetta, Pino Luca. "Aspetti Conflittuali del Dialogo Ecumenico con le Religioni degli Immigrati." Paper presented at the CESNUR International Conference, Turin, Italy, September 9, 2010. Online. http://www.cesnur.org/2010/to-luca-trombetta.htm.

Ufficio Nazionale per l'Ecumenismo e il Dialogo Interreligioso (UNEDI), and Ufficio Nazionale per i Problemi Giuridici della CEI. *Vademecum per la Pastorale delle Parrocchie Cattoliche Verso gli Orientali non Cattolici*. Bologna: EDB, 2010.

8

Climate Justice Is for All: Making Peace with the Earth

GRACE JI-SUN KIM

AN UNTAPPED RESOURCE FOR addressing the world's pressing problems is the energy of religiously committed people who hunger for social justice. In our day, it is crucial that theologians and faith-based organizations are energized to inspire churches to advocate climate justice. This is one issue on which Christians can unite. No issue so grievously violates the core of Christian convictions as jeopardizing human life and God's creation through human-induced climate change. To work for justice and make peace in the world, we need to address global issues such as the distribution of medical resources, food, and water; the enforcement of fair land usage; the reduction of excessive deforestation; the safety of migrants and refugees; and creating spirituality.

In Christian scriptures, we recognize God's commandment to be peacemakers. To make peace on earth, the World Council of Churches (WCC) reminds us that we need to make peace *with* the earth. Humanity sees itself as the center of creation, viewing the earth as an object to be dominated and exploited. Such a view is destroying the earth's natural resources at a rate faster than what the earth can replenish without our cooperation. With such human destructiveness, we are now in an Anthropocene period that is abusing the earth and misusing its precious resources. It grows increasingly important to change our ways and work towards peace in order to end the alienation between humanity and creation. This chapter will examine the theological underpinnings of ecumenical efforts to be caretakers of creation. Making peace with the earth will not be easy, but now is the time for leaders with insight into the value of creation left in our charge to make tempering climate change their priority.

Climate Change

Climate change is a great social issue of our time. It affects all people, but scientific reports confirm that climate change disproportionately affects the people who are most vulnerable to its changes. It interacts in devastating ways with issues of land, food, human work, and human dignity. It often robs people of their land and forces them to migrate to other areas that are less devastated by climate change. Their rights are being violated as the threats to human beings and to all life on our planet grow.[1] The earth suffers under the strain of climate change with deadly storms[2] becoming more frequent. The earth is ravaged by thoughtless human lifestyles. We can no longer ignore the earth's cry and warning; we must take some action to reverse the adverse trends that we have created.

The planet is warming at an alarming rate. Climatologists agree that Earth's average temperature has increased by 0.06 degrees Celsius since the mid-nineteenth century.[3] The Earth's temperature is variable, but the long-term upward trend is clear, especially the rapid rise at the end of the twentieth century.[4] This will affect the water, land, and air and have consequences on all life as the rise in the Earth's temperature continues to play havoc on weather, sea levels, precipitation, and human livelihood.

Global warming results mostly from burning fossil fuels, deforestation, and other human activity. If we do not change our ways, the consequences will be disastrous. Climate change will cause severe weather patterns, including droughts and flooding. It will dry lands and make them uninhabitable. This will cause mass migrations of both wild animals and human populations. We need to change our lifestyle habits and use of fossil fuels, otherwise the earth's temperature can rise by 6 degrees Celsius. Consequences of global warming are apparent in extreme weather, melting glaciers, and altered ecosystems that exacerbate human suffering from the Irrawaddy River Delta to Darfur.[5] Hurricanes Harvey and Irma were, re-

1. Kim, *Making Peace with the Earth*, xii–xiii.
2. Riebeek, "Rising Cost of Natural Hazards."
3. Schneider et al., *Climate Change Policy*, 4.
4. Schneider et al., *Climate Change Policy*, 5.
5. Brainard et al., *Climate Change and Global Poverty*, 10.

spectively, Category 4 and 5 hurricanes that caused massive destruction in the southern US and in the Caribbean. As Hurricane Irma ripped through the Caribbean, it devastated the islands; powerful winds tore down trees, plants, electrical wires, buildings, and homes. The severity of these storms is intensified due to climate change. It isn't just human suffering but all of creation, including plants, animals, and everything in the air, that suffers. Changing weather patterns will destroy ecosystems which rely on the migration of butterflies, which pollinate flowers to bear fruit.

Another problem that arises from global warming is the rise in sea level. There is a misconception that the rising sea level is due to the melting Arctic ice, but the ice floating on the oceans has little effect on sea level if it melts. However, the glaciers and large sheet ice covering Greenland and Antarctica are a different story, as they do contribute to the increase of sea level. The primary cause of increasing sea levels is the thermal expansion of seawater. This is the same process that drives up the liquid in a mercury- or alcohol-based thermometer. The sea level rose some ten to twenty centimeters during the twentieth century. Some believe that it may rise fourfold, resulting in a rise most likely near half a meter. This rise adds to the highest tides and to the surges associated with major storms. This is not good news to many, as much of the world's population lives close to sea level. Even a half-meter rise will have serious consequences in places such as Bangladesh, which does not have the resources and infrastructure to adapt to rising sea levels.[6] As the sea level continues to rise, people will lose their homes and their ways of life which will contribute to climate refugees and migrants. This is a huge problem for which the world needs to prepare itself.

Reducing greenhouse gas emissions is essential to stabilize the climate. It is an enormous global task which will require the transformation of economic and energy paradigms worldwide. Gases warm the planet for many years after they are emitted. It is a cause for concern as the emissions legacy of prior years and the emissions of tomorrow mean more climate change. Preventing the risk of a future climate catastrophe means reducing emissions immediately, with a long-term goal of continual emissions reduction to help stabilize the climate. We have passed the point of preventing the consequences of climate change in the decades ahead. The challenge now is to avoid the unmanageable and manage the unavoidable[7] before we have catastrophic results.

Although climate change is a global threat, it is especially taking a toll on the world's poor. As the temperature rises globally, climate change

6. Schneider et al., *Climate Change Policy*, 33, 34.

7. Brainard et al., *Climate Change and Global Poverty*, 12.

impacts water, food, health, and living standards. The impact will be greater in the areas that are already struggling, such as the Pacific islands and many parts of Asia and Africa. This results in climate refugees, damage to traditional cultures, and increasingly frequent and severe floods and droughts.[8] We see this in the Syrian crisis, where the droughts have caused farmers to migrate into the cities as their livestock were dying and the vegetable crops were not growing. With the massive surge into the cities of people looking for jobs and a lack of assistance from the government, there was civil unrest. With the civil crisis mounting, many fled Syria and became climate refugees in neighboring countries.

Climate change will result in a worldwide humanitarian disaster. As the poor lose their homes, livelihood, and family members, the unthinkable happens. The surviving spouse without a good job to sustain their young family may resort to selling their children to work in factories or the sex trade. The havoc of severe storms has already forced some to resort to this as a means of survival. These consequences are usually more acute for poor women rather than poor men.

As we enter this sensitive time, we are faced with two important challenges: lifting up the lives of the global poor and stabilizing the Earth's climate. The way we confront these challenges will determine the lives of our children and the generations to come.[9] Our actions or inactions today will have damaging effects on our future generations. As we live in a globalized world, what happens across the ocean will affect us and vice versa; knowing that how we live will affect so many around the world should pivot us to move towards climate justice. Let us turn to the issue of water and how water affects the work of sustainability and climate justice.

Water Issues

When I was growing up, it was common for us to drink tap water. It was considered safe enough to drink and put into portable containers to take to school. Now, we see bottled water being sold and purchased in all parts of the world. We have come to a time where water is on sale in bottles, jugs, and dispensers all over the world. This shift from drinking tap water to bottled water—and this commodification of water—is having grave consequences on the earth. The plastic bottles are polluting not only the ground that we walk on but the oceans as well, killing marine life.

8. Brainard et al., *Climate Change and Global Poverty*, vii.
9. Brainard et al., *Climate Change and Global Poverty*, 10.

For centuries, communities relied on free-flowing rivers and streams as sources of water for their well-being, including daily living needs and agriculture. Now, water is offered for sale to the highest bidder. With the commodification of water, it may be easier to see where water rights have been bought and indigenous people blocked from using a source of water.

Many of the rich believe that they can do whatever they want, wherever they want, and to whom or whatever they want. They need to understand that they, too, must observe the constraints of a good citizen. In the absence of protective laws, the law protects the owners of property. Thus, the police should be protecting the Native Americans and not the rich oil companies. The difficulty is that this pattern of favoring the rich has been a reality since the dawn of civilization on the Euphrates and the Nile. This isn't just happening here in the US but also elsewhere around the globe.

When we look at the composition of the earth, we find that two-thirds is covered with water. We also find that 97 percent of that water is in the briny oceans, while 3 percent of that is fresh water. Furthermore, 69 percent is frozen in glaciers. This leaves only 1 percent, and out of that, only 0.03 percent is available in all the rivers and lakes in the world.[10] Understanding this, we come to see that water is a very precious resource, something which humanity depends on for life.

However, the global water crisis is not due to scarcity but rather to unjust distribution. It is not about the lack of water; there is still enough for everyone. It is about how the water is distributed. Each of us needs to rethink our own water use—how we can drink, bathe, and clean. We must reimagine the ways we use water to do what we need to do.

The World Health Organization (WHO) says that almost two billion people drink water that is contaminated with feces, which puts them at risk for cholera, typhoid, and polio.[11] This is a health crisis that we need to face head-on. Children are the most vulnerable victims of the water crisis; statistics show that five thousand children around the world die every day because of dirty water. That translates to the deaths of nearly two million children a year from contaminated water and improper sanitation. Furthermore, the poor around the globe pay more for water than people in Britain or the US, for example. The United Nations has reported that 1.1 billion people do not have safe water and 2.6 billion suffer from inadequate sewerage.[12] The scarcity and the cost of water for poor people is creating an imbalance which needs to be addressed. Having access to clean water

10. USGS, "Where Is Earth's Water Located?"

11. "Two Billion People Drinking Contaminated Water."

12. Seager, "Dirty Water."

is a human right; it is what keeps us alive. But the lack of clean water is a crisis for people around the globe which requires immediate attention. With the change in climate, this crisis is only going to worsen as droughts and flooding will be more common, creating massive havoc for people around the globe. And tied in with water is the production and availability of food; we cannot talk about these in isolation.

The issue of virtual water, for example, is one that links both food and water. Virtual water is used to create the goods and services that we consume and use.[13] When we think about saving water, we tend only to think of things like leaking taps or taking short showers, and we fail to discuss the virtual water that is used to create food or services for our consumption and use. Virtual water is more than the actual water that we use. To give an example: on average, taking a shower may require one hundred and twenty liters of water, while a burger requires two thousand liters of water to feed and process the cow which yields the hamburger. We can calculate the virtual water for most of the materials that we consume, and we end up eating much more water than we drink. Therefore, to help us move towards sustainability, we must rethink our diet and look for items which require less virtual water.

In North America, much of our food gets wasted. The statistics reveal that approximately one third of the food produced is wasted—about 1.3 billion tons of food gets thrown out.[14] Keeping in mind creation care and how the ground produces food that keeps us alive, we need to find ways to avoid wasting our resources and draining our lands. We cannot afford to continue wasting our food; to prevent it from being thrown out, we need to redistribute it. People are going to bed hungry, not because there isn't enough food but rather because food is unjustly distributed. We need to produce food for *all* people, not just for a select group of people who can easily afford to pay more for their hamburger. It is imperative that we find creative ways to produce and distribute food which will reduce waste.

World Council of Churches and Water Justice

The World Council of Churches (WCC), along with other organizations, is doing its part to speak out against the injustices which are damaging the earth. Many Christian churches around the world connect climate change

13. "Virtual water is the amount of water required to produce a product, from start to finish and is a mainly neglected and hidden component of production" (Sonesson et al., *Environmental Assessment*, 261).

14. FAO, "Key Facts."

and climate justice, recognizing that the latter may be broadly configured to include. racial justice, gender justice, and human rights. The WCC is taking seriously the issue of water's just distribution in different parts of the world. In 2008, it founded the Ecumenical Water Network (EWN) that advocates for water justice in the Middle East, especially Palestine. Israelis living in illegal settlements in the occupied Palestinian territories have access to clean water for drinking and sanitation, while Palestinians in Gaza do not.[15] Contaminated water leads to waterborne diseases like cholera and other health problems,[16] such as skin and digestion issues; thus, there is a constant struggle for equitable water distribution so that those in the occupied territory have the same access, per capita, to clean water as Israel does.

Water is the source and sustainer of life, but it has become a commodity, subject to being owned, bought, and sold. Today, as through the centuries, access to it is a cause of conflict. We may argue about climate change against the very convincing conclusions of science, but surely no reasonable person can deny that we all need and have a right to access water. When some people have access to clean water and others do not, it leads to the deterioration of society.[17]

On July 28, 2010, through Resolution 64/294, the United Nations General Assembly explicitly recognized the human right to water and sanitation, acknowledging that clean drinking water and sanitation are essential to the realization of all human rights. The Resolution calls upon states and international organizations to provide financial resources, capacity-building, and technology transfer to help countries, in particular developing countries, to provide safe, clean, accessible, and affordable drinking water and sanitation for their citizens.[18]

As Protestant churches around the world celebrate five hundred years since the Reformation, many are wondering how we can continue to reform the church, to continue to make a difference in people's lives and an impact on the world. One important question among the churches during this five hundredth anniversary is how the churches deal with sustainability and climate change.

According to Caroline Bader, youth secretary of the Lutheran World Federation (LWF),

> One of our thematic approaches to the commemoration of five hundred years of Lutheran Reformation is the theme

15. Kim and Sipilainen, "Lack of Water Justice."
16. Kim and Sipilainen, "Lack of Water Justice."
17. Kim and Sipilainen, "Lack of Water Justice."
18. Kim and Sipilainen, "Lack of Water Justice."

"Creation—Not for Sale." When Luther spoke out in the sixteenth century on God's redeeming love, he was not thinking
about the environment. Ecological challenges were not in the
forefront at that time. However, today many parts of the world
face critical environmental challenges. In Africa, for example,
many communities face tremendous pressure to find safe drinking water, while all around them huge expanses of communal
land are being sold off or leased to the highest bidder. Water
and land—resources that for centuries have sustained communities and which pastoralists have held in common—are now
moving into the marketplace. Communities that have relied on
them have been forced to migrate, often to urban slums where
there are few or poor services. Luther's intervention at the time
of the Reformation reminds us that there are aspects of life on
this planet which, for the sake of both earthly and eternal life,
should not be commodities and should never be for sale. That
includes the good creation God has given us to watch over.[19]

The churches must work towards a greener future that encourages
more sustainable living. We must stop selling God's creation for our own
personal profit. We must recognize how creation was freely given to humanity to care for rather than destroy and dominate it. It is critical for us to
reimagine God's creation as part of God's body. Digging into the ground to
put in pipelines which will eventually burst will not only kill the soil and the
animals but also kill us. We cannot keep digging, building, and destroying
God's creation as it all takes time to replenish, and we are not giving it time
to replenish. It is time to rework, rethink, and reimagine.

Stewards of the Earth

The creation story in Genesis gives us a good view of creation and how it is
supposed to be. "Then God looked over all he had made, and he saw that it
was very good!" (Gen 1:31a, NLT). As Randy Woodley writes, "We see that
God created everything, and everything that God created is described in
Hebrew not just as good, but as 'really good!'"[20] God found joy in creation;
it was beautiful, good, and pleasing to God. This indicates that creation was
important to God and that we are creatures who were created by a loving
God. We should look at creation and find joy in it, but instead we have
begun to destroy it and, ultimately, our planet. We have somehow confused

19. Interview with Caroline Bader, LWF Youth Secretary, November 4, 2016.
20. Woodley, *Shalom and the Community of Creation*, 41.

being stewards of the earth with being dominators of the earth. Rather than taking care of creation, we have become greedy, taking what we want from the earth without considering the need to replenish and restore what we have taken and used.

All of humanity is related to one another and to this creation. Understanding this idea opens us to the possibility of once again becoming the family we already are. By realizing the connectedness of humankind to all animal life, we become aware of new possibilities for learning and maintaining concern for the preservation of all living things. A worldview based on reciprocity and familial relatedness also has tremendous ecological implications. In humanity's dependence upon the earth, we allow ourselves renewed opportunities for sustaining our planet and finding fresh prospects for developing food, water, and renewable energy. All of this and more are contained in our simple prayers—like the Lakota phrase, *Mitakuye Oyasin* (which means all are related)[21]—that describe the interrelatedness of all creation. Harmony or balance is the key to all happiness, health, and well-being.[22]

As we read in Genesis 1:28, we were commanded by God to take care of all that God had created on this earth. That included the animals, plants, and the environment. Christianity has misread this passage, and it has done so as a justification for exploitation and as a way of legitimizing greed. This passage has become a foundation for supporting more corporate greed and disregard towards the poor around the globe. We have deemed it our right to dominate the world and take from it what we want. This causes a tremendous burden on the land, as we continue damaging it to satisfy our greed. We have not stopped mining or conventional drilling. To extract oil from the land, we are now fracking (hydro-fracturing), which leaves that land in tatters. The damage we are causing may be irreversible. We have rationalized it away by telling ourselves that the world will replenish itself. But this is nonsense: the world can only replenish renewable resources (plants, animals, and their ecosystems) as long as we don't allow species to become extinct or irreparably damage these ecosystems through pollution or overuse. We are exceeding the earth's speed of self-replenishing at an alarming rate.

21. International Council of Thirteen Indigenous Grandmothers, "Mitakuye Oyasin."

22. Woodley, *Shalom and the Community of Creation*, 81.

Steps Towards Climate Justice

As Christians, we need to be aware of our participation in despoiling the earth. We have played into a dualism which devalues the earth and its resources, perceiving reality within a framework of two opposing rudiments, such as spirit and flesh, mind and body, male and female, mind and matter, or good and evil.[23] We have envisioned the earth as feminine, imagining that we can therefore dominate it just as men tend to dominate women.

In a dualistic worldview, only the spirit is considered to be good; creation (the material world, including our own bodies) is considered to be either evil or less spiritual. In Christianity, we can easily view the departure from a holistic worldview by discussing the "soul." We speak of Jesus saving our souls, of reaching souls for Christ, and of our souls going to heaven. Most often, however, the way we use these terms is a departure from biblical Christianity; in Scripture, Jesus "saves" our whole person.[24]

The participants in the WCC's tenth assembly adopted a message that asked churches and Christians to join in a "Pilgrimage of Justice and Peace." Part of this journey and pilgrimage involves practicing environmental justice and treating the earth with respect, which require working on the pressing issue of climate change.[25]

Churches and other faith-based communities are called to address this issue that is affecting so many people and vulnerable communities in various parts of the world. Some Christians fail to recognize the reality of climate change, however, because of their views on the Bible and faith as Christians; they have misinterpreted, for example, scriptural passages about dominating the earth, such as Genesis 1:28. Others do not believe in climate change because of culturally conditioned climate skepticism and an attitude which devalues the evidence of science. Yet others believe that it is not the role of faith communities to address climate change, feeling that it is not religion's job to engage any political issues.[26]

Religions Need to Respond to Climate Change

Here are some of the questions that Christians, churches, and faith communities face when addressing climate change:[27] Why should churches

23. Woodley, *Shalom and the Community of Creation*, 101.

24. Woodley, *Shalom and the Community of Creation*, 101–2.

25. Kim, *Making Peace with the Earth*, xi.

26. Kim, *Making Peace with the Earth*, xii.

27. Kim, *Making Peace with the Earth*, xii.

address environmental issues? Why should Protestants join Orthodox and Roman Catholics in caring for creation? Why should Christians look to join interfaith work with Jews, Muslims, Hindus, Buddhists, and other faith traditions? Why advocate for climate justice and peace with the earth?

Taking these questions into consideration, the WCC is addressing climate change for two reasons. First, churches in various parts of the world recognize how the consequences of climate change are affecting the lives and livelihoods of their communities. To respond to these consequences, churches are helping to develop resilient communities, equipped to adapt to climate change, and these churches benefit greatly by learning from the work of other faith communities around the world. Second, at the local level, churches of many denominations are coming together to respond to the impact of climate change and to advocate policies that respond to the needs and rights of vulnerable populations at both the local and national level. In both instances, the WCC has a unique ability to build relationships between churches around the globe, and to enhance their work.[28]

Advocacy for the earth must become a priority for faith-based organizations. For example, we must all work towards preventing Earth's temperature from rising more than two degrees Celsius. Unlimited carbon pollution must be stopped. Wealthy countries must mitigate their carbon dioxide emissions so as not to leave developing countries suffering from a burned-out planet through no fault of their own. All of these steps are crucial in addressing climate change.[29]

Environmental justice is intimately related to economic justice. The environment affects our economy, and those who live in poverty are the most affected. To emphasize and illustrate the link between these two issues, the WCC adopted the term eco-justice. Conditions of eco-injustice, such as the access to water by the Palestinians, are a source of conflict. The WCC's International Ecumenical Peace Convocation, held in Kingston, Jamaica, in 2011, clearly stated that there can be "no peace on earth without peace with the earth." The way we have related to the earth, however, is with little conservation and no restraint. We have lost any tradition of being stewards of the earth. This path of violence and domination may not lead to open war, but it contributes to the destruction of the earth.[30]

The earth needs us to work together toward climate and environmental justice. We need to advocate for the earth and be at peace with the earth. We need to come together to greet our strangers and welcome our friends. We

28. Kim, *Making Peace with the Earth*, xii.
29. Kim, *Making Peace with the Earth*, xiii.
30. Kim, *Making Peace with the Earth*, xiii.

need to bring Christians, Hindus, Buddhists, Muslims, individuals, communities, politicians, churches, and corporations together so that all can challenge each other to live a life of stewardship rather than one of greed, domination, and destruction. We all need to turn to the God of life and ask God to lead us to social justice and peace.[31] There are groups such as "Religions for Peace" which bring people of different faiths together to work together on how to live sustainably. Other organizations such as Sojourners, 350.org, and Green Faith work on climate justice in various communities and political organizations.

Perhaps we can work towards *shalom* and work for peace on earth. Shalom is both personal (emphasizing relationships) and structural (replacing systems where shalom has been broken). In shalom, the old structures are replaced with new structures. God expects us to make the old way of living new. The Creator requires us to reshape the world we know into the world God has intended.[32]

Part of creation care can come in the form of a Sabbath year, which was a way of life for the ancient Israelites and even mentioned in Exodus and Leviticus. As Randy Woodley explains,

> One purpose of the Sabbath year was to allow the land to rest and grow what it would naturally produce on its own without planting. On the Sabbath year, no one was to work the land. On normal years, a person's land was divided into seven sections. Each year, one-seventh of the land was left unplanted so that it would rejuvenate and so the poor of the community could raise food for themselves. (Another provision for the poor was the command to leave the edges of the fields uncut so the poor could harvest something for themselves.) All of these injunctions were concerned about the well-being of the land; the poor; livestock and wild creatures; and the landowner.[33]

However, we have forgotten how we are to take care of the earth and practice Sabbath in our own lives.

Even climate change skeptics must join in the journey for the earth's protection and sustainability. We must all continuously provide imaginative possibilities for how the church, faith communities, individuals, and the academy can move forward to help save God's creation.[34] All people of faith need to work together to bring peace on earth so that the earth will survive.

31. Kim, *Making Peace with the Earth*, xiii.

32. Woodley, *Shalom and the Community of Creation*, 10.

33. Woodley, *Shalom and the Community of Creation*, 29.

34. Kim, *Making Peace with the Earth*, xiii–xiv.

We need the earth to flourish, and this will happen if humanity learns to live sustainably and for the good of all.

Bibliography

Brainard, Lael, et al. *Climate Change and Global Poverty: A Billion Lives in the Balance?* Washington, DC: Brookings Institution, 2009.

Food and Agriculture Organization of the United Nations (FAO). "Key Facts on Food Loss and Waste You Should Know!" *Save Food: Global Initiative on Food Loss and Waste Reduction.* Online. http://www.fao.org/save-food/resources/keyfindings/en.

International Council of Thirteen Indigenous Grandmothers. "Mitakuye Oyasin (All My Relations." Online. http://www.grandmotherscouncil.org/mitakuye-oyasin-all-my-relations.

Kim, Grace Ji-Sun, ed. *Making Peace with the Earth: Action and Advocacy for Climate Justice.* Geneva: WCC, 2016.

Kim, Grace Ji-Sun, and Ilkka Sipilainen. "Lack of Water Justice Endangers Peace and Good Life: The World Council of Churches Climate Change Meeting." *Huffington Post,* May 12, 2016. Online. http://www.huffingtonpost.com/grace-jisun-kim/lack-of-water-justice-end_b_9885618.html.

Riebeek, Holli. "The Rising Cost of Natural Hazards." *NASA: Earth Observatory,* March 30, 2005. Online. https://earthobservatory.nasa.gov/Features/RisingCost/rising_cost.php.

Schneider, Stephen, et al. *Climate Change Policy: A Survey.* Washington, DC: Island, 2002.

Seager, Ashley. "Dirty Water Kills Five Thousand Children a Day." *The Guardian,* November 10, 2006. Online. https://www.theguardian.com/business/2006/nov/10/water.environment.

Sonesson, U., J. Berlin, and F. Ziegler. *Environmental Assessment and Management in the Food Industry: Life Cycle Assessment and Related Approaches.* Philadelphia: Woodhead, 2010.

"Two Billion People Drinking Contaminated Water: WHO." *PHYS.org,* April 13, 2017. Online. https://phys.org/news/2017-04-billion-people-contaminated.html.

US Geological Survey (USGS). "Where Is Earth's Water Located?" Online. https://water.usgs.gov/edu/pdf/earthwherewater.pdf.

Woodley, Randy S. *Shalom and the Community of Creation: An Indigenous Vision.* Grand Rapids: Eerdmans, 2012.

global South and throughout Asia more widely. The
also been pressed that, in such contexts, all that mat-
e "Life and Work" agenda of shared witness, worship,
e.[2]

s all plays very neatly into a long-running debate and
in the World Council of Churches and sits particularly
rtain forms of Protestant ecclesial and ecumenical in-
m that one can also find being made in Catholic circles,
e surprising given that it is more difficult to accommo-
lic theological and ecclesiological framework.
ally, at first hearing at least, there is some cogency to the
ical dialogues focused upon attempts to resolve historic
rinal divisions (e.g., justification by faith) are of limited
l South contexts, in which such issues have not been live
on.[3] However, from a Catholic perspective, it is far more
hat this also applies to tradition-dividing ecclesiological
ues, concerning the shape and structure of the Church and
nterrelationship with the church's witness and mission, are
Catholic understanding and practice and not simply in aca-
cal debates in the global North.
d by this presupposition that the specifically ecclesiological
formal ecumenism are of abiding relevance within global
cism, even while allowing for significant contextual differ-
nasis and relative priority, this chapter is concerned with prob-
holic ecumenism might look like if the Catholic Church were
usly the move towards being a genuinely world church. This is
ed by the Second Vatican Council and definitively symbolized
cy of Pope Francis, the first global South pope. How can the
rience and insights of the diverse, local Catholic churches of the

rther discussion on the distinctiveness and necessary interrelationship of
ork" ecumenism and "Faith and Order" ecumenism, see Murray, "In Search

"at first hearing" as I believe that, once discussion of justification and sanc-
noves out of the register of the conceptual coherence of differing conceptual
d linguistic frameworks for the action of saving grace in the life of the indi-
instead connects with the underlying existential, spiritual, and pastoral con-
n which these schema deal (i.e., the experienced fact of our utter dependence
forgiving embrace and gracious lifting of us, together with the experienced
od's grace as being both reliable and transformative), then we see that these
global North concerns have universal contemporary resonance and are not
f historic parochial and regional concern.

PART FOUR

Receptive Ecumenism

9

Formal Ecumen
the Diverse Loc
Communion

Paul D. Murray

Introduction: Thematic and

In the context of the overall focu
World Church," this chapter explo
ism (e.g., multilateral "conciliar"
ecumenical dialogue) play out in th
The chapter specifically explores w
has come to be known as Receptive E
regards.[1]

The "Faith and Order" ecumenism
has typically focused, on the one hand,
such matters as *sola fide* and Eucharistic s
differences in church structure, order, and
claimed that these standard Faith and Or

1. See Murray, "Receptive Ecumenism and Ca
Murray, "Receptive Ecumenism and Ecclesial L
Ecumenism."

to the churches of the
related claim has often
ters ecumenically is th
and mission for justic

At one level, th
point of conflict with
comfortably with ce
stinct. But it is a cla
which is all the mo
date within a Cath

More specific
claim that ecumen
global North doc
relevance to glob
issues of content
difficult to see t
matters. Such iss
their necessary
live throughout
demic theologi

So, guide
dimensions o
South Catholi
ences of empl
ing what Cat
to take serio
a move mark
by the papa
diverse exp

2. For fu
"Life and W
of a Way."

3. I say
tification
schema ar
vidual an
cerns wit
on God's
fact of C
historic
merely

world properly inform and reshape Catholic ecumenism for the twenty-first century?

As for my own personal perspective and shaping influences, I grew up as part of the UK Liverpool Irish in the 1960s and 1970s. This was a community strongly conscious of being a largely immigrant, misfit Catholic minority in a historically Protestant country, with pictures of Italian popes on our walls, grandparents with clear and frequently rehearsed memories of religious discrimination, a sizeable Polish-language community in our parish with its own Mass, and frequent visits of religious to our school with fascinating stories of our Catholic sisters and brothers in Africa, Asia, and South America. This all contributed to my growing up with an inchoate but nevertheless real sense of sharing, by virtue of being Catholic, in a world-wide communion with the center of one's identity not being the nation-state with its Protestant queen but somewhere else. I recall my father expressing his appreciation that the Mass, even in the vernacular, offered a common liturgical currency such that one could go anywhere in the world and still be able, regardless of linguistic comprehension, to understand what was going on and to situate oneself within it. So, even in my parochial, tribal, northern, insular existence, the Catholic imaginary in which I was formed had a certain global orientation to it, even if this was in a somewhat vague and under-defined manner.

Many years later, one of the strongest affective experiences I had of the world church was during my first pilgrimage to Rome, which I made with Andrea, my wife, in 2005. We spent eight days living beside the basilica of St. Paul's Outside the Walls and traveling each day to the center point of St. Peter's. This daily back-and-forth communicated a sense of the pulsating rhythm of Catholicism as being one of living between the Pauline instinct for outward-facing mission and locality and the Petrine instinct for holding this rich pluriformity in centered communion. Our week culminated in participation in the Wednesday general papal audience, for which we had been given tickets on the raised area immediately beneath the steps of St. Peter's. Our vantage point gave us a wonderful perspective on the Square as it filled up with groups of pilgrims seemingly from every nation on earth, many sporting their national colors, banners of patron saints, or the names of their diocese, parish, or school, and all intent on making their presence felt. It seemed as though the whole world was gathered there in the embrace of Bernini's colonnades. There was something deeply appropriate in the real power of the audience residing not in the cult of personality of the pope but in the pluriform pilgrim people, and this sense of the global Catholic communion gathered in celebration, prayer, and joy. After all, the true function of the papacy is to be the structural and sacramental focus of the communion of the dispersed, diverse People of God.

Another experience of the vibrant catholicity of the world church—albeit one significantly less institutionally Catholic—was when I was invited to be an independent observer at the 2009 meeting of the World Council of Churches' Faith and Order Plenary Commission in Crete.[4] There was a quite remarkable diversity of ethnicity, national context, and ecclesial affiliation represented there—indeed, the richest such mix I have ever experienced. There was a correspondingly strong sense of fraternal and sororal appreciation across this diversity, a sense which I fully shared. But there was also something of a sense of the gathering as lacking either a center or any great depth of communion.

The theological conversations tended to focus either on case studies in theological ethics relating to particular practical issues arising in various ecclesial and missiological contexts or on somewhat minimalist discussions of what could be said together in the then-prospective convergence document, *The Church: Towards a Common Vision* (2013). There was little to no space or explicit encouragement given to working theologically *from out of* the diverse particularities gathered there and the challenges and possibilities which they represented for each other. With that, the rather small, Vatican-appointed formal Catholic delegation was remarkably global North and Caucasian in make-up.

The importance, then, of the global Catholicism initiative here at DePaul in Chicago, from which this volume stems, is that here there is a dual concern in evidence to take both the particularity of Catholicism and its immense global diversity equally seriously. With this, there is also a concern to pursue live issues in Catholic conversation in a manner that is attentive both to this internal plurality and to what can be learned from the distinctive particularities and experience of the other Christian traditions. These are also the themes and questions with which this chapter grapples. More specifically and as noted earlier, it explores the distinctive strategy of Receptive Ecumenism and its potential relevance for the global reach of the Catholic Church.

Perhaps the first thing to note is that, while Receptive Ecumenism *is* understood as representing a distinctive strategy in contemporary ecumenism, it is one with deep Catholic roots and precedent and strong Catholic resonance. With that, and as it might imply, Receptive Ecumenism is also understood as being intentionally in service of what I have referred to as

4. Although the Catholic Church is not a member church of the World Council of Churches, it is a fully participating member of the Faith and Order Commission and sends a delegation of formal representatives appointed by the Vatican.

"formal ecumenism." As should be clear by now, by "formal ecumenism," I mean theological and ecclesial ecumenism, not just forms of practical and relational ecumenism focused on doing things together.

The exploration is pursued through four stages: (1) the necessity and challenge of formal-theological-ecclesial ecumenism; (2) the basic vision and principles of Receptive Ecumenism; (3) Receptive Ecumenism in practice—i.e., potential Catholic learning from Anglican tradition; and (4) key questions regarding formal ecumenism, Receptive Ecumenism, and global South Catholicism. Throughout, three major questions percolate away and come to focus in the final section:

- Where and how is formal-theological-ecclesial ecumenism evidenced in global South contexts?

- How does the Catholic instinct for the need to hope for and work towards full structural and sacramental communion engage with such contexts?

- How might the thinking, instincts, and practice of Receptive Ecumenism take specific root and variously come to particular flower in the diverse ecclesial-cultural-regional contexts of global Catholicism?

The Necessity and Challenge of Formal-Theological-Ecclesial Ecumenism

As already indicated, by "formal-theological-ecclesial" ecumenism, I do not simply mean any and all structured gatherings of representatives of diverse Christian traditions. With this cumbersome phrase, I specifically refer, first, to the classical Faith and Order concern to seek full structural and sacramental communion between the traditions. With that, I refer, second, to the concern to seek to overcome any dividing differences between the traditions, as distinct from non-dividing distinctions.[5]

There are, of course, many important gatherings of representatives of Christian traditions which do not make the search for full structural and sacramental communion a key focus of their work. This is exemplified in the Life and Work movement, which is focused on the need for Christian communities to present a united witness and proclamation to the world, regardless of the abiding substantive differences of structure, doctrine, and

---

5. Regarding "dividing differences" and "non-dividing distinctions," Congar, following Möhler, referred to "contradictions" (*Widersprüche*) and "contrasts/oppositions" (*Gegensätze*). See Congar, *Diversity*, 151–52; Möhler, *Unity*, 194–48 (§46) as well as 157–60 (§32), 201–5 (§48).

practice which pertain between the traditions which they represent. More recently, there is the Global Christian Forum, the primary purpose of which is to encourage into ecumenical engagement the myriad new evangelical and Pentecostal churches which do not usually engage with conciliar ecumenism and bilateral dialogues.[6]

In some respects, such Life and Work-style initiatives in interecclesial fellowship, prayer, and witness are the very oxygen and lifeblood of Christian ecumenism. Unless we are meeting together, praying together, and growing to love and value each other, then little else is possible. Equally, however, no matter how many such initiatives we have, on their own they are incapable of resolving the ecumenical problem. For at root, the ecumenical problem consists in the broken sign-value we give to the world when we proclaim reconciliation in Christ but live structural and sacramental divisions in Christ's ecclesial body, wherein we cannot fully recognize and share in each other's ministry, authoritative teaching, and sacramental life. For this, we need more than fraternal and sororal feeling; more than shared prayer and action; and more than reconciled diversity without structural and sacramental communion. Going beyond all this, we also need grace-filled repentance met by grace-filled conversion: repentance of the deep sin of division into which God has given us up; repentance of our own tradition's complicity in this divided state of the Church; repentance of our blindness to the dreadful significance of these divisions; and repentance, too, of our blindness to the particular character of our own tradition's sinful complicity in such divisions.[7]

Now, of course, recognition of the scandalous significance of the Church's divided state and the commensurate importance of this "formal-theological-ecclesial ecumenism" is by no means an exclusively Catholic trait. It is, however, strongly resonant with the core Catholic instinct for living and thinking "according to the whole." It is also the case that it was given a remarkable boost by Catholicism's entrance into the ecumenical project at Vatican II. A host of bilateral dialogues were subsequently established, each focused on identifying and seeking to overcome perceived historic causes of division. Over the decades, a range of strategies have been employed in service of this aim. There has been:

- the ecumenism of repentance of tribalism and of narrowed vision;

6. See Beek, *Revisioning Christian Unity.*

7. For a searing analysis of the complicity of each of the Christian traditions in the divisions of the Church and the need for radical repentance on behalf of each, see Radner, *End of the Church.*

- the ecumenism of charitable representation and the overcoming of misunderstandings;

- the ecumenism of openness to fresh understanding, both of the other and of the common tradition;

- the ecumenism of recognition of legitimate and necessary difference in communion;

- the ecumenism of sharing one's gifts: not hoarding them as family treasures but offering them freely;[8]

- the ecumenism of hope-filled imaginings of possibilities which are not yet but which might be and, perhaps, one day will be;

- the ecumenism of loving desire for that which appears good and attractive in the other, recognizing that, at its heart, ecumenism is a process of falling in love with what God's grace has nurtured in the other;[9]

- the ecumenism of recognition of our own need for help: looking to the other not simply as potential recipient of what God's grace has nurtured in one's own tradition but as a potential resource for the growth and healing of the difficulties and limitations in one's home tradition;[10]

- the ecumenism of patient faith and realism: recognizing that we are servants, not architects; recognizing that it takes time to grow, both personally and even more so at the level of institutions and traditions.

Taken together, these form the multi-stranded cord of formal ecumenical activity. While these various strands are not all equally operative in any given context, they can each be seen to have been variously operative over the years. Of particular importance in the classical bilateral dialogues have been the first four. Think of the *Joint Declaration on the Doctrine of Justification*: through overcoming mistaken, caricatured understandings of each other forged through polemic and by also recognizing that the richness of

---

8. O'Gara, *Ecumenical Gift Exchange*.

9. See Murray and Murray, "Roots, Range, and Reach."

10. This theme was expressed by Pope Francis during the 2014 Week of Christian Unity: "It is beautiful to recognize the grace with which God blesses us and, still more, to find in other Christians something we need, something that we could receive like a gift from our brothers and our sisters. The group from Canada who prepared the texts for this Week of Prayer did not invite communities to think about what they could give to their neighbor Christians, but urged them to meet with one another in order to understand what they all can receive each from the others" (Francis, "General Audience").

Christian truth does not need always to be expressed in the exact same way in all contexts, Lutherans and Catholics came to see their teachings as compatible and complementary.[11] More broadly, in Anglican–Roman Catholic dialogue, the combined use of such strategies proved successful in showing how to navigate a way beyond case after case of historic division, such as the issue of Eucharistic sacrifice.[12] This led to high hopes of unity being just around the corner.

Such hopes were, however, to be disappointed. In recent decades, formal ecumenism has experienced a significant energy drain, frequently finding itself in an apparent impasse. The strategies which previously seemed so powerful appear to have reached the limits of their effectiveness as they moved through the softwood and came up against hardwood issues of real difference which cannot be explained away as differing but complementary ways of dealing with the same reality. For example, in the Anglican–Roman Catholic context, we might think of the fundamentally different structures and practices of ecclesial authority and global communion. The Anglican Communion is a communion of self-governing provincial churches which, through historical circumstance and by definition, are autonomous but exist in relationships of interdependence and ecclesial communion.[13] While ecclesial tradition is focused around provincial autonomy, Catholic ecclesial tradition is focused around a strongly centered model of authority through communion with the Bishop of Rome.

In relation to such matters of substantive difference, the strategies of clarification and complementarity alone cease to be effective. Here, we need to draw out some of the other strands within the ecumenical cord in order to expose each tradition to the challenge and promise of the different ways of understanding and organizing things to be found in the other traditions. That is, we need strategies aimed more at the medium-term substantive conversion of the traditions, so they can each journey somewhere genuinely new, rather than strategies aimed simply at a more immediate conceptual harmony. This is what Receptive Ecumenism seeks to do. It seeks to offer a constructive way forwards for formal ecumenism at a time when it can seem that we have ended up in a cul-de-sac.

Before turning, however, to a lengthier exposition of Receptive Ecumenism, some initial words of clarification might be in order.[14] Long-

11. Lutheran World Federation and the Roman Catholic Church, "Joint Declaration"; Murray, "St. Paul and Ecumenism."

12. See Murray, "Reception of ARCIC."

13. See Avis, *Anglican Understanding of the Church* as well as *Identity of Anglicanism*; *Vocation of Anglicanism*.

14. In this and other respects, I am grateful to conversations with Paul Avis, both

term substantive reconciliation and rich, complex convergence—in ways allowing for appropriate diversities of emphasis, articulation, and performance—continue to be envisaged here as permanent core aspirations of formal ecumenism. Indeed, it is intended that this long-term aspiration for full structural, sacramental, and theological communion in diversity itself be served and furthered by what is emphasized here as the more immediate concern to expose each tradition to the real challenge and promise of the others' differences. The hope is that, by indicating the possibility of fresh ways of proceeding in relation to difficulties within one's own tradition, real attentiveness to the challenge and promise of others' differences will promote continuing conversion, development, and ecclesial reform within each of the traditions, thus making more achievable the long-term realization of differentiated substantive convergence—the gathering of all things in the complex simplicity of communion in Christ. From this perspective, the two-fold concern with focusing prematurely on the attempt to achieve conceptual harmony is (1) that this appears to leave no way forward in relation to areas of apparent real substantive difference (e.g., as to whether or not the communion of the Church requires a centered authority) and (2) that even where it is possible to draw differing theological languages into harmonious conversation with each other—as in the *Joint Declaration on the Doctrine of Justification*—there is a danger that too immediate an emphasis on harmonious convergence will dull respective attention to what continues to be interestingly and significantly different in the other in ways that might be of potential grace for one's own tradition.

Receptive Ecumenism: Basic Vision and Principles

As the previous section might indicate, at the heart of Receptive Ecumenism is the conviction that further progress is indeed possible on the way towards full structural and sacramental unity. But this progress is only possible if a fundamental, counter-instinctual move is made *away* from the traditions

---

at and subsequent to DePaul's 2017 World Catholicism Week. This has helped me to clarify the nature of my cautionary concern about focusing, potentially prematurely, on achieving ecumenical convergence on the basis of conceptual-doctrinal harmonization alone. My concern is that this can end up effectively leaving each tradition unchanged rather than allowing for a changed appreciation for the others' beliefs (as less alien than previously imagined), without ever properly engaging the challenge and promise of the others' significant differences. With this, however, it has also helped clarify my conviction as to the abiding, long-term importance of harmonious "convergence" across differences of doctrine, life, structure, and practice as the nonnegotiable long-term goal of formal ecumenism—with "convergence" understood here as "convergence into pluriform communion."

wishing that others could be more like themselves and *towards* each asking what it can and must learn, with dynamic integrity, from the respective others in ways that can help to address the specific challenges with which they themselves struggle. We are all familiar with the famous John F. Kennedy reversal: "Ask not what your country can do for you. Ask rather what you can do for your country." There is a similar reversal at work in Receptive Ecumenism: ask not what your others should learn from your tradition; ask rather what your own tradition can learn from these others. Pope Francis expresses something like this in *Evangelii Gaudium* §246, where he says: "If we really believe in the abundantly free working of the Holy Spirit, we can learn so much from one another! It is not just about being better informed about others, but rather about reaping what the Spirit has sown in them, which is also meant to be a gift for us." Such receptive ecclesial learning is envisaged as operating not only in relation to such things as hymnody, spirituality, devotional practices, and pastoral strategy but also as extending to doctrinal self-understanding and, even more so, respective structural and ecclesiological-organisational realities—what Denis Edwards refers to as "institutional charisms."[15]

With that articulation of the basic vision of Receptive Ecumenism in view, it is now helpful to draw out more explicitly some of the key principles which are in play:

1. Receptive Ecumenism believes that, in the context of the more mature dialogues, the convergence concern to overcome historic divisions through such means as clarifying misunderstandings, using fresh concepts to say together what, previously, could only be said apart, and recognizing the validity of distinct but compatible theological frameworks has, on the whole, now gone as far it can, at least for the time being. For all the real achievements of processes such as those leading to the *Joint Declaration on the Doctrine of Justification*, Receptive Ecumenism recognizes that some seemingly insuperable obstacles and substantive ecclesial differences still stand in the path of full sacramental and structural communion—obstacles and difficulties which do not lend themselves to being explained away, either as misunderstandings or as alternative ways of articulating the same reality.

2. Consequently, Receptive Ecumenism recognizes that we are going to be living with some substantive theological, procedural, and structural differences between the churches for a longer time than some

15. See Edwards, "Receptive Ecumenism."

earlier generations of ecumenists had hoped and believed to be the case. Commonality and full communion in understanding, practice, and structure are simply not within our tangible grasp. For the sake of clarity, it is important to say again that, in recognizing this, Receptive Ecumenism is not saying this is a good thing. Nor is it saying we should just reconcile ourselves to this being permanently the case. It is simply saying that we need to be realistic about recognizing that this *is* the current situation in which we find ourselves, whether we like it or not. Sure, it is a situation for which we need to repent and from which we need conversion, but it is where we are and there is no benefit to be had from pretending otherwise. So, Receptive Ecumenism represents a move away from ecumenical idealism and ecumenical optimism and towards a hope-filled ecumenical realism.

3. Receptive Ecumenism believes that what is now needed is a strategy which prioritizes the need for significant ecclesial conversion *within each tradition* in the face of its ecumenical others rather than strategies which seek for immediate ecumenical convergence *between the traditions*.[16] The assumption is that the others' differences represent valuable gifts from which we are called to learn and receive in ways that can help to heal the specific sinful distortions in our own tradition. With this, the further assumption is that acting in this way will both enrich our own tradition and help to create the conditions in which full ecclesial communion will eventually become possible. So, Receptive Ecumenism proceeds by bringing to the fore the dispositions of self-critical hospitality, humble learning, and ongoing conversion that have always been quietly essential to good ecumenical work, and by turning them into the explicit required strategy and core task of contemporary ecumenism.

4. There is an urgent and somewhat self-interested practicality about Receptive Ecumenism, which relates to a sharpened recognition within each of our traditions that, for all our gifts, we nevertheless each have our own particular wounds, difficulties, and sinful distortions, which we cannot easily resolve through our own resources alone. Coincidentally, then, as we have moved to a period of greater ecumenical realism, so also *within* the traditions we have each come to have a more realistic perception of our own limits, difficulties, and distortions. This has happened not because we have become more virtuous but

16. "In any case, full communion cannot be achieved by convergence alone but by conversion, which implies repentance, forgiveness, and renewal of the heart" (Kasper, "*Justification*," 21).

rather because we have been confronted by the reality of such wounds, whether we like it or not—as, for example, through the clerical sexual abuse crisis—and have thereby been disabused of some of the illusions we might have had about ourselves. Furthermore, given that these are difficulties and wounds within our current thought and practice, it is not easy to see how they can be resolved simply by staying within the logic of such existing thought and practice. They show our need for fresh resource and fresh perspective from without. In this regard, then, the immediate value of Receptive Ecumenical learning is that the different gifts and perspectives of our ecumenical others offer the promise of providing us with this fresh resource that we need in order to be able to address our own intractable difficulties. It is in this way that Receptive Ecumenism is a somewhat self-interested call to conversion and transformation: out of things that are narrowing and confining us in various ways and into greater life in Christ.

5. Much ecumenical engagement is a matter of getting out the best china tea service: of showing ourselves, somewhat formally, in the best possible light to our distant relatives who are coming to visit rather than allowing the more "warts-and-all" self-understanding we keep locked behind the closed doors of the intimate family space to come into view. In contrast, rather than the ecumenism of the best china, Receptive Ecumenism represents an ecumenism of the wounded hands: of being prepared to show our wounds to each other knowing that we cannot heal or save ourselves and asking the other to minister to us from the particular gifts and grace given to them.

Putting all of that together, we could say that Receptive Ecumenism is intended as an instrument of ecclesial reform and renewal, which could be well understood as a practice of *ressourcement* against the lost gifts of Christ and the Spirit in the other traditions. However, one clarification is in order, for what makes this a formal, theologically-driven mode of ecumenical engagement is that Receptive Ecumenism does *not* think that a purely instrumentalist, mix-and-match adoption of various interesting-looking practices in other traditions is adequate. Rather, Receptive Ecumenism believes that the respective operative webs of understanding, habit, procedure, and structure within each of the traditions need to be brought into conversation with each other, with a view to pursuing a theologically rigorous process of testing as to how, with dynamic integrity and appropriate transposition, the host tradition might coherently receive from the donor tradition on the basis of a combination of creative expansion, retrieval, and reconfiguring.

Receptive Ecumenism in Practice: Potential Catholic Learning from Anglican Tradition

The third phase of work (2011–present) of the Anglican–Roman Catholic International Commission (ARCIC III) has been addressing respective Anglican and Roman Catholic understandings and practices concerning the relationship between the local, regional, and universal dimensions of the Church. This process has highlighted a number of areas of Catholic practice which are comparatively undeveloped and which could benefit from some receptive learning from Anglican tradition. Here, I briefly highlight four such areas, concerning (1) the role of lay people in ecclesial governance and decision-making; (2) the need for more open Catholic conversation; (3) the possibility of a broader range of models for ordained ministry; and (4) the role of regional bodies in helping to shape the thinking of the universal church.

To take the first of these: it is Catholic teaching that all the faithful, both ordained *and* lay, participate in different ways in the *tria munera* of Christ, to which belong the tasks of teaching, sanctifying, and governing. It is notable, however, that Catholic lay people are restricted to nondeliberative, consultative roles in ecclesial decision-making and discernment processes. This has a negative impact on the quality of the thinking and practice of the Church given that it limits the extent to which lay experience and understanding can effectively contribute to its shaping. It also means that clerical exercise of governance is largely devoid of checks and balances by those governed in a manner that can give rise to problems. By contrast, Anglican lay people routinely share in the *munera* of ecclesial governance in a more determinative way. The question is consequently raised as to whether the Catholic Church might look to the roles accorded to the lay faithful in Anglican parochial, diocesan, and regional conciliar structures as models that could be transposed into the Catholic context in such a way as would still preserve the respective executive roles of parish priests and bishops.

To take the second point about the need for more open Catholic conversation: there is an instinct for unity and participation in a greater whole which is a deeply embedded value within Catholicism. This common and deep instinct for unity is arguably the main gift that Catholics bring to the ecumenical table. But it comes at a price—at times, an unnecessarily and unacceptably high price—for the instinct for unity can tend too easily towards uniformity, with the suppression of legitimate difference, self-policing, and the avoidance of contentious issues in open conversation. The quality of Catholic conversation at parochial, diocesan, national, and international levels could be enriched by learning from Anglican openness to honest debate while the church is in process of coming to a common mind.

Regarding the third point concerning the need for a wider range of models of ordained ministry: the closure and merging of parishes throughout the global North due to an insufficient number of ordained presbyters is a source of pain and grief. This is causing people to ask whether other forms and models of ministry might not enable established worshipping communities to continue. The global South equivalent lies in the massive insufficiency of the numbers of ordained ministers relative to the great needs of the Church. Now, while we recognize that some decisions regarding ministry made by provinces of the Anglican Communion are deemed not to be open to the Catholic community, others *could* feasibly be explored in the Catholic context. Here we might name the possibility of a married presbyterate, together with the possibility of various forms of part-time and non-stipendiary ministerial service; a female diaconate; and the role of lay readers licensed to preach.

Regarding the fourth point, concerning the need for a stronger role for regional bodies in shaping the thinking of the universal church, it is Catholic teaching that the primary locus of authority in the Church is the College of Bishops in communion with the Bishop of Rome as the chair of the college. Reflecting this, teaching emanating from Rome is meant to be articulated in relation to the perceptions and concerns of the diverse local Catholic churches throughout the world. In reality, however, the strongly centered nature of Catholic polity in the organs of the universal church limits the extent to which Catholic teaching and practice *are* effectively articulated within the diversities of Catholic cultural contexts. Compounding this is the fact that we are still struggling to articulate a theological basis for the nature and extent of the teaching authority of national and regional episcopal conferences as part of the ordinary teaching magisterium.

Consequently, while recognizing the significant asymmetry that exists between Anglican and Roman Catholic tradition in relation to the status of the regional church and the inability simply to transfer across in any direct way, ARCIC III has been reflecting on the way in which Catholics could nevertheless profit from looking closely at what there is to be learned from the theology and associated principles of the provincial church in Anglican tradition. It is significant, for example, that Anglican provincial synods provide a regular forum not only for deliberation amongst the bishops of a province but also for the clergy and the laity. With this, Anglican models from Lambeth Conferences and Primates' Meetings could be drawn upon in order to develop the Synod of Bishops from being a purely consultative body to being a deliberative body which could function as an effective organ of collegiality.

Formal Ecumenism, Receptive Ecumenism, and Global South Catholicism: Key Questions

As noted in the introduction to this chapter, it is not uncommon to hear the claim that formal bilateral ecumenism is irrelevant to the churches of the global South. I want to push this a bit in order to try to get a sense of what is going on here. This will take the form of a series of questions.

First, does this reflect the kind of prioritizing of Life and Work ecumenism over Faith and Order ecumenism that was encouraged during Konrad Raiser's period in office at the World Council of Churches?[17] If so, I find myself reflecting, as indicated earlier, that while this fits fairly comfortably with evangelical and Pentecostalist dispositions, which take Christian freedom in Christ to give positive value to ecclesial independence, it sits less comfortably with the core Catholic instinct for the structural and sacramental unity of the Church. Here, ecclesiological matters pertaining to differing patterns and structures of authority, decision-making, and order and the respective formal theologies which diversely apply in these regards surely continue to be of significance regardless of geographical context.

Indeed, while considerable swathes of Protestantism—both in the global North and in the global South—have become increasingly impatient with the Faith and Order orientation towards structural communion and with the related claim that structural ecclesiological differences can be properly communion-dividing, for formal Catholic understanding throughout the world, it remains the case that such ecclesiological differences do matter. Moreover, this fact stands about the character of formal Catholic understanding, irrespective of whether it uniformly corresponds to the variegated understanding of Catholic devotees on the ground.

What shape, then, might this core Catholic instinct for ecclesial communion take in global South contexts? Is it still a gift, a witness, that can usefully be brought to the table of ecumenical ecclesial interaction? Perhaps it is, but also perhaps it just is neither the most pressing of the challenges facing the church in global South contexts nor felt to be the most important of the contributions which Catholicism can make there. How, then, will the

17. See Raiser, *Ecumenism in Transition.*

experience and insights of the diverse local Catholic churches of the world serve to reshape Catholic ecumenism in their respective contexts?

Perhaps the intensely pressing nature of the need to work for economic justice, social care, environmental concern, and the priority of basic human solidarity simply serve to displace and reframe any interecclesial concern for formal ecumenism?[18] And perhaps this is all the more true in contexts in which the Christian communities collectively are a tiny minority relative to the prevailing culture?[19]

Perhaps the classic topics of bilateral ecumenical dialogue are felt to be alien to the churches of the global South, products of a global North history and experience which do not need to be reproduced in and imposed on the churches in the South?[20] Indeed, perhaps the denominational divides are themselves experienced as being part of the colonial legacy and associated territorialism that need to be resisted?

Perhaps the relative scarcity of ordained ministers in the mainline traditional Christian denominations leads to a natural fluidity and permeability of ecclesial identity such that Christians in some global South contexts find themselves already anticipating what it might mean to be one people of God?[21] Thus viewed, might formal ecumenism appear as a necessary tidying-up exercise which must urgently be addressed elsewhere so that the scandal which prevents the people of God more widely from living this communion can be overcome?

What might we say about the possible role of Receptive Ecumenism in the face of such questions and challenges? Can it in any way be a resource for the churches in such contexts? What might Receptive Ecumenism come to look like if developed in these diverse, particular contexts?

The first thing I would say is that Receptive Ecumenism and the basic disposition it represents—of self-critical receptive learning—are not a "one-size-fits-all" reality. It is like a virtuous virus which adapts to context and circumstance. Consequently, it is for the diverse local churches of the global Catholic communion each to ask for themselves what the specific challenges

18. See Chia, "Asian Ecumenism," 69.

19. Chia, "Asian Ecumenism," 66.

20. "The divisions of Christendom were writ large on missionary maps" (Isichei, *History of Christianity*, 76). See also Chia, "Asian Ecumenism," 70 and also 66: "Formal ecumenism is important and makes sense mainly for those who grow up with constricted and exclusive views of faith."

21. See Chia, "Asian Ecumenism," 70: "By the time they realize that their faith is different, such as Protestants having different views of the sacraments, or that Catholics understand the Bible differently, their relationships would have been so deep that their differences don't matter anymore."

and opportunities for receptive learning might be in their own context, confident that there will indeed be such challenges and opportunities.

A second point is that a commitment to receptive ecumenical learning does not depend on reciprocity. It can be a unilateral initiative. I can choose to attend to what I can learn from you even if you have no interest in learning from me.

Following this, the third thing to consider is that the worldwide growth of Pentecostalism, particularly in global South contexts, represents a vital opportunity for receptive Catholic learning in this specific regard. On the one hand, it requires us to think through, more explicitly than we frequently tend to do, the realm of the spirit world and of evil as a personal force. Here, the challenge is to think this through in a way that is intelligent, not silly, and not damaging. On the other hand, it requires us to rethink the relationship between the Holy Spirit and the entire Church as one of constantly renewed promise and gift rather than secure possession and delegated power.

Much more needs to be said about each of these two points in relation to Pentecostalism, but it is interesting to note that they each represent characteristic features of Pope Francis's teaching, as, too, do the seriousness and matter-of-factness with which he engages Pentecostalism. It is also interesting to note that the second point takes us right into an issue which lay at the theological core of the Lutheran Reformation: that is, the Lutheran occasionalist approach to grace, emphasizing the need for active trust in relation to the Spirit, compared with the more typical Catholic emphasis on there being God-given stable structures of grace both within the individual and within the Church. So, perhaps these historic global North issues are not as irrelevant to the churches of the global South as we might assume? Just as the church of the global North is learning how deeply it needs to attend to and learn from the experience of the church in the global South, so also, perhaps, the church of the global South should not be too quick to dismiss as irrelevant the sites of historic dispute and learning in the global North experience. Or, alternatively stated: just as the global Church will rightly continue to learn from the disputes, experience, and insights of the ante-Nicene and post-Nicene North African church, so can we all—indeed, so *must* we all—attend to and learn from the sites of theological learning at issue in the European reformations.

Bibliography

Avis, Paul. *The Anglican Understanding of the Church: An Introduction.* 2nd rev. ed. London: SPCK, 2013.

———. *The Identity of Anglicanism: Essentials of Anglican Ecclesiology*. London: T. & T. Clark, 2007.

———. *The Vocation of Anglicanism*. London: T. & T. Clark, 2016.

Beek, Huilbert van, ed. *Revisioning Christian Unity: The Global Christian Forum*. Studies in Global Christianity. Oxford: Regnum, 2009.

Chia, Edmund Kee-Fook. "Asian Ecumenism from a Roman Catholic Perspective." In *The Asian Handbook for Theological Education and Ecumenism*, edited by Hope Antone et al., 66–71. Oxford: Regnum, 2013.

Congar, Yves. *Diversity and Communion*. Translated by John Bowden. London: SCM Press, 1984.

Edwards, Denis. "Receptive Ecumenism and the Charism of a Partner Church: The Example of Justification." *Australasian Catholic Record* 86.4 (2009) 457–67.

Francis, Pope. *Evangelii Gaudium*. Vatican City: Vatican, 2013. Online. http://w2.vatican.va/content/francesco/en/apost_exhortations/documents/papa-francesco_esortazione-ap_20131124_evangelii-gaudium.html.

———. "General Audience." St. Peter's Square, January 22, 2014. Online. https://w2.vatican.va/content/francesco/en/audiences/2014/documents/papa-francesco_20140122_udienza-generale.html.

Isichei, Elizabeth. *A History of Christianity in Africa: From Antiquity to the Present*. Grand Rapids: Eerdmans, 1995.

Kasper, Walter. "*The Joint Declaration on the Doctrine of Justification*: A Roman Catholic Perspective." In *Justification and the Future of the Ecumenical Movement*, edited by William G. Rusch, 14–22. Collegeville, MN: Liturgical, 2003.

Lutheran World Federation, and the Roman Catholic Church. "Joint Declaration on the Doctrine of Justification." October 31, 1999. Online. http://www.vatican.va/roman_curia/pontifical_councils/chrstuni/documents/rc_pc_chrstuni_doc_31101999_cath-luth-joint-declaration_en.html.

Möhler, Johann Adam. *Unity in the Church or the Principle of Catholicism: Presented in the Spirit of the Church Fathers of the First Three Centuries*. Translated by Peter C. Erb. Washington, DC: Catholic University of America Press, 1996.

Murray, Paul D. "In Search of a Way." In *The Oxford Handbook of Ecumenical Studies*, edited by Geoffrey Wainwright and Paul McPartlan. Oxford: Oxford University Press, 2017. Online. https://www.oxfordhandbooks.com/view/10.1093/oxfordhb/9780199600847.001.0001/oxfordhb-9780199600847-e-45.

———. "Introducing Receptive Ecumenism." *The Ecumenist: A Journal of Theology, Culture, and Society* 51 (2014) 1–8.

———. "The Reception of ARCIC I and II in Europe and Discerning the Strategy and Agenda for ARCIC III." *Ecclesiology* 11.2 (2015) 199–218.

———. "Receptive Ecumenism and Catholic Learning: Establishing the Agenda." In *Receptive Ecumenism and the Call to Catholic Learning: Exploring a Way for Contemporary Ecumenism*, edited by Paul D. Murray, 5–25. Oxford: Oxford University Press, 2008.

———. "Receptive Ecumenism and Ecclesial Learning: Receiving Gifts for Our Needs." *Louvain Studies* 33 (2008) 30–45.

———. "St. Paul and Ecumenism: Justification and All That." *New Blackfriars* 91.1032 (2010) 142–70.

Murray, Paul D., and Andrea L Murray. "The Roots, Range, and Reach of Receptive Ecumenism." In *Unity in Process*, edited by Clive Barrett, 79–94. London: DLT, 2012.

O'Gara, Margaret. *The Ecumenical Gift Exchange*. Collegeville, MN: Liturgical, 1998.

Radner, Ephraim. *The End of the Church: A Pneumatology of Christian Division in the West*. Grand Rapids: Eerdmans, 1998.

Raiser, Konrad. *Ecumenism in Transition: A Paradigm Shift in the Ecumenical Movement?* Translated by Tony Coates. Geneva: WCC, 1989.

World Council of Churches. *The Church: Towards a Common Vision*. Faith and Order Paper 214. Geneva: WCC, 2013. Online. https://www.oikoumene.org/en/resources/documents/commissions/faith-and-order/i-unity-the-church-and-its-mission/the-church-towards-a-common-vision.

10

The Elusiveness of Consensus and a Pathway to Deeper Communion

PAUL AVIS

A BEMUSED COLUMNIST AT *The Tablet* recently wrote: "In theology there is much talk of 'difference' and how good it is and how God contains an infinite lot of it. This seems very puzzling to the outsider. . . . Difference between what and what?" she asks.[1] One can certainly sympathize. My aim in this paper is not to indulge in a frivolous celebration of unexamined "difference" or to advocate an uncritical pluralism of doctrine and practice in the Church. It is rather to examine the concept of difference in an ecclesial perspective—that is, between churches and within churches—and to probe the place of difference on the challenging road to the kind of theological agreement that can provide one of the building blocks of ecclesial communion.[2]

---

1. Grey, "Carmody Grey's Student Voice," 5.

2. Prior to the conference at DePaul University in May 2017, earlier versions of parts of this paper were given at a conference on Anglican-Baptist theological dialogue, convened by Professor Paul Fiddes at Regents Park College, Oxford, in November 2016, and to my fellow members of the Inter-Anglican Standing Commission on Unity, Faith, and Order, at its meeting in Larnaca, Cyprus, in December 2016. I am especially grateful to Mary Tanner, John Gibaut, Sarah Rowland Jones, and Paul D. Murray for comments on earlier drafts.

Facing Difference

The search for Christian unity is fundamentally a quest for the reunification of what belongs together but has come apart. A favored word in ecumenical theology for the process of churches drawing closer together—gravitating towards one another—is *reconciliation*. Reconciliation need not necessarily imply that the parties concerned have been living in a state of mutual enmity or hostility, though this has certainly often been the case in the past and is not entirely absent today. Reconciliation, in a milder sense, is still needed even when churches or groups within them already tolerate and even respect one another—perhaps consulting and cooperating with each other to some extent—but remain out of full sacramental communion with the result that the fragmentation of the one Church of Christ is still unhealed. Reconciliation is often called for between friends and between lovers who have become estranged. It is the pathway that we follow within the ecumenical movement towards the goal of ecclesial communion. Mathematical equations are also reconciled, I believe. To be reconciled can mean to interface, to stand four-square with each other, to be positioned *vis à vis*. This is the sense of reconciliation that seems to me particularly relevant to the state of ecclesial rapprochement today.

When we are reconciled with another at the personal level, we come close enough to look the other person in the face and see their true humanity. Then we realize our common destiny in the fragile human condition. It is brought home to us that we are both finding our way, equally negotiating our course as frail and fallible human beings through this world. In the face of the other as a person, we behold ourselves reflected back, as in a mirror.[3] The real otherness of the other is no longer regarded as alien or threatening, certainly not as something to be eliminated, but is recognized as belonging to the integrity of their personhood—of our common personhood. We now share the same personal space.[4]

A similar dynamic is at work in the reconciliation of churches. Through theological dialogue, accompanied by joint practical discipleship, we begin to see the presence of the one Church of Jesus Christ in each other's churches. We see that other churches are imperfect, struggling, and fallible, just as we know our own church to be. But we also see that the other churches have gifts and graces that we would like to share, insights and practices from which we can learn. Ecumenical reconciliation works for sufficient agreement in faith, order, and practice for two or more churches

3. At this point, I am indebted to the thought of Emmanuel Levinas. See Morgan, *Discovering Levinas*.

4. Zizioulas, *Communion and Otherness*; Crewdson, *Christian Doctrine*.

to begin to live, worship, decide, and act *as one*, for their mutual enrichment and empowerment, though they remain different. This is what I understand by the ecclesiological term "full visible communion."[5]

Like "the elephant in the room," the imperative of reconciliation is so familiar, so taken for granted, so overlooked, that it may be best to spell it out. It is this. Within the fellowship of the worldwide Christian Church, there exist churches or Christian communions who hold apparently incompatible beliefs. So, when the churches face one another in dialogue, formal or informal, they are confronted by deeply entrenched, divergent, and sometimes overtly opposed positions on faith and order. Moreover, these positions have generally developed within specific traditions precisely over against other churches or Christian communions in order to distinguish and separate the one from the other. The extent of the differences sometimes appears intractable: "A great gulf fixed" (Luke 16:26, KJV). These differences may focus on gender issues, human sexuality, and biblical interpretation or they may be concerned with matters of authority, governance, and ministry structures. The chasm between the parties sometimes seems so deep that we may be tempted to despair of ever reaching a common mind and sharing a common life. The path to unity can appear to be a "no through road." But to give up the quest is not an option. As recent popes and others have insisted, the quest for church unity is a street with no exit. Why so? ·

There can be no turning back from the quest for Christian unity, no losing hope, because as Christians and churches, we are called to the apostolic ministry of reconciliation (2 Cor 5:18). Pursuing the cause of unity involves a ministry of reconciliation with regard to the beliefs and practices of parties who seem to stand far apart on certain matters. Such a ministry of reconciliation is an inescapable stage on the path that leads to the ultimate goal of ecclesial communion (*koinonia*) or sacramental fellowship (*communicatio in sacris*). Christian unity presupposes agreement, to the degree that is mutually required, in faith and order, doctrine and practice. What the extent of that agreement—"the degree that is mutually required"—might be and how it might be arrived at is the question at the heart of this paper.

At the root of this all-too-familiar impasse is a fundamental problem of empathy (though that is not all there is to it). Can we truly understand one another? Are we cut off from each other by opposing mindsets? Can we ever realize within ourselves what it must be like for others to hold certain convictions that we may find alien, bizarre, or even detestable—and not only to hold but to live and die by them? This is the fundamental problem of

---

5. Here, I am very much in tune with the "Receptive Ecumenism" project. See Murray, *Receptive Ecumenism*; Avis, "Are We Receiving Receptive Ecumenism?"

mutual understanding, of rightly interpreting the other, of mutual indwelling. Every process of reconciliation involves a hermeneutic of unity, of what it means for two churches, each with its history, traditions, practices, and authoritative texts, to enter into sacramental communion.[6] The art and science of hermeneutics—that is, of understanding and interpreting a text or a tradition or the mind of a community—is at the heart of the problem of ecclesial convergence and reconciliation.

But to be deterred from the outset in our quest for unity and communion by the sheer fact of obvious and serious differences would reveal a serious misunderstanding of the nature of the Church and its unity. We should never say, "We are very different, therefore we cannot do business with each other," or "We are very different; therefore, we cannot come closer together." In truth, the fact of obvious difference is not a roadblock on the way; it is the way that we travel itself, and that is how we should learn to understand it. Unity and difference are not opposites; communion and diversity are not antithetical. The Christian Church on earth, in fact, exists as a collection, a concatenation, of differences. The Church is actually made up of interacting differences and is constituted as a reality by them. The fabric of church life is a tissue of diverse perceptions, convictions, and practices. Take away difference and the Church would cease to exist. Why so?

Differences and disagreements in Christian experience are generated by the interaction of the revelation of God in Jesus Christ with history, society, and culture. Divine revelation becomes embedded in an environment of this-worldly factors and can only be received and known within that context. Karl Barth taught that divine revelation comes to us clothed in the garments of creaturely reality.[7] The creaturely reality of which Barth spoke is, by definition, a contingent reality. That is to say, it depends on an almost infinite range of possibilities that might or might not come to pass. Creaturely reality could always be different to what it is. In the world as God has created it, there is an infinite potentiality for difference. People are different; cultures are different; and traditions are different. They interact; they absorb elements from one another, and they strive one against the other. Newman put the matter like this: "Christianity is faith; faith implies a doctrine; a doctrine, propositions; propositions, yes or no; yes or no, differences. Differences, then, are the natural attendant on Christianity, and you cannot have Christianity and not have differences."[8] It is a fallacy, but a common one, to imagine that, if only we could overcome our differences and all

6. Avis, *Reshaping Ecumenical Theology*, 60–79; Larini, "Text and Contexts."

7. Barth, *CD* 2/1:§25–27.

8. Newman, "Tamworth Reading Room," 197.

think alike, we would have attained unity. What we would, in reality, have attained is a gross impoverishment of Christianity, an anodyne uniformity, and an advanced state of entropy in the Church.

Moral communities, sustained by vibrant traditions, are constituted by ceaseless, ongoing, passionate argument and debate about the vision of the good at the heart of their tradition.[9] Such internal differences are the life-blood of societies and of the traditions, beliefs, and values that they embody. The Christian Church is no exception. Debate, argument, and even strife about differences convey energy to the Body. They raise consciousness, sharpen awareness. We know we are Christians and church people because we are passionately engaged in discussion, debate, and argument about the faith once given and how to apply it today. As T. S. Eliot put it, "We shall not cease from exploration / And the end of all our exploring / Will be to arrive where we started / And know the place for the first time."[10]

Medieval theologians talked about "the principle of plenitude." This meant that the infinite divine creativity found expression in the prolifera-tion of as much variety and richness as the world could contain.[11] It was a manifestation of the infinite generosity, almost exuberance or *jouissance*, of the divine energies. Without denying that there is truth in that view and also reinterpreting plenitude in the light of evolutionary necessities, we can now add something: plenitude—and with it diversity, pluriformity, and difference—is an ineradicable fact of cultural as well as of natural life. It characterizes our intellectual, emotional, artistic, and spiritual existence. We need difference simply in order to be what we are—as human beings, as Christians, as churches. The Church can be seen as the *plenitude* of divinely-inspired, adoring, faith-full responses to the grace of God in Jesus Christ.[12] In the Church of Christ, we should not feel uncomfortable about difference as such. So, can we learn to think about difference *differently*?

There may be help at hand in some concepts borrowed from contem-porary ecumenical theology. Ecumenical theology specializes in questions of difference. Difference is its *métier*. Much of the work of ecumenical the-ology is located in the conceptual space, the tension, between unity and diversity. Within ecumenical theology, reflection on the Church wrestles with the question, "How can the Church be *one* when it is thoroughly per-meated by different, even apparently incompatible, beliefs and practices

9. MacIntyre, *After Virtue.*

10. Eliot, *Collected Poems*, 222.

11. Lovejoy, *Great Chain of Being.*

12. Congar applies the notion of plenitude to the Church in Congar, *Diversity and Communion*, 152.

understood as diverse human, social, historical responses to the definitive Christ event?" The assigned territory of ecumenical dialogue is precisely the realm of difference. Difference is our business in dialogue, but so is agreement. In dialogue, we set out to explore the interface between different ecclesial traditions, to clear up misunderstandings (especially those based on semantic or cultural differences), to locate common ground, and to identify any remaining real (cognitive) differences and what we might call neuralgic practices—practices within the cult that cause offence to the dialogue partner—that require further study and ongoing conversation.

Elusiveness and Convergence

Significant, even astonishing, progress has been made in ecumenical dialogue over the past fifty years since the Second Vatican Council. Walter Kasper, former president of the Pontifical Council for Promoting Christian Unity, states "that many prejudices and misunderstandings of the past have been overcome, that bridges of new mutual understanding and practical cooperation have been built." Cardinal Kasper adds: "In many cases, convergences and consensus have been found, and old—though unfortunately still existing—differences have been better identified."[13] Differences are precisely what ecumenical theologians work with; they are the essential *milieu* of dialogue. There are some differences that will continue to divide churches for the present, but in the experience of dialogue, insights from diverse starting points may unexpectedly converge. It is the potential convergence of insights, the closing of the gap, the homing in on a truth that is greater than all our formulations that constitutes progress in ecumenical dialogue.[14]

I have wrestled all my working life as a theologian with the problem of the elusiveness of consensus, the intractability of cognitive agreement. One of my first books was entitled *Ecumenical Theology and the Elusiveness of Doctrine*.[15] It was critical of some aspects of the Anglican–Roman Catholic International Commission's *Final Report* of 1982 for its apparent lack of ideological awareness, particularly of the factors that make for the *elusiveness* of the goal of dialogue: doctrinal consensus. My concerns were not fueled by some kind of misplaced Anglican confessionalism but rather by my reading of modern Roman Catholic theologians, particularly Rahner, Lonergan, and Küng. I had been especially struck by Rahner's essay,

13. Kasper, *Harvesting the Fruits*, 2.

14. From a Christian philosophical point of view, the definitive study of insight is, of course, Lonergan, *Insight*; he touches on convergence of insight (see 300, 303).

15. Avis, *Ecumenical Theology and the Elusiveness of Doctrine*.

"Pluralism in Theology and the Unity of the Creed in the Church." Pluralism, even within the Roman Catholic Church, has reached such a pitch, Rahner argues, that "the representatives of the different schools cannot achieve, even indirectly, a position in which they can explain to one another consciously and unambiguously in what precisely the difference between their respective intellectual outlooks consists."[16] Rahner's is a deeply pessimistic analysis, and I would not follow him all the way, but it points out the fact that there is a huge mountain to climb if we are to enter empathetically into the minds, the worlds of discourse, of those from whom we differ markedly in our views.

The roots of the elusiveness of the meeting of minds are twofold:

(a) There are obvious—and sometimes glaring—differences of belief and practice between all human communities, including churches: they live differently and think differently. The differences between churches and between the traditions that they represent have historical, social, political, cultural, and psychological dimensions, and these cannot be reconciled by theologians around a table coming up with a formula or a form of words.

(b) The deeper issue is the incommensurability of the "language games," the mismatch of the worlds of discourse that stand behind the differences of belief. Can we take the measure of one another's linguistic worlds? Can we speak each other's language and think each other's thoughts? Can we inhabit each other's *habitus* and indwell each other's sphere of thinking, feeling, and doing? If not, what price convergence on the path to reconciliation?

The English word "convergence" derives from the Latin for "to incline together," to approach nearer to one another, to lean towards each other. Convergence is a dynamic process conducive to potential consensus (general agreement). It would be a fantasy to imagine that complete consensus—unanimity—could ever be attained in this world. What a strange place the world would be if everyone thought in an identical way! It would be utterly boring but would also be intellectually and culturally sterile. In fact, the world could not exist under those conditions and neither could Christianity. The Church lives by difference and debate about difference. But differences and disagreements must not be allowed to paralyze its life and mission. They must be turned to advantage—made to generate the energy that fuels the vitality of the Church and the momentum of its mission. Doing this

16. Rahner, *Theological Investigations*, 11:3–23. My approach was also very much in tune with Congar, *Diversity and Communion*.

requires pastoral and political skills, as well as theological understanding, in church leaders.

All communities seek sufficient convergence of beliefs, values, and behavior to make common action feasible. Consensus is a vital facet of our common life and shared discourse. Cicero translated *homologia* (or *koinōnia*) *tōn anthropōn* into Latin as *consensus* (*omnium*).[17] To the question, "How is society possible?" we must answer, "On the basis of consensus."[18] Consensus can be the fruit of convergence. Convergence draws us together in pursuit of a common goal. When convergence in the Church on faith and order questions amounts to a consensus in basic truths, it can become a platform for witness, for proclamation, to the world. Without a basic consensus, the Christian proclamation is fragmented, contradictory, and dissipated. While the Christian Church is unreconciled within itself, its witness is fundamentally flawed, intrinsically unpersuasive; its mission is contradictory. So, while we need difference in order to *be*, we need convergence in order to *act*. Convergence has its perfect work when it attains a degree of consensus, sufficient agreement for Christian churches to speak and act *as one* on the path to full visible communion.

While convergence is obviously a dynamic process, consensus may look like a stable state. But it is, in fact, an equally dynamic and volatile one. Consensus presupposes a process of convergence, and that process continues even when a workable degree of consensus has been reached. Neither of these two concepts represents a fixed position; both convergence and consensus are continually being renegotiated and evolving into a further stage—or perhaps, on the other hand, unravelling and falling back to previous, less convergent positions. As the Swiss Reformed ecumenist Lukas Vischer put it, "Consensus is never something static but is *a constantly evolving process*."[19] Vischer continues: "New historical experiences create new conditions. Questions arise that call for answers. Things which once stood unchallenged are suddenly called in question, and the consensus has to be established all over again."[20]

17. Hess, *Early Development of Canon Law*, 31.

18. Partridge, *Consent and Consensus*, 72. Obviously, I am applying the notion of consensus in a very limited sphere and not discussing political, social, or moral consensus and cohesion.

19. Vischer, "Consensus," 222.

20. Vischer, "Consensus," 222.

Differentiated Consensus

A nuanced concept of consensus that has proved of great heuristic value in recent ecumenical dialogue is "differentiated consensus." The role of differentiated consensus in dialogue is to enable structured exploration of agreement and difference and the relation between the two. As a tool of dialogue, differentiated consensus can point beyond *convergence* to a kind of *consensus* (general agreement), but that will be precisely a consensus that is incomplete and that calls for further joint study.

The essence of differentiated consensus is that it makes a positive statement about the reality of consensus while acknowledging that the consensus is incomplete. Consensus rarely equates to unanimity but rather represents the agreement of the group concerned to move ahead after all voices have been heard and the best solution for the group as a whole has been identified. The term "consensus" is often applied to the act of decision-making in representative bodies that follow a consensual process, guaranteeing space for minority voices to be heard (the World Council of Churches and the Canadian Council of Churches are two bodies that, to my knowledge, employ this professional practice). But the word "consensus" can equally apply to the search within a diverse community for agreement about values, priorities, and policies that can be owned by the community as a whole—which is, after all, a decision of a kind.[21]

Differentiated consensus, as it operates in ecumenical dialogue, is a consensus that recognizes and includes the reality of difference; it allows for unresolved issues and accommodates them within the basic agreement. That is a notion that is counterintuitive; it stretches our minds, if not our credulity. But differentiated consensus can help us to take a "glass half-full" rather than a "glass half-empty" approach to problems of unity and agreement in the Christian Church. The differences that remain unresolved at any particular time are not seen as alien intrusions into a fundamental harmony and, therefore, to be resented but rather as signs of beliefs and practices that have been held dear within a tradition over time and still play a role in the making of it. They are acknowledged to belong to the identity of the dialogue partner. So, they are not there to be smoothed over by a slick formula, a form of words that can be interpreted by the two sides in incompatible ways; instead, they are to be respected, understood, and discussed in a measured way when both partners are ready, precisely within the new context created by the basic consensus on essential truths. By taking *a different view of difference*—setting an alternative theological valuation on it

---

21. For an introduction, see Sandelin, "Basics of Consensus."

in a dialogue—we will have something concrete to build on, patiently and step-by-step, as far as we can go at any particular time, as we move towards some kind of consensus.

The notion of differentiated consensus has emerged in ecumenical method through reflection on the difficulties involved in moving from convergence to consensus. Convergence is a dynamic term, suggesting movement towards a closer relationship between the parties; it does not necessarily suggest closure. Railroad tracks appear to converge as they run towards the horizon, but in fact they never meet. On the other hand, consensus (general agreement), suggests on the face of it a state of affairs, a goal that has been reached: *stasis*. The train is standing at the station. But, as we have already noted, that *stasis* would be an illusion. No consensus is ever complete; no agreement is final. The relationship, including the agreement on which it is based, is continually evolving. So, the notion of differentiated consensus reflects ecumenical realism. Can there ever be complete agreement between churches whose traditions, languages, teachings, and practices have been formed over the centuries in diverse contexts and in separation from one another? All genuine agreement will inevitably be qualified in some way. The fact is that *undifferentiated* consensus is almost impossible to achieve; the only kind of consensus normally available to us is a differentiated one.

The 1982 benchmark Faith and Order multilateral document *Baptism, Eucharist, and Ministry (BEM)* was the result of many decades of dialogue and mutual engagement, but the progress that it revealed, though real, remained limited. *BEM* marked a significant degree of progress in convergence on the three topics of its title: three profoundly contested ecclesiological sites. But responses from a number of churches worldwide signaled a reluctance to see it as representing an actual consensus; for them, it did not go that far. *BEM* incorporated a tacit method of differentiated consensus by employing a "sidebar" commentary, which recognized areas of continuing difference.[22]

In the case of any historic communion of the Church—say, the Roman Catholic Church or the Anglican Communion—there is a previously existing theological consensus, explicit or implicit (if there were not, it could never have become a communion, capable of a thick, empirical description). But the consensus within the major Christian traditions is

22. WCC, *Baptism, Eucharist, and Ministry*. The more recent WCC document, *The Church: Towards a Common Vision*, explicitly announces itself as a "convergence" text, though it does not have demarcated areas of text for the discussion of unresolved issues. In effect, though not claiming to be so, it shows significantly greater approximation to consensus than does *BEM*.

now fragile, threatened by passionately held divergent convictions and the clash of vested interests. All the major church families are riven by internal disagreement over theological and ethical principles and by related power struggles. What is needed in such circumstances is a method of facilitating convergence in order to repair the historic consensus—a sort of internal ecumenism. The skills that have been honed in inter-church dialogue are equally relevant to the challenge of intra-church reconciliation.[23]

What kind of language is needed to facilitate the movement from convergence to consensus? Theological dialogue between the Roman Catholic Church and the Anglican Communion has sometimes stumbled over the question, "Are we looking for *identical* doctrinal language or *consonant* doctrinal language? Are we asking whether the terminology of a particular text matches the terminology of our official statements, or are we asking ourselves whether we can recognize within it the faith of the Christian Church through the ages? Do we have that intuitive sense of the whole that is greater than the sum of its parts in all their diversity?"[24] When *BEM* was commended by the Faith and Order Commission for study and response in 1982, the churches were asked to discern "the extent to which your church can recognize in this text the faith of the Church through the ages." The guided process of reception of *BEM* throughout the world rightly highlighted the need for active discernment.[25]

The response in 1991 of the Congregation for the Doctrine of the Faith to the *Final Report* of ARCIC I took a less helpful approach. The Anglican–Roman Catholic International Commission (ARCIC) had looked for consonance, but the Vatican wanted identity—identity with the definitive formulations of the magisterium, including the doctrine of transubstantiation.[26] But because language always reflects a lived culture, and a culture presupposes a structured community with a history, a tradition, and a complex of practices in daily life, identical language is simply unachieveable, except on one condition: that one partner in the dialogue should be willing to subsume its historic communal identity completely into that of the other partner—in other words, submit itself to become absorbed into the history, tradition, culture, and practices of the other partner—and that goes against

23. Hinze, *Prophetic Obedience*.

24. For a helpful exposition of my perception of the relation of parts and wholes and the possibility of an intuitive grasp of the latter, see Polanyi, *Personal Knowledge*; *Tacit Dimension*.

25. Church of England, *Towards a Church of England Response*, 5. The Anglican Consultative Council (and, therefore, the Church of England) sometimes used the word "congruent" rather than "consonant" but without any apparent difference of meaning.

26. Hill and Yarnold, *Anglicans and Roman Catholics*, 156–66, esp. 166.

the very nature of dialogue. Yves Congar, drawing on J. A. Möhler, insisted that "there is nothing more contrary to true Christian unity than the quest for unification. This always consists in wanting to universalize one particular form, to endorse life in one of its expressions."[27]

In the semi-official Malines Conversations of the 1920s, between representatives of the Roman Catholic Church and of the Church of England, the key to ecumenical advance was found in the title of the paper, "L'Église anglicane *unie non absorbée*," later identified as the work of Dom Lambert Beauduin. In 1960, following Pope John XXIII's recent announcement of an ecumenical council, Geoffrey Fisher made the first visit of an archbishop of Canterbury to a pope since the Reformation. When the pope expressed a hope that Anglicans would "return to the Mother Church," the archbishop intervened: "Your Holiness, not *return*." Pope John was puzzled; any other way of looking at the matter had not occurred to him, but after a further exchange, he accepted the correction.[28] It is fatally unrealistic to hope to achieve an exact correspondence between two positions in ecumenical formulations. The absorption of the vernacular doctrinal language of one tradition—which is the tip of the iceberg of its liturgical and theological life—into that of another is never going to happen. But what is possible is what we might call an emergent differentiated consensus, composed of complementary discourses, which can be said to be consonant with each other, not in the sense that they agree all the way down the line but inasmuch as they have a common intention and focus on a common object. They are not the same, but they roughly match up. They do not need to exclude actual oppositions—some intractable cognitive differences may remain—but this can only be known after deep, protracted, and sincere exploration in dialogue; it should not be assumed from the start. These discourses can be placed side-by-side, and they can talk to each other; they are not incommensurable. And that in itself should be sufficient for an incremental step in Christian unity, as growth in theological agreement goes hand in hand with growth in lived, albeit partial, communion.[29]

It is utopian and illusory to imagine that partners in dialogue could jointly arrive at a completely fresh—*de novo*—re-description of Christian doctrine on matters that have, historically, been the cause of controversy and separation. ARCIC's founding language came close to suggesting that this was possible. The "Common Declaration" of Pope Paul VI and Archbishop

27. Congar, *Diversity and Communion*, 150. See the exposition of Congar's ecumenical theology in Murray, "Expanding Catholicity through Ecumenicity."

28. Carpenter, *Archbishop Fisher*, 737.

29. For the notion of partial communion, see Haight, *Ecclesial Existence*, 275–80.

of Canterbury Michael Ramsey in 1966, which set up the ARCIC commission, committed the dialogue to begin from "the Gospels and the ancient common traditions." In their preface to the *Final Report* of 1982, the co-chairs stated that the commission had avoided "the emotive language of past polemics" and had sought to pursue together a contemporary restatement of doctrine that would serve the imperative of unity.[30] But ARCIC found that it could not pursue its aim without rehearsing the traditional positions of the two communions on such sensitive questions as eucharistic doctrine, ordination, and justification. In the first report of ARCIC II, *Salvation and the Church* (1987), historic positions were wheeled out to clarify where the parties to dialogue were coming from. Avoidance of polemic is one thing and is entirely necessary, but to look for a fresh language with no historical baggage is another—merely a mirage. When Pope Saint John Paul II gave an audience to ARCIC members in 1980, he nuanced its method in a more realistic direction. The pope noted that ARCIC sought to "go behind the habit of thought and expression born and nourished in enmity and controversy" and "to clothe it in a language at once traditional and expressive of the insights of an age which no longer glories in strife." Here, John Paul drew attention to the unavoidable claims of tradition. We are not looking for a freshly-minted doctrine but a restatement of received doctrine that, while drawing on tradition, looks for convergences and has its sights on what will serve the Gospel and the unity of the Church in a new age. The more recent work of ARCIC has made much of the "reception" and possible "re-reception" of aspects of the tradition.[31]

Several different expressions have been used in ecumenical dialogue to indicate agreement that is qualified, that is to say, not total (and what agreement ever is?).[32] Claims of "substantial agreement," "agreement on essential points," and "fundamental agreement" are formulae that have sometimes been favored by ecumenical dialogues such as ARCIC but without being very clear about what they meant.[33] What these turns of phrase suggest to

30. ARCIC, *Final Report*.

31. Cf. Sherlock and Sagovsky, "Doctrinal Methods of ARCIC II," in Denaux et al., *Looking Towards a Church Fully Reconciled*, 257–59. In truth, "re-reception" is simply a highlighted episode in the long process of reception.

32. Evans, *Method in Ecumenical Theology*, 182–218.

33. ARCIC, *Final Report*, 11, 16–17, 38. The report also uses the terms "consensus," "consonance," and "convergence." See also ARCIC II, *Salvation and the Church*, 26: "We believe that our two communions are agreed on the essential aspects of the doctrine of salvation and on the Church's role within it." Chadwick, "'Substantial Agreement,'" suggests that "agreement in substance" should be seen in the light of Vatican II's notion of the hierarchy of truths, both terms pointing, by means of different metaphors, to what is primary in faith. This gives "substantial agreement" and "agreement in substance"

me is that a method approximating that of differentiated consensus had been found necessary and had been employed, though in a tacit rather than an explicit way. (ARCIC's methodological consciousness has never been high; the dialogue between the World Methodist Council and the Roman Catholic Church has been more methodologically aware and consistent.) We noted that *BEM* made tacit use of differentiated consensus. A clearer example is the synopsis of the work of ARCIC provided by the ARCIC Commission for Unity and Mission (IARCCUM) with its frequent use of shaded areas of text to register remaining differences.[34]

Clearly, the method of differentiated consensus, in a broad sense, has been widely used in ecumenical dialogue in a tacit and implicit way but without being held up to examination until recently. However, it is a further step to name the method as "differentiated consensus" and to reflect systematically on its meaning, uses, and limitations. We can begin to do this by taking a look at the jewel in the crown of ecumenical agreement and the only ecumenical declaration to have been signed by the Roman Catholic Church, the *Joint Declaration on the Doctrine of Justification* (*JDDJ*).

The Joint Declaration on the Doctrine of Justification

The *Joint Declaration on the Doctrine of Justification* was signed by the Roman Catholic Church and the Lutheran World Federation on Reformation Day, October 31, 1999, in Augsburg, the birthplace of the 1530 Lutheran Augsburg Confession (*Confessio Augustana*). In its day, the *Augustana* was an irenic, conciliatory text *vis à vis* the Roman Catholic Church and has remained foundational for Lutheran confessional identity. The *JDDJ* goes a long way (if not all the way) in laying to rest a particular issue that had been the cause of bitter distrust, division, and hostility between Lutherans and Roman Catholics since the sixteenth century.[35] Let us briefly examine its method as the prime example of differentiated consensus.

The road traveled was hermeneutical. A differentiated consensus became achieveable in the *JDDJ* because the dialogue built on decades of Roman Catholic-Lutheran dialogue, especially in Germany and the US. These

(the adjective and the noun, particularly) rather different meanings. Strangely, Chadwick does not give any examples from the work of ARCIC, on which he served for many years.

34. IARCCUM, *Growing Together in Unity and Mission*.

35. For Roman Catholic views, see Kasper, *That They May All Be One*, chapter 6; Witte, *Doctrine, Dynamic and Difference*; Rinderknecht, *Mapping the Differentiated Consensus*; and for a Protestant but not Lutheran view, see Lane, *Justification by Faith*. The historical background is provided in McGrath, *Iustitia Dei*.

dialogues had probed differences of interpretation in opposing theological-cultural contexts (though there had never been a communion-to-communion formal agreement). In other words, the *Declaration* built on immense hermeneutical efforts that had uncovered deep linguistic differences and exposed diverse theological presuppositions. But it had also discovered, through the same hermeneutical explorations, profound commonalities of intention. The different traditions were aiming to say something very similar but in different language. Though following different trajectories, they were homing in on the same target. The *JDDJ*'s essentially hermeneutical character—one that explicitly acknowledges diverse perspectives and interpretations but sees beyond them and requires all the arts of interpretation of texts and of the collective minds and worlds that lie behind them—is not always given its due.

A sophisticated but skeptical analysis of the *JDDJ* has been made by Daphne Hampson.[36] Hampson argues that Lutheran and Roman Catholic theologies are separated by opposing structures of thought and that their respective views of salvation, including justification, reflect these structures. The distance between them cannot be bridged; therefore, she concludes, there can be no consensus. Hampson helps her case by presenting the Lutheran and Roman Catholic positions in their more hard-edged and least nuanced forms. The diversity of both Lutheran and Roman Catholic theology means that examples that are closer together than those she uses are available from both traditions. In fact, Hampson misunderstands key aspects of the two traditions and, thus, inadvertently caricatures them and exaggerates the differences.[37]

Hampson's study highlights the problem of cultural relativism—in its strong form, cultural incommensurability. The assumption that traditions are locked out of each other's mindsets has worrying implications that reach well beyond the sphere of ecumenical dialogue. It calls into question the possibility of empathetically understanding any culture that is radically—or perhaps only significantly—different from our own in order to discover common ground between them. If true, such a conclusion would signal the end of a wide range of established academic disciplines in the human sciences, the disciplines that are essentially hermeneutical and require the arts and skills of empathetic insight—not only theology and philosophy, with their diverse traditions and schools of thought, but also anthropology, history, the study of languages, and various other forms of intercultural studies.

36. Hampson, *Christian Contradictions*. See also Sagovsky, "Christian Contradictions?"

37. Rinderknecht, *Mapping the Differentiated Consensus*, 67–69, 235–40. See also Williams, "Ramsey Lecture."

It is an issue with which thinkers have wrestled since the Neapolitan philosopher Giambattista Vico (1668–1744) achieved a breakthrough in this area, and it underlies the whole development of humanistic hermeneutics in modern philosophy.[38] Isaiah Berlin showed that even though systems of beliefs and values are incommensurable (which he insisted on), it does not follow that we cannot understand each other, that we cannot talk across cultures. In his prolific studies in several departments of the history of ideas, Berlin showed that profound study, infused with a passionate empathy, can do exactly that.[39]

In an exhaustive analysis of consensus in ecumenical theology, Minna Hietamäki points out that the problem of incommensurability is not alien to the *JDDJ* but is precisely the point of it. The *Declaration* recognizes, at least implicitly, that the Roman Catholic and Lutheran doctrinal traditions talk a different language and inhabit different worlds of discourse. It is precisely because diverse perspectives are involved that any consensus has to acknowledge remaining differences—differences that require further work. It would not make sense to say that differentiated consensus embraces contradictions. It embraces not contradictions but *apparent, ostensible,* or *seeming* contradictions, which is a rather different matter.[40] Differentiated consensus does not set out to defy the most basic rule of logic, the law of contradiction. However, the main point is that, even though we are dealing with alternative structures of thought, different worlds of discourse, it does not follow, as Hampson would have it, that some kind of qualified consensus is impossible: hermeneutical insight, born of empathy and intellectual humility, can bridge the gap.[41]

But the hermeneutical path, the path of mutual understanding in the context of difference, takes us beyond the quest for merely cognitive, intellectual agreement, into the realm of faith lived in community, and beyond the matching of propositional assertions to a potential rapport between communities and their traditions as trust is built up.[42] Consensus must be

38. For Vico's significance in this respect, see chapter 6 in Avis, *Foundations of Modern Historical Thought.*

39. For example, Berlin, *Vico and Herder; Against the Current.*

40. Rinderknecht, *Mapping the Differentiated Consensus,* 26, 77–78, 95, 97, 245, 247–48, 263.

41. Hietamäki, *Agreeable Agreement,* 54–55. Kasper, *That They May All Be One,* 128, 130–32, outlines some remaining problems, both within the doctrine of justification itself and in the sphere of ecclesiology. Kasper also comments that, while differentiated consensus excludes contradictory positions, it can embrace "complementary oppositions"; this gambit needs careful probing which is not possible here.

42. Hietamäki, *Agreeable Agreement,* 10, 221, drawing on Lindbeck's cultural-linguistic model of doctrine, Lindbeck, *Nature of Doctrine.*

lived as well as thought. Hand in hand with differentiated (cognitive, intellectual) consensus must go differentiated (lived, practiced) *participation*.[43] Here, I believe, we need to draw on the insights of modern personalist philosophy as applied to persons in relation.[44] Human life is certainly full of differences, but much of the time we successfully negotiate them. We know that we are interdependent and have the making or marring of one another. Human relationships are essentially hermeneutical in character: we "read" others and seek to understand their minds, interpreting the signals that they give in word and act, gesture and demeanor. Sometimes we meet halfway in an agreement that is sufficient to get along together. Human community is possible through qualified consensus and negotiated participation, based on hermeneutical insight and lived out in practice.[45]

The method of differentiated consensus only works in situations where both parties have lost their ideological innocence. To lose one's ideological innocence means seeing, for the first time, a disconcerting truth about our deeply cherished beliefs and practices and taking it to heart. It is the perception that the beliefs and practices that we share with co-religionists within our own community and church—which we probably regard as "the best there is" or, at least, "the best we know"—have been shaped in history by powerful political, social, economic, geographical, linguistic, and cultural factors. A further step in the shedding of ideological innocence is the realization that these "non-theological" factors serve certain interests, economic or political, that have to do with power in the form of dominance, security, or advantage. It means becoming conscious, in a self-aware and self-critical way, that those same hard-won and deeply entrenched beliefs and attitudes have also been shaped by our personal biography and psychology. By the same token, however, we can then come to recognize that the beliefs and practices held dear by members of another community of faith—our opposite numbers—have also been shaped by similar processes and factors, external and internal. Neither of us has received our views and practices from on high, inscribed on tablets of stone. To cease to absolutize our own convictions and spiritual pathway is perhaps the first step towards

43. Meyer, "Differentiated Participation"; Rusch, "Structures of Unity."

44. Macmurray, *Persons in Relation*.

45. My approach is more personalist and hermeneutical than Lindbeck's cultural-linguistic model. I do not accept that the *function* of doctrines is to make cultural-linguistic statements. I believe, with Pannenberg, that the function or purpose of doctrines is to make heuristic statements about reality—truth claims that are to be tested—but I believe that cultural-linguistic awareness is essential to *understanding* and *interpreting* doctrines, especially those of a community other than our own. See Lindbeck, *Nature of Doctrine*; McGrath, *Genesis of Doctrine*; Pannenberg, *Theology and the Philosophy of Science*; *Systematic Theology*, vol. 1, chapter 1.

mutual understanding. Such self-knowledge should conduce to some theological humility.

While some historical differences between Roman Catholic and Protestant versions of the doctrine of justification can be put down to differences of emphasis and misunderstandings due to semantic ambiguity, there remain real theological—that is to say, cognitive—differences of approach. There is no facile appeal to "complementarity." The reality of stubborn differences is clearly acknowledged in the *Joint Declaration*. This carefully claims no more, but no less, than "a consensus on [*or* in] basic truths of the doctrine of justification." The *JDDJ* makes a very bold claim in using the word "consensus," but it immediately qualifies it with the expression "in basic truths." While a cynic might allege that "a consensus in basic truths" is an oxymoron, containing a contradiction in terms, the *JDDJ* is careful not to claim a full or complete consensus but rather one that has been recognized as differentiated. A differentiated consensus is one that is compatible with remaining areas of difference that need further study (one acknowledged area in the *JDDJ* is the biblical basis of the doctrine of justification, though this had, in fact, been thoroughly explored in regional dialogues, notably in the US).[46] The Vatican's hesitations at the penultimate stage of the *JDDJ* process and the Lutheran World Federation's ensuing insistence on further reflection before the *Declaration* could be signed were met by the distinction between basic consensus and the need for further work.

While the *JDDJ* itself does not use the expression "differentiated consensus" (the term has frequently been applied to the *JDDJ* in research literature), the idea is certainly latent in the language that it does use: "consensus on basic truths" with "remaining differences" or "differing explications." The *JDDJ* makes no claim to have achieved complete doctrinal agreement, but it offers an agreement that is substantial enough and fundamental enough to ensure that the remaining differences on this key doctrine, as articulated in the document, should no longer be regarded as church-dividing. The expression "differentiated consensus" has now become identified with the *JDDJ* during the course of its reception and evaluation by theologians.[47]

A key aspect of the method of differentiated consensus in the *JDDJ*, one that probably enabled the project to be brought to a successful conclusion, is the way that Lutheran and Roman Catholic voices are allowed

---

46. US Lutheran-Roman Catholic Dialogue, "Justification by Faith."

47. A seminal text profiling the concept of differentiated consensus is Meyer, "Die Prägung einer Formel." The method of differentiated consensus has also been used in the work of the joint Roman Catholic-Reformed Groupe des Dombes; see "*Un Seul Maître.*" For an exposition, see Gaillardetz, "Doctrinal Teaching Office." See also Legrand, "Receptive Ecumenism."

to speak for themselves in the "Explication" of the *Declaration* (Section 4). Thus, this section proceeds through each of seven areas of the doctrine of justification in a threefold way. First, there is a summary paragraph that always begins: "We confess together . . . " This is followed, in each case, by a Roman Catholic statement and a Lutheran statement, varying the order of presentation. Each of the two traditions has the opportunity to say how it sees the doctrine and how it prefers to articulate it in its own terms. But it is explicitly affirmed in the *Declaration* that these "confessional" statements "are in their difference open to one another" (§40) and do not detract from, or undermine, what has been said jointly in the *Declaration*.

In the search for agreement between separated or opposing groups, there are often things, however basic, that can be said together. Saying them together may in itself constitute a major hermeneutical breakthrough. Giving both sides an equally formal, equally public opportunity to state matters in a way that is authentic to each, alongside what they are able to say together, can reassure the parties that they are not being manipulated, put in a false position, or asked to renounce what is important to them. Their historic stance is respected; there is a desire to hear what they have to say in their own words and their own way. As they articulate again what they stand for as churches in a specific area of doctrine, they cannot help but be aware that they are addressing a particular audience, one that is different in culture, language, and institutional assumptions from their domestic audience "back home." They are engaging the other, and they will almost certainly temper their discourse accordingly. It will be nuanced in a way that helps it to be heard and understood, that enables "the penny to drop." This hermeneutical method is surely a key factor among the conditions that make it possible for the parties eventually to say something meaningful together. This particular aspect of the method of differentiated consensus that made the *JDDJ's* breakthrough possible was, in my view, a masterstroke.

Conclusion

Ecumenical dialogue has already experienced remarkable convergence, and in some cases—notably in the *JDDJ*—it has achieved a consensus in some basic truths of salvation. This is no surprise to historical theologians, who are aware of the complexity and interconnectedness of Christian thought and practice, but it may come as a revelation to many lay Christians, and even clergy, who uncritically imbibe from sermons, catechesis, and the church-press-stereotyped and -caricatured versions of Christian traditions other than their own. The uncritical retailing of inherited distortions of the ecclesial other is possibly the greatest barrier to progress towards deeper communion. So, let the churches continue steadfastly to seek through dialogue ever deeper avenues of convergence. Let them keep working to close the hermeneutical gap of mutual understanding step by step until, God willing, we arrive at a broader consensus on historically contested doctrines. Though such a basic consensus will be shot through with remaining differences, it should prove a sufficient foundation for a life lived more and more closely together as Christians and as churches. Then, theology will be married to practice, thought to life, and differentiated consensus to differentiated participation. In such a way, we may enter ever more deeply into communion with one another, which is inseparable from our communion with God the Holy Trinity.

Bibliography

Anglican-Roman Catholic International Commission (ARCIC). *The Final Report.* London: CTS/SPCK, 1982.

Avis, Paul. "Are We Receiving Receptive Ecumenism?" *Ecclesiology* 8.2 (2012) 223–34.

———. *Ecumenical Theology and the Elusiveness of Doctrine.* London: SPCK, 1986.

———. *Foundations of Modern Historical Thought: From Machiavelli to Vico.* 2nd ed. Oxford: Routledge, 2016.

———. *Reshaping Ecumenical Theology: The Church Made Whole.* London: T. & T. Clark, 2010.

Barth, Karl. *Church Dogmatics.* Vol. II/1, *The Doctrine of God, Part 1.* 12 vols. Edinburgh: T. & T. Clark, 1957.

Berlin, Isaiah. *Against the Current: Essays in the History of Ideas.* Oxford: Oxford University Press, 1981.

———. *Vico and Herder: Two Studies in the History of Ideas.* London: Hogarth, 1976.

Carpenter, Edward. *Archbishop Fisher: His Life and Times.* Norwich: Canterbury, 1991.

Chadwick, Henry. "'Substantial Agreement': A Problem in Ecumenism." *Louvain Studies* 16.3 (1991) 207–19.

Church of England. *Towards a Church of England Response to BEM and ARCIC, the Final Report of the Anglican-Roman Catholic International Commission.* GS/ Church of England Series 661. London: CIO, 1985.

Congar, Yves. *Diversity and Communion.* Translated by John Bowden. London: SCM, 1984.

Crewdson, Joan. *Christian Doctrine in the Light of Michael Polanyi's Theory of Personal Knowledge: A Personalist Theology.* Lampeter: Edwin Mellen, 1994.

Denaux, Adelbert, et al. *Looking Towards a Church Fully Reconciled: The Final Report of the Anglican-Roman Catholic International Commission 1983–2005 (ARCIC II).* London: SPCK, 2016.

Eliot, T. S. *Collected Poems 1909–1962.* London: Faber & Faber, 1974.

Evans, G. R. *Method in Ecumenical Theology: The Lessons So Far.* Cambridge: Cambridge University Press, 1996.

Gaillardetz, Richard R. "Does a Doctrinal Teaching Office Have an Ecumenical Future? Assessing the Groupe des Dombes Document 'One Teacher' (2005)." In *Where We Dwell in Common: The Quest for Dialogue in the Twenty-First Century*, edited by Gerard Mannion, 161–83. Basingstoke: Palgrave Macmillan, 2016.

Grey, Carmody. "Carmody Grey's Student Voice: 'As I Put the Question to God, I Remember This Way of Thinking Rests on a Lie.'" *The Tablet* 271.9200 (2017) 5.

Groupe des Dombes. *"One Teacher": Doctrinal Authority in the Church*. Translated by Catherine E. Clifford. Grand Rapids: Eerdmans, 2010.

———. *"Un Seul Maître": L'Autorité Doctrinale dans l'Église*. Paris: Bayard, 2005.

Haight, Roger. *Ecclesial Existence*. Vol. 3 of *Christian Community in History*. London: Continuum, 2008.

Hampson, Daphne. *Christian Contradictions: The Structures of Lutheran and Catholic Thought*. Cambridge: Cambridge University Press, 2001.

Hess, Hamilton. *The Early Development of Canon Law and the Council of Serdica*. Oxford: Oxford University Press, 2002.

Hietamäki, Minna. *Agreeable Agreement: An Examination of the Quest for Consensus in Ecumenical Dialogue*. Ecclesiological Investigations 8. London: T. & T. Clark, 2010.

Hill, Christopher, and Edward Yarnold, eds. *Anglicans and Roman Catholics: The Search for Unity*. London: SPCK, 1994.

Hinze, Bradford E. *Prophetic Obedience: Ecclesiology for a Dialogical Church*. Maryknoll, NY: Orbis, 2016.

International Anglican-Roman Catholic Commission for Unity and Mission (IARCCUM). *Growing Together in Unity and Mission: Building on Forty Years of Anglican-Roman Catholic Dialogue; An Agreed Statement of the International Anglican-Roman Catholic Commission for Unity in Mission*. London: SPCK, 2007.

Kasper, Walter. *Harvesting the Fruits: Basic Aspects of Christian Faith in Ecumenical Dialogue*. London: Continuum, 2009.

———. *That They May All Be One: The Call to Unity Today*. London: Burns and Oates, 2004.

Lane, Anthony N. S. *Justification by Faith in Catholic-Protestant Dialogue: An Evangelical Assessment*. London: T. & T. Clark, 2002.

Larini, Riccardo. "Text and Contexts: Hermeneutical Reflections on Receptive Ecumenism." In *Receptive Ecumenism and the Call to Catholic Learning: Exploring a Way for Contemporary Ecumenism*, edited by Paul D. Murray, 89–101. Oxford: Oxford University Press, 2008.

Legrand, Hervé. "Receptive Ecumenism and the Future of Ecumenical Dialogues: Privileging Differentiated Consensus and Drawing its Institutional Consequences." In *Receptive Ecumenism and the Call to Catholic Learning: Exploring a Way for Contemporary Ecumenism*, edited by Paul D. Murray, 385–98. Oxford: Oxford University Press, 2008.

Lindbeck, George A. *The Nature of Doctrine: Religion and Theology in a Post-Liberal Age*. London: SPCK, 1984.

Lonergan, Bernard J. F. *Insight: A Study of Human Understanding*. London: Darton, Longman, and Todd, 1958.

Lovejoy, Arthur O. *The Great Chain of Being: A Study of the History of an Idea*. The William James Lectures delivered at Harvard University, 1933. Cambridge, MA: Harvard University Press, 1936.

Lutheran World Federation, and the Catholic Church. "Joint Declaration on the Doctrine of Justification." October 31, 1999. Online. http://www.vatican.va/roman_curia/ pontifical_councils/chrstuni/documents/rc_pc_chrstuni_doc_31101999_cath-luth-joint-declaration_en.html.

MacIntyre, Alasdair. *After Virtue.* 2nd ed. London: Duckworth, 1985.

Macmurray, John. *Persons in Relation: Being the Gifford Lectures Delivered in the University of Glasgow in 1954.* London: Faber, 1961.

McGrath, Alister E. *The Genesis of Doctrine.* Oxford: Blackwell, 1990.

————. *Iustitia Dei: A History of the Christian Doctrine of Justification.* 2 vols. Cambridge: Cambridge University Press, 1987.

Meyer, Harding. "Die Prägung einer Formel: Ursprung und Intention." In *Einheit aber Wie? Zur Tragfähigkeit der ökumenischen Formels "differenzierten Konsens,"* edited by Harald Wagner, 36–58. Freiburg: Herder, 2000.

————. "Differentiated Participation: The Possibility of Protestant Sharing in the Historic Office of Bishop." *Ecumenical Trends* 34 (2005) 10–14.

Morgan, Michael L. *Discovering Levinas.* Cambridge: Cambridge University Press, 2007.

Murray, Paul D. *Receptive Ecumenism and the Call to Catholic Learning: Exploring a Way for Contemporary Ecumenism.* Oxford: Oxford University Press, 2008.

Murray, Paul D., ed. "Expanding Catholicity through Ecumenicity in the Work of Yves Congar: *Ressourcement,* Receptive Ecumenism, and Catholic Reform." *International Journal of Systematic Theology* 13.3 (2011) 272–302.

Newman, John Henry. "The Tamworth Reading Room." In vol. 2 of *Essays and Sketches,* edited by C. F. Harrold, 171–214. New York: Longman, 1948.

Pannenberg, Wolfhart. *Systematic Theology.* Vol. 1. Translated by G. W. Bromiley. Edinburgh: T. & T. Clark, 1991.

————. *Theology and the Philosophy of Science.* Translated by Francis McDonagh. London: Darton, Longman, and Todd, 1976.

Partridge, P. H. *Consent and Consensus.* London: Macmillan/Pall Mall, 1971.

Polanyi, Michael. *Personal Knowledge.* London: Routledge and Kegan Paul, 1958.

————. *The Tacit Dimension.* London: Routledge and Kegan Paul, 1967.

Rahner, Karl. *Theological Investigations.* London: Darton, Longman, and Todd, 1965.

Rinderknecht, Jakob Karl. *Mapping the Differentiated Consensus of the Joint Declaration.* Basingstoke: Palgrave Macmillan, 2016.

Rusch, William G. "Structures of Unity: The Next Ecumenical Challenge—A Possible Way Forward." *Ecclesiology* 2.1 (2005) 107–22.

Sagovsky, Nicholas. "Christian Contradictions? Hampson, Jüngel, and Lane on Justification and the Structure of Lutheran and Catholic Thought." *International Journal for the Study of the Christian Church* 4.1 (2004) 91–101.

Sandelin, Rob. "Basics of Consensus." http://nica.ic.org/Process/Consensusbasics.php.

Second Anglican-Roman Catholic International Commission (ARCIC II). *Salvation and the Church: An Agreed Statement by the Second Anglican-Roman Catholic International Commission.* London: Church House, 1987.

US Lutheran-Roman Catholic Dialogue. "Justification by Faith." *Origins* 13 (1983) 277–304.

Vischer, Lukas. "Consensus." In *Dictionary of the Ecumenical Movement,* edited by Nicholas Lossky et al., 221–25. Geneva: WCC, 1991.

Williams, Rowan. "Ramsey Lecture, Durham: 'The Lutheran Catholic.'" Lecture given in Durham Cathedral, Durham, NC, November 23, 2004. Online. http://aoc2013.brix.fatbeehive.com/articles.php/2102/ramsey-lecture-durham-the-lutheran-catholic.

Witte, Pieter de. *Doctrine, Dynamic, and Difference: To the Heart of the Lutheran-Roman Catholic Differentiated Consensus on Justification.* Ecclesiological Investigations 15. London: T. & T. Clark, 2012.

World Council of Churches (WCC). *Baptism, Eucharist, and Ministry (BEM).* Faith and Order Paper 111. Geneva: WCC, 1982.

———. *The Church: Towards a Common Vision.* Faith and Order Paper 212. Geneva: WCC, 2013.

Zizioulas, John. *Communion and Otherness.* London: T. & T. Clark, 2006.

II

Past Divisions and Present Ecumenical Dialogues: Are These Elements of God's Providential Plan?

VIMAL TIRIMANNA, CSsR

DIVISIONS IN THE FOLD of those who believe in Jesus Christ are not new. They go back to New Testament times and were mostly based on doctrinal or moral issues, though often human weaknesses, such as misunderstanding, error, not listening to the other, etc., were the proximate causes. At face value, divisions among human groups—let alone those among Christians—that isolate one another can never be considered as something positive. The divisions within the Christian fold, especially in Christianity's early centuries, were surely unfortunate, often based on trivialities that could have easily been ironed out if some control of passions, some common sense, and some readiness to listen to the other had prevailed.[1] However, could such divisions be perceived exclusively as negative? Could they not also be perceived as the means by which a providential God, in mysterious ways, achieves his own eternal plans of salvation for all humankind?

This paper is an effort to examine briefly whether those unfortunate divisions among Christians in history and the present efforts in ecumenism (particularly, receptive ecumenism) could be perceived as elements which God absorbs into his own wider plan of humanity's salvation—i.e., not that God directly wished such unfortunate divisions, but God, in his divine providence, may be using human (even Christian) divisions themselves to

---

1. See, for example, Pongratz-Lippitt, "Reformation Triggered by 'Trivial' Issue."

achieve his own eternal plans. In what follows, I will first briefly describe what divine providence is and then highlight how, in salvation history (as revealed in the Bible), God has providentially used the even seemingly negative effects of free human acts to achieve his own designs. Thereafter, using the comparatively "new" concept of "Receptive Ecumenism," I will try to demonstrate how God preserves his fullness of revelation to the apostles (revealed in and through Jesus of Nazareth) by not allowing historical divisions among later generations of Christians (which are often a result of human weakness and error) to damage the main elements of his revelation contained in the original Apostolic faith.

Divine Providence

Cameron describes "providence" as follows:

> The beneficent outworking of God's sovereignty whereby all events are directed and disposed to bring about those purposes of glory and good for which the universe was made. These events include the actions of free agents, which while remaining free, personal, and responsible are also intended actions of those agents. Providence thus encompasses both natural and personal events, setting them alike within the purposes of God.[2]

Providence can also be viewed as "the divine care of the world, God's guidance of history and human affairs toward the achievement of his purpose."[3] Even though we do not meet the term "providence" as such in the Bible, "the idea of a wise, loving, and powerful God who is everywhere at work in the world pervades the entire Bible."[4] The idea of divine providence is closely related to that of God's continuous activity in the world, expressed by the Hebrew word *bara* which means basically "to create" (Exod 34:10; Num 17:20; Isa 43:1, 15; 45:7; 48:7). It implies God's "continuous creation through preservation and governance of all that is created."[5]

Down through the centuries, some of the perennial theological questions related to the concept of divine providence have been: if God (the Creator) is in control of the affairs of this world (his creation) and if he always intends the good of human beings, how can one explain the evil that pervades our world? Is God responsible also for the evil in the world?

2. Cameron, "Providence," 541.
3. Wright, "Providence," 815.
4. Wright, "Providence," 816.
5. Masterman, "Providence of God (In the Bible)," 780.

Moreover, if God is in control of the world and of all that happens therein, where is the space for human freedom? In responding to these unavoidable questions, the Christian concept of divine providence has consistently maintained a delicate but sensible balance between God's ever prevailing free will and the freedom of human beings. St. John Damascene (645–749), for example, suggested a way of conceiving what divine providence would amount to, based on the biblical view of providence, when he made a distinction between "the antecedent will of God" and "the consequent will of God."[6] This distinction enables one to speak of an antecedent and a consequent plan of God's providence:

> The antecedent plan provides for all the possibilities of the world. It includes what God wants to happen as well as what he is willing to let happen in view of human freedom. It includes the total initiative of divine grace. It determines how each event can somehow be made to further his love, if only humans are willing. The consequent plan is that aspect of the antecedent plan which God actually puts into execution in view of human free choices.[7]

In other words, God can use even those free human choices that apparently deviate from his own "original" designs, for he is the one who can write straight even using the crooked lines (of human beings). That is to say, God respects human freedom and the actions which ensue from that freedom, even when those actions bring about evil, contrary to God's will.[8] God thus permits evil which emanates exclusively from free human actions,[9] but ultimately, he uses even those "evil" acts and their consequences to further his own plans. St. Paul's statement that "we know that in everything God works for good with those who love him" (Rom 8:28) would also corroborate this point.

In fact, in salvation history one notices how God uses even non-Israelites and their activities to achieve his purposes for the good of Israel. Accordingly, in Second Isaiah, Cyrus of Persia, though a non-Israelite, is used by God to achieve his own purposes, namely, to bring salvation to his chosen one, Israel (Isa 45:1–7). Similarly, in the New Testament, even the betrayal of Jesus by Judas was meant to fulfill God's own plans to redeem humanity (Matt 26:20–24a; John 13:21–30). Thus, in the Bible, "where evil is encountered, it is always presented as serving the order of God's providence.

6. John of Damascus, "Exact Exposition of the Orthodox Faith," 263.

7. Wright, "Providence," 817.

8. See Hidber, "Il Male, Onnepotenza di Dio e Libertà Umana," 507–11.

9. See Journet, Il Male: Saggio Teologico.

Even in the seeming irrationality of the prosperity of the evildoers and of the suffering of the righteous, God's providence is effective."[10] One of the most colorful biblical illustrations in this regard is the story of Joseph in the book of Genesis. Joseph, the favorite son of Jacob, is sold to some slave traders by his envious brothers. He is taken to Egypt by them, and as time passes, he acquires a reputation for interpreting dreams, which draws the attention of the pharaoh when the latter himself has a disturbing dream. Joseph's interpretation of this dream so impresses the pharaoh that he appoints him vizier of the kingdom of Egypt.[11] McKenzie describes the rest of the story succinctly as follows:

> When the famine touched Canaan, Jacob sent his sons to Egypt to purchase grain; they did not recognize Joseph. He tested them by accusing them of spying, by holding Simeon as a pledge, and by returning their money, and learned that they were sorry for their treatment of him, but he demanded they bring his own uterine brother, Benjamin, on their next trip (Gen 43). When they brought Benjamin, he tested them again by accusing Benjamin of stealing his cup and when Judah offered to substitute himself for Benjamin's punishment, Joseph revealed his identity and told them to bring their father and his family to Egypt (Gen 44–45).[12]

As is well known, the consequence of this chain of events was that the family of Jacob was not only reunited in Egypt but also saved from the deadly famine in Canaan, and so, God ensured Israel's continuity, thus making sure that they ended up as the chosen people of God which would later be liberated from the clutches of slavery in Egypt and be brought to the promised land. In this story, therefore, one notices how God uses the evil schemes of Joseph's brothers to achieve his own salvific ends, keeping his promise to Abraham (Gen 12:1–3; 15:1–6). The divisions caused by human evil are providentially used by God to further his own plan of salvation by uniting Jacob's family (Israel) once again, thus laying the basis for the chosen people of God's existence and continuation.

---

10. Masterman, "Providence of God," 780.

11. See McKenzie, *Dictionary of the Bible*, 455.

12. McKenzie, *Dictionary of the Bible*, 455.

Contemporary Religious Pluralism and Divine Providence

Writing in the very different context of those theologians who work in the field of the contemporary reality of the plurality of religions, Claude Geffré says:

> Without claiming to know the reason for the multiplicity of ways to God, these theologians are simply seeking to interpret an apparently insurmountable pluralism in the light of what we know of God's universal will of salvation. This pluralism cannot be simply the sign that, after twenty centuries, the Church's mission has met defeat. Hence, it is theologically permissible to interpret it as a pluralism that corresponds to a mysterious divine design.[13]

Geffré's point is that the undeniable phenomenon of religious pluralism that exists in our contemporary world could be interpreted as "a mysterious design of God, the ultimate significance of which is beyond us."[14] For him, further proof of this point is the Second Vatican Council text, which states that the Holy Spirit offers everyone the possibility to participate in Christ's paschal mystery "in a way known to God."[15]

Taking the parallel case of the many divided churches in our world today, could we also extend Geffré's ideas above and dare say that, in the mysterious design of God known only to him, there could be a providential way in which he uses even those human-made Christian divisions to achieve his eternal plan for the salvation of all humanity? (Of course, we must keep in mind the undeniable nuances of the serious difference between the phenomenon of the presence of different religions in the world and that of the presence of different churches who believe in the same Jesus Christ.) God cannot be simply perceived to will unity among Christians (John 17:21) and then, at the same time, be a mere helpless spectator in the face of divisions which destroy that which he himself willed! Rather, he may be perceived as the One who uses those very divisions to achieve his own eternal plan, in his own mysterious, providential ways.

13. Geffré, "From the Theology of Religious Pluralism," 50.

14. Geffré, "From the Theology of Religious Pluralism," 50.

15. Geffré, "From the Theology of Religious Pluralism," 50. The text he refers to is *Gaudium et Spes*, 22.

Christian Unity Is Not Uniformity

It is true that Jesus earnestly prayed for the unity of those who believed in him (John 17:21). However, one needs to keep in mind that genuine unity is not uniformity, a fact that has been conveniently ignored by different churches all throughout history. It is the unity in diversity that is to be upheld if one were to be serious with regard to what is indicated in the New Testament itself. There was no one uniform Church as such, even among the primitive Christians of Apostolic times. But certainly, they were one in faith in the one Lord Jesus Christ and all shared in one Baptism in the name of the Trinity. The diverse ways of living the one Christian faith in diverse communities are expressed clearly in the diverse texts of the New Testament which emerged in those respective communities. Thus, in his erudite study on the different Christian communities of the first century as evident in the New Testament texts, Raymond Brown could write about the diversity of Christian communities (churches) within the city of Ephesus itself as follows:

> More likely, Ephesus had different churches with different theologies. We must remember that the Christian situation in a large city would have involved a number of house churches where twenty or thirty people met together, and so there is no reason why there could not have been, in the one city, house churches of different traditions—for example, of the Pauline tradition, of the Johannine tradition, of the Petrine or apostolic tradition, and even of the ultraconservative Jewish-Christian tradition. Even though the house churches of one tradition probably had *koinonia* with those of another tradition, Christians may not have transferred easily.[16]

The absence of any sense of uniformity in expressing their one faith among the early Christians is further illustrated by Brown when he writes:

> There was no evidence in these works that a consistent or uniform ecclesiology had emerged. Rather, writings addressed to different New Testament communities had quite diverse emphases. Even though each emphasis could be effective in the particular circumstances of the writing, each had glaring shortcomings that would constitute a danger were that emphasis isolated and deemed to be sufficient for all times. Taken

---

16. Brown, *Churches the Apostles Left Behind*, 22–23; see also 29.

collectively, however, these emphases constitute a remarkable lesson about early idealism in regard to Christian community life.[17]

But Brown is also quick to demonstrate how this situation does not tally well in later history with our own Christian divisions which have given occasion to put more emphasis on and deepen those very diversities along the course of the centuries:

> No one can show that any of the churches I have studied had broken *koinonia* or communion with another. Nor is it likely that the New Testament churches of this Sub-Apostolic Period had no sense of *koinonia* among Christians and were self-contained conventicles going their own way. Paul is eloquent on the importance of *koinonia*, and in the Pauline heritage, concern for Christian unity is visible in Luke/Acts and the Ephesians. Peter is a bridge figure in the New Testament, and the concept of the people of God in 1 Peter requires a collective understanding of Christianity. For all its individualism, the Fourth Gospel knows of other sheep not of that fold and of Jesus's wish that they be one. Matthew has a concept of *the* church and expands the horizon of Christianity to all nations. Most of the New Testament was written before the major break in *koinonia* detectable in the second century, and so New Testament diversity cannot be used to justify Christian division today. We modern Christians have broken *koinonia* with each other, for, explicitly or implicitly, we have excommunicated each other and/or stated that other churches are disloyal to the will of Christ in major issues. Such a divided situation does not have New Testament approbation.[18]

So, while acknowledging the vast difference between the expressions of the one Christian faith in the first-century apostolic Church and the expressions of that same faith in our present day's churches whose divisions occurred later in history and are often man-made, one can still highlight the crucial point that unity does not at all mean uniformity. That is to say, unity in diversity and, also, diversity in unity can well be living human characteristics of the one Christian faith, which different Christian churches today ought to take note of.

---

17. Brown, *Churches the Apostles Left Behind*, 146–47.
18. Brown, *Churches the Apostles Left Behind*, 147–48.

Christian Divisions and Receptive Ecumenism

As the Aristotelian-Thomistic concept of human beings asserts, we humans live in society with others. We are social beings. In fact, in Gen 2:18, God himself says that it is not good for man to be alone. In other words, any isolation that ensues from human divisions is not healthy for us. While any and every division that isolates humans (or pits one against the other) is to be looked at with contempt, such divisions among those who believe in the One Lord Jesus Christ (who prayed for unity among all his followers) are surely to be condemned all the more, simply because this is not what Christ himself willed for his followers.

Due to our Christian church communities' separations from each other for centuries, there have been separate developments based on different emphases on the Christian scriptures and tradition within the respective traditions of the different churches. That is to say, our varied Christian church traditions have developed diverse ways of living the gospel of Jesus Christ by emphasizing certain aspects of the original apostolic faith while neglecting other aspects of the same. As a result, today, different churches have well preserved various traditional Christian elements (some even coming from apostolic times). These can surely enrich the other churches and thus enable them to return (within their respective church communities) to the fullness of early churches' apostolic faith. In a way, one could easily talk of a complementary nature among the churches, at least with regard to certain traditional Christian elements once found in the apostolic churches. Long ago, the renowned Roman Catholic theologian Yves Congar, in his *Diversités et Communion*, demonstrated convincingly that if we are serious about the presence of the Holy Spirit among other Christians, then we are bound to listen carefully to what they are saying, for such listening would surely lead us to take note of the fact that some issues perceived as divisive are, in fact, only differences of expression of the same reality.[19] This is the basis for what has now come to be known as "receptive ecumenism."[20] Denaux describes succinctly what "receptive ecumenism" in the discussions of ARCIC III basically amounted to, when he writes:

> It is a dynamics of receiving and giving gifts, of receiving and giving elements of the Apostolic Tradition, which might have

19. See Congar, *Diversity and Communion*, 171–72.

20. See Murray, *Receptive Ecumenism and the Call to Catholic Learning*. See also Murray, "Receptive Ecumenism and Ecclesial Learning," 30–45; "Introducing Receptive Ecumenism," 1–8.

been obscured or forgotten in the course of our wounded histories.[21]

Paul Murray, the pioneer of receptive ecumenism, describes its central aim as follows:

> The central aim of Receptive Ecumenism is to take seriously both the reality of the contemporary ecumenical moment— wherein the once widely held hope for structural unification in the short-medium term is, in general, now widely recognized as being unrealistic—and the abiding need for the Christian churches precisely in this situation to walk the way of conversion towards more visible structural and sacramental unity. The aim is to seek after an appropriate ecumenical ethic and strategy for living between the times; for living now orientated upon the promise of and calling to being made one in the Trinitarian life of God.[22]

In fact, the Second Vatican Council, while speaking on the People of God, also spoke of how different parts of this People brought together by one baptism share their diverse gifts with each other and thus enrich the One Church of Christ.[23] Developing this idea further, in his 1995 encyclical, *Ut Unum Sint*, Pope John Paul II taught: "Dialogue is not simply an exchange of ideas. In some way, it is always an 'exchange of gifts.'"[24] The main implication here is that other Christian traditions are not to be seen as erroneous or "heretical" but rather inspired by the Spirit in their own way, so they should be perceived as "gifts" to be appreciated and experienced. Later, following this same line of thought, Pope Francis would often talk of things that we can learn from each other, especially from the elements that one church tradition has lost but another has preserved or even deepened:

> If we really believe in the abundantly free working of the Holy Spirit, we can learn so much from one another! It is not just about being better informed about others, but rather about reaping what the Spirit has sown in them, which is also meant to be a gift for us. To give but one example, in the dialogue with our Orthodox brothers and sisters, we Catholics have the opportunity to learn more about the meaning of episcopal collegiality and

---

21. Denaux, "Ecclesial Repentance and Conversion," 319.

22. Murray, "Receptive Ecumenism and Ecclesial Learning," 32.

23. See Paul VI, *Lumen Gentium*, 13; *Unitatis Redintegratio*, 4, 6.

24. John Paul II, *Ut Unum Sint*, 28.

their experience of synodality. Through an exchange of gifts, the Spirit can lead us ever more fully into truth and goodness.[25]

Addressing the Pontifical Council for Christian Unity in its plenary session in November 2016, Francis said:

> The different theological, liturgical, spiritual, and canonical traditions which have developed in the Christian world, when they are genuinely rooted in the apostolic tradition, are a wealth for and not a threat to the unity of the Church. Seeking to suppress this diversity is to counter the Holy Spirit, who acts by enriching the community of believers with a variety of gifts.[26]

Last but not least, during his groundbreaking visit to Sweden to mark the Reformation's five hundredth anniversary, the pope addressed those gathered at Lund, saying that the half a millennia of separation between the two faith groups has "enabled us to understand better some aspects of our faith," and he noted specifically: "With gratitude we acknowledge that the Reformation helped give greater centrality to sacred Scripture in the church's life."[27]

Ecclesial Repentance and Conversion in Action

In his elucidating essay, "Ecclesial Repentance and Conversion," Denaux talks, in the context of ecumenism, of a process in which "receptive ecumenism" forms an indispensable part in our contemporary reality.[28] Accordingly, such conversion is integral to the ecumenical movement. He points out the need "to see clearly that the heart of the ecumenical problem lies in disunity of the institutional dimension of the Church."[29] If the will of God is the unity of Christians, then obviously disunity or the division into separate churches is against that will; therefore, it is a sin: "One could say that the divided churches are in a state of sin, in as far as they stick to their

---

25. Francis, *Evangelii Gaudium*, 246.

26. "Pope's Address to Pontifical Council."

27. McElwee, "Marking Reformation."

28. See Denaux, "Ecclesial Repentance and Conversion," 304–25. Using Pope John Paul II's 1984 apostolic exhortation, *Reconciliatio et Paenitentia*, 16. Denaux points out how such a conversion consists of both personal and institutional structural elements. In other words, such a conversion involves not only the individual adherents of different churches but also the very structural institutions of those churches. See Denaux, "Ecclesial Repentance and Conversion," 306–9.

29. Denaux, "Ecclesial Repentance and Conversion," 306.

confessional identity without the will to change. Hence a more corporate form of conversion, i.e., an ecclesial conversion, is also needed."[30]

Denaux also refers to the International Theological Commission which in 2000 wrote:

> Indeed, in the entire history of the Church there are no prec-
> edents for requests for forgiveness by the Magisterium for past
> wrongs. Councils and papal decrees applied sanctions, to be
> sure, to abuses of which clerics and laymen were found guilty,
> and many pastors sincerely strove to correct them. However,
> the occasions when ecclesiastical authorities—pope, bishops, or
> councils—have openly acknowledged the faults or abuses which
> they themselves were guilty of, have been quite rare.[31]

As the same document points out, Pope Paul VI will be remembered by history as the first pope to express a request for pardon addressed as much to God as to a group of contemporaries. In his address at the opening of Vatican II's second session, he asked "pardon of God . . . and of the separated brethren" of the East who may have felt offended "by us" (the Catholic Church) and declared himself ready for his part in pardoning offenses received.[32] Later, Vatican II also would follow the same path of calling for a change of heart with regard to other Christian churches.[33] At the turn of the third millennium, Pope John Paul II, following Paul VI and Vatican II, would again renew the same request and would also ask for forgiveness:

> Not only did John Paul II renew expressions of regret for the
> "sorrowful memories" that mark the history of the divisions
> among Christians, as Paul VI and the Second Vatican Council
> had done, but he also extended a request for forgiveness to a
> multitude of historical events in which the Church, or individ-
> ual groups of Christians, were implicated in different respects.
> In the Apostolic Letter, *Tertio millennio adveniente*, the pope
> expresses the hope that the Jubilee of 2000 might be the occa-
> sion for a purification of the memory of the Church from all
> forms of "counter-witness and scandal" which have occurred in
> the course of the past millennium.[34]

---

30. Denaux, "Ecclesial Repentance and Conversion," 306.

31. International Theological Commission, "Memory and Reconciliation," 1.1.

32. International Theological Commission, "Memory and Reconciliation," 1.1.

33. See Paul VI, *Unitatis Redintegratio*, 7.

34. International Theological Commission, "Memory and Reconciliation," 1.3.

For his part, Pope Francis has actively engaged himself during the past two years with many other Christian church communities. In the process, he has often asked their pardon for what the Catholic church community has done in the past, indicating ecclesial conversion on the part of the Roman Catholic church community afresh.[35] That same sentiment is seen in the joint statement made by Francis and leaders of different Christian churches.[36]

Similarly, other church leaders have also expressed their sorrow for past mistakes and their eagerness to embark on a journey of receptive ecumenism. For example, in a joint message sent to Anglican communities on the occasion of the five hundredth anniversary of the Reformation, the archbishops of Canterbury and York, Justin Welby and John Sentamu, said:

> This year is a time to renew our faith in Christ and in Him alone, remembering the Reformation should also lead us to repent of our part in perpetuating divisions. Such repentance needs to be linked to action aimed at reaching out to other churches and strengthening relationships with them.[37]

So, at this point of history, most of the Christian churches have been one in voicing their need to be one flock of Jesus, first of all, by asking forgiveness from each other, an essential step in the process of Christian unity toward healing bitter ecclesial memories. Some have even taken the next obvious step of this process, namely, to follow the concept of "receptive ecumenism"—to learn, unlearn, and re-learn, as necessary, in their relationships with other Christian churches. In other words, there are genuine and realistic efforts to amend past mistakes where possible in relation to other churches. It is precisely here that receptive ecumenism enters, forcefully and effectively, the ecumenical arena.

The concepts and practices of "ecclesial repentance" and of "receptive ecumenism" have their own specific characteristics which could be complementary. Ecclesial repentance focuses on past sins and faults, honestly confessed and for which forgiveness is asked. Through this, the hope is to come to a purification of memories. Receptive ecumenism is more oriented towards recognizing present difficulties in one's own tradition, and by doing

35. See, for example, his statement during his meeting with Eugenio Bernardini, the moderator of the Waldensian Church on June 22, 2015, in Turin, Italy.

36. For example, see the joint statement between Francis and the Russian Orthodox Patriarch Kirill, of Moscow and All Russia, on February 12, 2016, in Havana, Cuba, as well as the joint statement with Bishop Munib Yunan, president of the Lutheran World Federation on October 31, 2016, in Lund, Sweden.

37. Bernadelli, "Welby on the Reformation."

this, becoming open to learning from other traditions how to solve these difficulties (through an exchange of gifts). This requires, most importantly, focusing on the practical and organizational issues at stake.[38]

Denaux then says that both practices—namely, ecclesial repentance and receptive ecumenism—can be integrated into the more general concept of "ecclesial conversion." In the context of difficulties faced within Anglican-Roman Catholic relations, Denaux gives an illustration of such a conversion: on the Anglican side, the main difficulty is the principle of provincial autonomy, while on the Roman Catholic side, it would be the excessive centralization "resulting from a certain view of the primacy of the Bishop of Rome." If the two communions "are to overcome the impasse," then, both sides must go through an ecclesial repentance as well as an ecclesial conversion in the form of a practical receptive ecumenism, and Denaux enumerates this in four concrete steps.[39]

In the context of our own topic, we would maintain here that such ecclesial conversion on the part of Christian churches will not only create further space for divine providence to achieve its goal—namely, the unity of all those who believe in Jesus Christ—but it will also offer one way of cooperating with the same providential will of God for Christian unity. After all, as Pope Francis says, "Unity is not the fruit of our human efforts or the product built by ecclesiastical diplomacy, but it is a gift that comes from on high."[40]

Conclusion

In the past, there have been many divisions among our Christian churches, though they all continued to have one Baptism and to believe in one Lord Jesus Christ. Since those divisions had as their root causes various types of misunderstandings, human error, etc., they often were due to human irresponsibility. Consequently, these divisions went against the desire of Jesus that all his disciples be one. However, God who never ceases to achieve his own designs and plans can and does use ("in a mysterious way known to him") even those divisions to achieve those eternal ends of his. The original apostolic elements of faith that are present either fully or partially in the different churches could well be the connecting bridge that not only unites them into one flock of believers once again—a unity in diversity—but they could also be the very vehicle which God uses providentially to achieve his

38. Denaux, "Ecclesial Repentance and Conversion," 320–21.
39. See Denaux, "Ecclesial Repentance and Conversion," 322–23.
40. "Pope's Address to Pontifical Council."

plan for the same Christian unity. However, the ecumenical efforts of today in general and the concept of "receptive ecumenism" in particular beckon those very divided churches to go through a process of ecclesial repentance and ecclesial conversion, not only in words but also in action on both the personal and the institutional level. They are challenged to learn, un-learn, and re-learn from each other seriously so that the original elements of apostolic tradition may be seen in them once again, though, of course, in diverse ways. In fact, if heeded by the individual churches, this is one way—irrespective of human weakness and error which often caused (and may continue to cause) the divisions among the churches—of cooperating with God's providential way of realizing his own designs for the salvation of all humanity—i.e., unity in diversity among Christians.

Bibliography

Bernadelli, Giorgio. "Welby on the Reformation: Past Violence Must Not Be Forgotten." *Vatican Insider,* January 18, 2017. Online. http://www.lastampa.it/2017/01/18/vaticaninsider/welby-on-the-reformation-past-violence-must-not-be-forgotten-BCoubyrQTLKBXlCZHblYJI/pagina.html.

Brown, Raymond E. *The Churches the Apostles Left Behind.* New York: Paulist, 1984.

Cameron, N. M. de S. "Providence." In *New Dictionary of Theology,* edited by Sinclair B. Ferguson et al., 541–42. Downers Grove, IL: InterVarsity, 2005.

Congar, Yves. *Diversity and Communion.* London: SCM, 1984.

Denaux, Adelbert. "Ecclesial Repentance and Conversion: Receptive Ecumenism and the Mandate and Method of ARCIC III." In *Conversion and Church: The Challenges of Ecclesial Renewal,* edited by Stephen van Erp and Karim Schelkens, 304–25. Boston: Koninklijke, 2016.

Flannery, Austin, ed. *Vatican Council II: The Conciliar and Post-Conciliar Documents.* Dublin: Dominican, 1975.

Francis. *Evangelii Gaudium: The Joy of the Gospel.* Vatican City: Libreria Editrice Vaticana, 2013.

Geffré, Claude. "From the Theology of Religious Pluralism to an Interreligious Theology." In *In Many and Diverse Ways: In Honor of Jacques Dupuis,* edited by Daniel Kendall and Gerald O'Collins, 45–59. Maryknoll, NY: Orbis, 2003.

Hidber, Bruno. "Il Male, Onnepotenza di Dio e Libertà Umana." *Rivista di Teologia Morale* 124 (1999) 507–11.

International Theological Commission. "Memory and Reconciliation: The Church and the Faults of the Past." December 1999. Online. http://www.vatican.va/roman_curia/congregations/cfaith/cti_documents/rc_con_cfaith_doc_20000307_memory-reconc-itc_en.html.

John of Damascus. "An Exact Exposition of the Orthodox Faith." Book 2, Chapter 29. In *The Fathers of the Church: A New Translation,* edited by Bernard M. Peebles et al., 260–63. Translated by Frederic H. Chase. Washington, DC: Catholic University of America, 1958.

John Paul II. *Ut Unum Sint: That They May Be One*. Vatican City: Libreria Editrice Vaticana, 1995.

Journet, Charles. *Il Male: Saggio Teologico*. Roma: Borla, 1963.

Masterman, M. R. E. "Providence of God (In the Bible)." In *New Catholic Encyclopedia*, edited by Bernard L. Marthaler et al., 780–81. Washington, DC: Thomson-Gale, 2003.

McElwee, Joshua J. "Marking Reformation, Francis Calls Lutherans and Catholics to 'New Common Path.'" *National Catholic Reporter*, October 31, 2016. Online. https://www.ncronline.org/news/vatican/marking-reformation-francis-calls-lutherans-and-catholics-new-common-path.

McKenzie, John L. *Dictionary of the Bible*. London: Geoffrey Chapman, 1965.

Murray, Paul D. "Introducing Receptive Ecumenism." *The Ecumenis: A Journal of Theology, Culture, and Society* 51 (2014) 1–8.

———. "Receptive Ecumenism and Ecclesial Learning: Receiving Gifts for Our Needs." *Louvain Studies* 33 (2008) 30–45.

———. *Receptive Ecumenism and the Call to Catholic Learning: Exploring a Way for Contemporary Ecumenism*. Oxford: Oxford University Press, 2008.

Paul VI. *Lumen Gentium: Dogmatic Constitution on the Church*. Boston: St. Paul, 1965. Online. http://www.vatican.va/archive/hist_councils/ii_vatican_council/documents/vat-ii_const_19641121_lumen-gentium_en.html.

———. *Unitatis Redintegratio: Decree on Ecumenism*. Boston: St. Paul, 1964. Online. http://www.vatican.va/archive/hist_councils/ii_vatican_council/documents/vat-ii_decree_19641121_unitatis-redintegratio_en.html.

Pongratz-Lippitt, Christa. "Reformation Triggered by 'Trivial' Issue." *Tablet*, June 23, 2016. Online. https://www.thetablet.co.uk/news/5743/reformation-triggered-by-trivial-issue.

"Pope's Address to Pontifical Council for Promoting Christian Unity." *Zenit*, November 10, 2016. Online. https://zenit.org/articles/popes-address-to-pontifical-council-for-promoting-christian-unity-2.

Wright, John H. "Providence." In *The New Dictionary of Theology*, edited by Joseph A. Komonchak et al., 815–16. Dublin: Gill and Macmillan, 1988.

PART FIVE

Plurality and Unity

12

Asian Ecumenism through a Postcolonial Lens

FELIX WILFRED

Introduction

I WOULD LIKE TO start by referring to how ecumenism is viewed by canon law. It is important to take note of this since canon law is what officially guides Catholics in the concrete practice of ecumenism. There is but a single canon,[1] Canon 755, which deals *ex professo* with ecumenism in the Latin Code, and it reads as follows:

> It is primarily for the supreme Church authority to foster and direct the ecumenical movement among Catholics, whose scope is the restoration of unity among all Christians . . . [and] it is for bishops and episcopal conferences to promote it according to norms of law.

What do we find? That it links ecumenism with the magisterium—with the teaching authority of the Church—the pope, the bishops. How helpful is this position? In spite of all the beautiful things said in the Vatican II documents *Unitatis Redintegratio* and *Orientalium Ecclesiarum* when it comes

---

1. The Eastern Code (CCEO), however, has seven canons on ecumenism (canons 902–8).

to the practice of ecumenism, the doctrinal preoccupations have pinned it down to the *magisterium*.[2]

Let us look at the word *restoration* in the above cited canon. What is implied as the goal of ecumenism is a going back to (restoring of) the unity that existed before the historical division of churches. Implied in this "restoration" is the goal of organic unity, for the Roman Catholic Church considers itself to be the true Church of Christ or sees this Church of Christ as "subsisting" in the Catholic Church.[3] Both of these notions have been problematic. While the ecumenical discourses and practices have advanced—and many models have been put forward, such as conciliar unity, reconciled diversity, receptive ecumenism, etc.[4]—the Roman Catholic Church's official position seems to have gotten stuck at organic unity. Similarly, while there are attempts to understand and interpret the statement that the true Church of Christ "subsists" in the Catholic Church, we note that Catholic fundamentalism in practice still seems to profess an equation of the Roman Catholic Church with the Church of Jesus Christ.

As a method, the cited canon manifests a top-down approach to ecumenism, and there is nothing concerning the faithful, the people of God, and their role in ecumenism and its practice. What we have in this canon is, then, *institutional ecumenism*, reflecting the hierarchical structure of the Roman Catholic Church.[5] With this canon, we do not come very far with ecumenism! Fortunately, the Eastern code has seven canons and more to say about the people of God when speaking of ecumenism. Canon 755, which I quoted from the Latin code, would explain why Rome is focused on bilateral institutional dialogue with other denominations and agreement on

2. Nedungatt, "Ecumenism and Canon Law," 53–62.

3. Paul VI, *Lumen Gentium*, 8. For a commentary on the background of this as well as on the debated term "subsistit," see the comments of Aloys Grillmeier in Vorgrimler, *Commentary on the Documents of Vatican II*, 146. Whereas "subsistit" became an important point of reference for the post-Vatican opening of the Roman Catholic Church, some of the subsequent documents seem to have set back the clock and, in an effort to maintain orthodoxy, tend to equate the Roman Catholic Church with the Church of Christ. See, for example, CDF, "Letter to the Bishops of the Catholic Church," issued by the Congregation for the Doctrine of the Faith in 1992; "Responses to Some Questions," made public by the Congregation for the Doctrine of the Faith on July 10, 2007; *Dominus Iesus*. Such a trend cannot but promote re-confessionalization and mean a "winter of ecumenism."

4. See Murray, *Receptive Ecumenism and the Call to Catholic Learning*; "Receptive Ecumenism and Ecclesial Learning."

5. One may celebrate as a great achievement the accord between the Roman Catholic Church and the Lutheran World Federation on the debated issue of justification. But then, we may be tempted to ask: how are the people of God part of this accord, and what does it signify for them? Is it not, perhaps, a case of "magisterial mutuality"?

doctrinal points, whereas developments in the field of ecumenism at bottom point in a different direction.[6]

What has been happening in Asia in the field of ecumenism, especially in the light of the experience with "wider ecumenism" (namely, interreligious relationships and the way postcolonialism looks at unity and plurality), could open up new spaces and avenues for ecumenical relationships. In this chapter, I will discuss (1) the Asian ecumenical path; (2) insights from interreligious relationships for a new ecumenical practice; and (3) the future of ecumenism from a postcolonial perspective. All three sections are tied together by the thread of postcolonialism because the Asian ecumenical path has been one that distinguishes itself from the prevalent understanding of the relationship among churches during the missionary and colonial periods. The postcolonial understanding and interpretation of Asian Christianity leads to a discussion of the relationship with peoples of other faiths, as this is an issue of the unity of humankind which the Churches are called to serve. The future of ecumenism is also envisaged from the postcolonial perspective. At the same time, delving into these issues of Asian ecumenism is a matter of realizing its contribution to world ecumenism.

Part I: Asian Ecumenical Path

From Denominations to Indigenous Churches

The same missionary movement that brought denominationalism into Asia was, ironically, also the source of ecumenism. The spirit of ecumenism was triggered by the need to bear common witness. The World Missionary Conference in Edinburgh in 1910 was the occasion for missionaries of different denominations to come together to affirm common Christian witness.[7] There was also a lesser-known movement that followed the Edinburgh Conference: the move from denominationalism to autonomous, indigenous churches with their own features. This was an attempt to break the traditional framework in mission of thinking and acting based on past denominational identities. Visionaries like Bishop V. S. Azariah (1874–1945), a participant at the Edinburgh Conference of 1910, already foresaw new forms of Christianities in Asia and on other continents—Christianities not bound by past historical divisions. It would appear that Bishop Azariah and others preferred to invest their energies in the future shape of Christianities in indigenous forms rather than be caught in the agenda of reconciling

6. See O'Grady and Scherle, *Ecumenics from the Rim*, 498.
7. See Radano, *Celebrating a Century of Ecumenism*.

the historical divisions that had occurred in Christianity. Similarly, Cheng Ching-Yi, a young pastor from China, told the conference that the Chinese Church should exercise its own agency to shape and sustain a Chinese expression of Christianity according to its genius and with a nondenominational identity.

Let me quote from the speech of Azariah:

> Through all the ages to come, the Indian Church will rise up in gratitude to attest to the heroism and self-denying labors of the missionary body. You have given your goods to feed the poor. You have given your bodies to be burned. We also ask for love. Give us friends.[8]

Through these words, Azariah indicated the importance of mutuality, inclusiveness, and dialogue in mission as well as among Churches and denominations—a dialogue based on respect for each other as indicated by the metaphor of *friends*. He touched a sensitive nerve—the relationship between the missionaries and the native peoples. For him, the Edinburgh Conference was a great opportunity to highlight the importance of mutuality, reciprocity, and friendship since the relationship of missionaries to the indigenous was characterized by aloofness, condescension, and lack of interaction. Implied herein is a postcolonial critique of power relationships in the mission and the Church. The postcolonial critique of Azariah, antedating contemporary postcolonial theories, called for reciprocal self-understanding. Where there is domination, there is no room to talk of friendship or equality. I tend to think that colonial mission was perhaps the greatest religious enterprise in human history, but it was an enterprise lacking in friendship and intersubjectivity. Addressing an assembly of over one thousand white Protestant representatives of various missionary societies at the height of the colonial period, Azariah spoke of how the missionaries never cared to visit the home of indigenous workers or share meals with them. He also apparently commented, in a lighter vein, on how missionaries prevented the local people from participating in deliberations on Church matters: "Too often you promise us thrones in heaven but will not offer us chairs in your drawing rooms." One cannot but admire Azariah's audacity; however, it seems these words were deleted from the official proceedings of the Edinburgh Conference.[9] There was indeed talk about cooperation

---

8. As quoted in Stanley, *World Missionary Conference*, 125.

9. Ariarajah, "Contribution of Asian Participation," 265. I must add that there were individual missionaries who were exceptions. But the point is that the *system as such* was, at best, patronizing and, at worst, arrogant and authoritarian, with little room for reciprocity and intersubjectivity.

and promotion of unity during the Conference. But it concerned mission agencies of different denominations cooperating and avoiding rivalry and duplication in the work of mission.

Thanks to this heritage of V. S. Azariah, Cheng Ching-Yi, and other Asian participants in the Edinburgh Mission conference, today there has been a shift of attention from denominations to indigenous forms of Christianities, in which the agency of the local people is evident.[10] In other words, what has been happening in Asia is similar to the process that early Christianity witnessed. Different cultures, histories, and worldviews led to the emergence of different ecclesial traditions; "ecumenical" referred to the communications among the various expressions of Christianity. The possibility of this process is foreshadowed in Vatican II's *Lumen Gentium* which, while speaking of regional bishops' conferences, points to their possible future development into churches of their own, similar to the development of churches in the East and the West in Christianity's early centuries:

> It has come about through divine providence that, in the course of time, different Churches set up on various places by the apostles and their successors joined together in a multiplicity of organically united groups which, whilst safeguarding the unity of the faith and the unique divine structure of the universal Church, have their own discipline, enjoy their own liturgical usage, and inherit a theological and spiritual patrimony. . . . In like fashion, the episcopal conferences at the present time are in a position to contribute in many and fruitful ways to the concrete realization of the collegial spirit.[11]

Since the early twentieth century, there has been a move in Asia towards nondenominationalism. In China, the National Christian Conference started in 1913 in Shanghai and became a common platform of Protestant churches.[12] The three principles of the Three-Self Patriotic Movement—*self-governance, self-support,* and *self-propagation of the Gospel*—have their roots in the nondenominational Christianity of the early twentieth century. Thinkers like T. C. Chao, L. C. Wu, and Y. T. Wu were at the forefront of reappropriating Christianity in the Chinese way. Belonging to one of the Western denominational groups in colonial times was to reinforce further the "foreign" image of Christianity in China. In one sense, the Three-Self

10. On the development of indigenous Christianities in Asia, see Bhakiaraj, "Forms of Asian Indigenous Christianities," 171–81. See also Mullins, *Christianity Made in Japan.*

11. Paul VI, *Lumen Gentium,* 23.

12. Chow, "Protestant Ecumenism and Theology," 167–80.

Patriotic Movement was interdenominational, in that it brought together the various Protestant denominations with a common mission in China. But in another sense, the development of an indigenous Church was transdenominational, focused on the concrete situation in China. The Korean War reinforced the importance of forging Christian identity with national identity. This interdenominational and transdenominational approach met with opposition, as one would suspect, on the part of the Roman Catholic Church, which threatened to excommunicate any Catholics joining this transdenominational movement in China.

In India, the formation of the Church of South India (CSI) in 1947 occurred with the merger of the Anglican (Episcopal), Congregational, Presbyterian, and Methodist denominations. It was the first example in the world of an organic ecumenical unity.[13] It was the result of a long process of maturation, beginning at the Tranquebar Conference of 1919, which saw the coming together of several denominations' leaders. Following the inspiration of CSI, the Church of North India (CNI) came into existence in 1970.

Ecumenical Forces in Asia

Asian Christians have long been aware that denominationalism is a real scandal in the midst of peoples of other faiths and that it is not good for the proclamation of and witness to the Gospel. As C. H. Hwang noted:

> The sad thing is that, before becoming first a confessing church in the missionary situation, the younger churches were prematurely projected into a 'confessional' situation which was not their own; before they became a Community of Christ, they were told to become a Presbyterian, Lutheran, Methodist, or Anglican church. They were divided without even being able to know why.[14]

In Asia, the meeting among the churches has not been so much a matter of faith and order (negotiating doctrinal differences) as a necessary response to the challenges of the world, promoting common mission and witness. This point has been put forward strongly by D. Preman Niles, who notes that "an important key for grasping theological concerns in the ecumenical movement in Asia is the fact that theological articulations in Asia, with some few exceptions, arise at the places where the church meets the world

---

13. Daughrity, "South India," 56–68.

14. See Fey, *1948–1968*, 72–73; Kinnamon and Brian, *Ecumenical Movement*, 3–4.

and the world challenges the church."[15] This point could be illustrated by the Asian nations' struggle for independence from the colonial yoke, followed by the program of nation-building. The Christian churches were so scattered and heavily controlled by missionaries that there was hardly any room for them to come together in the struggle for independence. Opinions were very much divided among the Christians themselves on national issues.[16] However, once independence was attained, the mood changed. The situation of newly independent nations called for all the Christians to come together on the basis of a common nationhood and contribute to the growth and development of the newly liberated countries. The objective of nation-building created the mood for ecumenical cooperation for the benefit and welfare of the people.

Another refreshing ecumenical force in Asia has been the subalterns—marginalized peoples, victims, and those at the periphery who are discriminated against. From them came new impulses for ecumenism and unity. Here, I name the Dalit movement, movements of indigenous and tribal peoples, and the discriminated Burakumin of Japan. Groups like the Dalits have suffered discrimination from all churches and at different levels. Hence, the ecumenical agenda for them is not reconciliation and unity among the churches but rather a challenge to all of them to overcome caste divisions and create unity among the people of God. All the churches are divided by caste, and this is the major source of disunity in the Church. In the face of this agenda of unity, which touches upon their life and dignity, denominational divisions seem to pale in significance. The challenge from the marginalized groups is a challenge of unity—a call to the unity of the Church without division on the basis of caste, race, language, etc. Denominational division stemming from past history seems to have had little impact on the Christian faith and life of the marginalized; the Dalits, for example, cut across different denominations. Whichever denominations they may belong to—an accident of mission history—their goal is unity in the Church and among the churches. Illustrative of this is the fact that, when deciding to convert to Christianity, the subaltern people's choice of church is not based on which one offers orthodoxy and purity of doctrines but instead on which one integrates them within the Christian community in the spirit of unity and respects their human and Christian dignity. "There is neither Jew nor Greek, there is neither slave nor free, there is neither male nor female; for you are all one in Christ Jesus" (Gal 3:28, RSV). This is the

---

15. See Koshy et al., *History of the Ecumenical Movement in Asia*, 2:26.

16. See John, *Indian Catholic Christians*; Jeyakumar, *Christians and the National Movement*.

unity which the Dalit people seek from the churches. Dalits and other subaltern groups are contributing to a new and fresh understanding of unity that is yet to come. This is different from institutional ecumenism. The victims, the Dalits, and the marginalized stimulate the churches to reconceptualize ecumenism from the periphery.[17] As Jude Lal Fernando observes,

> It is the churches' ability to listen to the multiple voices of suppressed others within its own tradition and in other traditions; among the poor, women, different ethnic, tribal, and caste groups; among the lives that have been made fragmentary and episodic and the ecosystem that is threatened—which is the memory of the eternal Other who is existing in each and every one of us—that could further the process of dialogue. The church discovers itself in the face of the other within the churches, among the churches, and in the world at large. The other has been the victim of petty ideological interpretation of doctrine and faith. It is, in fact, the voices of such victims who evoke the moral responsibility of the Church.[18]

Persecution of Christians and their harassment have led to a greater experience of Christian unity. For example, a recent study on the Christian communities in the states of Gujarat and Odisha in India concluded that the persecution and violence they suffered have been a force which has cemented the relationships, the coming together, among various denominations. It has also led these various denominations to rethink, jointly, the past ways of evangelization. This is an example of ecumenism from below.

The geopolitical situation in Asia has also prompted the coming together of the churches for the cause of peace and reconciliation. This is exemplified by the Tozanso process,[19] the ongoing dialogue and exchange among subregional groups that began in 1984 when churches of North Korea and South Korea met with churches from Japan and the United States. Meeting together since then on a regular basis has helped to develop the spirit of solidarity. One of the important concerns in the process is the involvement of the Asian churches for the reconciliation between North and South Korea. The Tozanso process created opportunities for church leaders—especially of South and North Korea—to make mutual visits and increase mutual understanding among a divided people. This process has also created momentum in the churches' resistance to military buildup in Korea.

---

17. See Clifton, "Ecumenism from the Bottom Up," 576–92; Sawyer, "Black Ecumenical Movements," 151–61.

18. Fernando, "Ecumenism in Modern and Postmodern Contexts," 87.

19. See Weingartner, *Tozanso Process*.

Institutional and Theological Initiatives

At the institutional level, from the nineteenth century onwards, the medical, educational, and philanthropic works by the different churches in Asia have provided an opportunity for mutual cooperation among them. Further, movements like the Young Men's Christian Association (YMCA), Young Women's Christian Association (YWCA), and World Student Christian Federation (WSCF) have played an important role in promoting ecumenical spirit, giving new impetus to the institutional initiatives of cooperation among the various churches. One important institution that has been spearheading ecumenism in Asia is the Christian Conference of Asia (CCA), comprising the Protestant and Orthodox churches. At the time of time of its founding in 1957, it was known as the East Asia Christian Conference (EACC); in 1973, it became the CCA. The CCA and the Federation of Asian Bishops' Conferences (FABC), the Roman Catholic body of Asian bishops, have been in collaboration and undertaken many major ecumenical initiatives.[20] To provide a structural means to carry out these cooperative efforts, these two bodies created a committee known as the Asian Movement for Christian Unity (AMCU), which has been functioning since 1996. The FABC, for its part, has a very actively engaged department dedicated to the issue of interreligious dialogue and ecumenism, the Office of Ecumenical and Interreligious Affairs (OEIA).[21] It is significant that the CCA and FABC have come together to think and act in the field of inter-religious relationships—one of the major concerns throughout Asia. In a 1986 CCA-FABC initiative in Singapore, a highly significant consultation of representatives of various church bodies met under the theme, "Living and Working Together with Sisters and Brothers of Other Faiths in Asia." One crucial point of discussion and agreement at this gathering concerned the relationship of mission and dialogue (evangelization and dialogue), something that was under debate in the various churches. The Singapore consultation brought greater clarity and nuance to this question of the interrelationship between mission and dialogue. It stated:

> We affirm that dialogue and mission have their own integrity
> and freedom. They are distinct but not unrelated. Dialogue is
> not a tool or instrument for mission and evangelization, but it

20. For a detailed historical account, see vol. 1 of Koshy et al., *History of the Ecumenical Movement*. See also Christian Conference of Asia et al., *Living and Working Together*, 107; Rouse and Neill, *1517–1948*; Gnanadason, "Contributions of the Ecumenical Movement," 134–44.

21. For OEIA statements from recent years, see Eilers and Federation of Asian Bishops Conferences, *For All the Peoples of Asia*.

does influence the way the Church perceives and practices mission in a pluralistic world.[22]

What about theologians? D. T. Niles, M. M. Thomas, Stanley Samartha, and other Asian thinkers have made substantial contributions to world ecumenism, drawing particularly from Asian experiences. This legacy lives on today among present-day Asian theologians. Theologians across denominations meet regularly at the Congress of Asian Theologians (CAT). Churches are developing jointly Asian theologies, going beyond doctrinal differences among the traditional denominations and oriented to reinterpreting the Gospel most effectively in the context of Asia, facing the challenges of the times. It is interesting to note that Asian theologians hardly ever meet to discuss the various Christian churches' and denominations' doctrinal differences. This is not a priority for them. Instead, the question is this: how can we be truly Asian in understanding and interpreting the Christian mission and message?

Finally, it should be pointed out here that Asian ecumenism had a wider impact on the political realm. The effort of churches in the various regions of Asia to come together and engage themselves in mission and witness has also contributed to create greater regional solidarity among Asian nations. It is difficult to measure this impact. The ecumenical movement in Asia has generated transnational cooperation and a sense of "Asianness"; it preceded political cooperation in this part of the world. We can surely say that bodies like the Association of South East Nations (ASEAN) and the South Asian Association of Regional Cooperation (SAARC) are strengthened through the Asian ecumenical movement.[23]

Part II: Insights from Interreligious Relationships for a New Ecumenical Practice

Casting the Ecumenical Net Wider

One of Asia's great contributions to the ecumenical movement is to have widened the concept of "ecumenism" to include within its horizon the relationship with peoples of other faiths and traditions. This came to be known as "wider ecumenism."[24] There were—and are—purists who resist such an issue and would restrict the word strictly to the relationship among the

22. Christian Conference of Asia et al., *Living and Working Together*, 104–6.

23. See Koshy et al., *History of the Ecumenical Movement*, 2:286.

24. Ariarajah, "Wider Ecumenism."

Christian churches. If the Church is the sign and sacrament of the unity of humankind as declared by Vatican II,[25] then ecumenism cannot but be affected by the issues that touch upon humanity and its unity. One such question is the relationship among different faiths. Churches are invited to move ahead toward the goal of greater understanding, harmony, and peace among religions.[26] By fostering relationships with peoples of other faiths, the churches are contributing to the unity of humankind, hence the importance of their coming together for this cause. As the Sri Lankan theologian Wesley Ariarajah notes:

> At the global level, there is an increasing recognition that the world's problems are not Christian problems requiring Christian answers but human problems that must be addressed together by all human beings. We know that whether it is the issue of justice, peace and human rights, or the destruction of the environment, we need to work across boundaries of religions, nations, and cultures.[27]

The involvement with peoples of other faiths through wider ecumenism is bound to help intra-church unity too. During the missionary epoch, this was not possible due to a negative theology of other religions. It is significant that most of the ecumenical meetings that framed the interreligious agenda were held in Asia. The ecumenical movement pioneered a different theology of religion than the one that had characterized the missionary period. The development of a more positive attitude towards other religions owes a lot to the global ecumenical movement. Dialogue with other religious traditions opened the eyes of Asian churches to see the unity of the Church in a much broader light. This would include the relationship with other religious traditions through interreligious dialogue as well as unity with the whole of creation.

However, there is a sense of unease, insecurity, and threat connected with the use of the term "wider ecumenism." The point is well-formulated by Konrad Raiser in the form of a series of questions:

> Can the churches and those responsible for ecumenical organizations agree on a sufficiently firm common base for the understanding of ecumenism? Does ecumenism in the proper sense relate only to the search for the communion among the Christian churches, or should it be opened up to relations with other

25. Paul VI, *Lumen Gentium*, 1.

26. See Wilfred, "Christianity and Religious Cosmopolitanism," 216–32.

27. Ariarajah, "Wider Ecumenism," 21.

religious communities—as is frequently advocated in Asia? Should the ecumenical movement reach beyond the churches to make alliances with other groups in civil society? What is the proper relationship between the commitment to church unity and to social justice? Are common witness and evangelism more important than church unity?[28]

Wider ecumenism need not be a threat to ecumenism among Christian churches. The experience of Asia has shown that relationships among churches and dialogue with religions are intertwined and mutually supportive. As a result, an effective intra-religious dialogue among Christian churches has strengthened the interreligious dialogue of the wider ecumenism. Conversely, interreligious dialogue has called for greater unity and collaboration among Christian churches and communities. What Andrew Pratt says about the issue in the United States serves to confirm the Asian orientation:

> The two ecumenical conversations, interfaith and intrafaith, are connected and may be mutually beneficial. The new religious pluralism in the United States could contribute toward a positive, shared Christian identity that, in turn, might contribute toward healthy and mutually enriching interfaith relationships.[29]

Learning from the Theology and Practice of Interreligious Dialogue

The Asian theology of religions and the practice of interreligious dialogue have turned out to be important sources for ecumenism. Interreligious dialogue has suggested a non-teleological approach in inter-church relationships. This means that one need not hurry with unity and consensus. That would reflect a view from the center. Rulers and administrators are very concerned about a unity that ensures that everything is in order and under control. This imperial model of unity is not what is envisaged for the churches. Such a mindset and the values attendant to it could also be transported into the practice of ecumenism and in the relationship among religious traditions. For a long time, fulfillment theory was in vogue in the theology of religions, and it is still the dominant theological approach in many churches, especially in the Roman Catholic Church. Consider what a more recent document, *Dominus Iesus,* says: "Objectively speaking, they [other religions] are in a gravely deficient situation in comparison with

28. Raiser, *To Be the Church,* 15.
29. Pratt, "Out of One, Many; Within One, Many," 144.

those who, in the Church, have the fullness of salvation."[30] If other religions have elements of goodness and truth, they are only in an unfulfilled state; hence, one may not rest but hasten toward fulfillment until it is reached. Such an approach, however, does not really value the richness and uniqueness that each religious faith represents or the value of the pluralism and the rainbow-like beauty they manifest. A predetermined idea of fulfillment simply turns them into rungs of a ladder leading to the top—fulfillment—with no other value in and of themselves. As for the relationship among churches, this kind of perspective sees ecumenism solely in terms of organic unity. In fact, for the Roman Catholic Church, the fullness of the Church is to be found in *it*, while other churches and communities have *elements* of the Church of Christ. This is what I would call a teleological approach to dialogue and ecumenism, an approach which seriously undermines each. If, in interreligious relationship, we need to focus our attention on the richness the various faiths represent, so it is in the case of inter-church relationships. True ecumenism calls for appreciation of the history and tradition of other Christian churches for the *value they hold in themselves*. The rush towards organic unity could seriously undermine this. *Dialogue is a value in itself*, not simply a means to a predetermined end. It should be continuously fostered, independent of any goal. Setting goals could affect negatively the quality of the dialogue, and this applies as much to interreligious relationships as to ecumenical practices.

Dialogue is what we can do. What comes out of it is not under our control. We need to approach the fruit of dialogue with *a sense of mystery*. Teleological thinking and pragmatic practices may condition our minds to set definite goals for our dialogues. Doing this robs dialogue of its true spirit. If we take dialogue as an end in itself, not a means, then it creates an atmosphere for mutual learning and enrichment.

In interreligious dialogue, there is much opportunity for mutual learning and enrichment from the internal sources of each religious tradition. However, the world also gives new impetus to interreligious dialogue. For example, all religions are challenged to contribute to justice and peace, to human dignity and rights, around the world. Similarly, ecumenical endeavors could be enlivened today by drawing from *nonreligious resources and traditions*. The conversations among churches need not be restricted to their

30. CDF, *Dominus Iesus*, 22. A similar view is also expressed from Africa; concluding his article on this subject, Method Kilaini writes: "The ecumenical effort cannot end with inter-Christian dialogue but must go beyond to interreligious dialogue. And this will bear more fruit for all—Christians, Muslims, and those following traditional religions—if it is done ecumenically" (Kilaini, "Ecumenism in a Multi-Religious Context," 364–65).

doctrines and worship. The ecumenical net should be cast wider into the sea of humanity to reach the intricate problems it is facing today. "Justice, Peace, and Integrity of Creation" is a program and invitation by the WCC Vancouver Assembly (1983) to all member Churches and became an expression of commitment of the Churches for the transformation of the world and protection of the environment. It sets out an important ecumenical agenda for many years to come. So, too, the concerns which form part of the WCC Commission of Churches on International Affairs.

Reconception of truth is another lesson we learn from interreligious dialogue. Truth as a set of doctrines to be believed offers no real clue or approach to other religious traditions. We need to begin from somewhere else. One of the realizations in interreligious understanding is what was expressed in Rig Veda—*ekam sat; vipraha bahudha vadanti*—truth is one, but sages have spoken of it in a plurality of ways.[31] If we follow the same line of thought in ecumenical dialogue, it would mean that, instead of resolving doctrinal differences to arrive at the goal of unity, we would go deeper into the different theological languages and accents in which the truth of the Gospel has been expressed. We would contemplate the rich truth of the Gospel as refracted through the prism of different denominations.

The understanding of ecumenism and the relationships among churches will be different if we employ new insights and the perspectives of contemporary hermeneutics.[32] With reference to ecumenism, we could highlight at least two important hermeneutical intuitions. First, every text needs to be placed in the overall context of a broader discourse. For example, Pope Paul VI made it clear in a speech at the beginning of the second session of Vatican II that the ecumenical relationship with the Christian churches and communities was an important goal of the Council. If so, it follows that not only *Unitatis Redintegratio* (the document speaking *ex professo* on ecumenism) but all the documents of Vatican II need to be read and interpreted from an ecumenical perspective as well. Second, every text is open-ended; namely, the meaning and significance of a text goes beyond the meaning intended by the author and could be reinterpreted and reappropriated anew every time and in different situations. This means, whether documents of Vatican II, the WCC, or other bodies, they need to be reinterpreted in relationship to the local context.[33]

31. Rig Veda 1.164.46.

32. In this connection, I would like to underline the importance of the hermeneutics of Vatican II—that is, not only diachronic but also synchronic; such a hermeneutic which relates the various teachings and insights with one another will have great impact in fostering ecumenical relationships.

33. See Wilfred, "Die Rezeption des II. Vatikanums in Asien," 426–66.

Further, we need to build on what Vatican II said about a "hierarchy of truths,"[34] which helped greatly to facilitate ecumenical understanding. For example, in Catholicism, Marian dogmas need not be the kind of obstacles they would have been had no one acknowledged a hierarchy of truths. Similar to a hierarchy of truths, we need a "hierarchy of laws" which will help pave the way for better ecumenical relationships.

Ecumenism and the Issue of Power

There is another set of issues which should also form part of any ecumenical engagement: the question of authority and power and their conception in the Church and in relationship to the world. Let us begin with the inner-church issue of power. For those who set their goals on doctrinal reconciliation among the denominations, it is good to remember that *one of the greatest obstacles in ecumenical understanding is the conception of power in the Roman Catholic Church and its juridicism.* Lukas Vischer, a leading ecumenist of his time, had already indicated where the real problem lies. In his words,

> The question about the proper "juridical form" of the Church is an eminently ecumenical problem. . . . The "juridicism" of the Roman Catholic Church is the object of earnest and radical criticism from the side of the Orthodox as well as from the Churches of the Reformation. They see in the premises as well as in the conclusions of canon law some of the deepest differences which divide them from the Roman Catholic Church.[35]

Let us reflect on the *issue of power in the Churches in relation to its exercise in the larger society.* Some Churches have an understanding of power that resonates with medieval and feudal models in total contrast to a *participatory approach* that is respectful of modern democratic aspirations and based on human dignity and rights. Churches embedded in the traditional conception of authority and power are increasingly being challenged by an approach to power in which checks and balances are an integral part. An example would be the call to make human dignity and human rights among the fundamental principles of canonical order in the Roman Catholic Church, hence its accountability and transparency in this matter.[36] But this move, unfortunately, is being resisted. The call from the world for

34. Second Vatican Council, *Unitatis Redintegratio,* 11.
35. Vischer, "Reform of Canon Law," 395, 398.
36. See Kirchschläger, "Human Rights and Canon Law," 65–77.

responsibility and transparency in the exercise of power and authority poses a challenge to all Churches in the *ecumene*. This issue may not be set aside. It needs to be faced by Christian Churches and communities. The source and channel of power in the Church and the mode of its exercise may not go against the order of creation in which every human being has dignity and inalienable rights. Ecumenical engagements need to grapple with this question.

To respond to the challenge of power posed by the modern world would be for all Churches a regression to the early Christian understanding of power and authority in the Church as service. The recovery of this truth will help loosen the rigorous conception of power and authority that follows the feudal model in the Church rather than the Gospel model of service. The model of authority in the Church as service implies, in an eminent way, the participatory exercise of power with due respect to human dignity and rights.

Part III: Future of Ecumenism from a Postcolonial Perspective

Postcolonialism helps us see the future of ecumenism from the perspective of difference *and plurality* rather than think of restoration of a broken unity.[37] There is certainly room to speak of unity, but this kind of unity, paradoxical as it may sound, is inextricably bound to difference. There is, of course, unity between man and woman when we think of their common humanity. And yet what constitutes deeper union are the *differences* man and woman represent. It is precisely the difference among them that becomes the basis of their deeper bonds of union. Could we use this analogy for interdenominational relationships? Are we not in an age when, through the ecumenical movement, we celebrate the *difference?* The ecumenical cause is lost when we interpret difference as *deviance*. The differences the denominations and Christian groups represent are a sign of the richness of Christianity and not a weakness to lament.

37. A vast amount of literature is available on this growing field of postcolonial studies. The following selected works will help identify some of the major concepts in postcolonial theories: Nayar, *Postcolonial Studies*; Dirlik, "Postcolonial Aura," 294–320; Mongia, *Contemporary Postcolonial Theory*; Gandhi, *Postcolonial Theory*; Said, *Orientalism*; Ashcroft et al., *Postcolonial Studies Reader*; Bhabha, *Location of Culture*; Barker et al., *Colonial Discourse, Postcolonial Theory*; Bilimoria and Al-Kassim, *Postcolonial Reason and Its Critique*; McLeod, *Beginning Postcolonialism*; Ashcroft et al., *Key Concepts in Postcolonial Studies*; McLeod, *Routledge Companion to Postcolonial Studies*; Parry, *Postcolonial Studies*; Kumar Das, *Critical Essays on Postcolonial Literature*; Loomba, *Colonialism/Postcolonialism*.

Besides helping us to value difference and pluralism, postcolonialism also gives us a *relational self-definition*. The colonizer and the colonized cannot be interpreted independently of each other. The one is comprised in the definition of the other. Thus, Catholics are implied in any understanding of Protestants and vice versa. They are relational concepts.

A good ecumenical practice would also presuppose a critical approach to the roles that language and discourses play in constructing the other—the other denomination, the other Christian belief. Postcolonialism helps us analyze how "the Catholic" and "the Protestant" are constructed through the use of language and discourses. It would be interesting to study, for example, how the discourse among Irish Catholics about Protestants is traditionally constructed and, conversely, how the discourses of traditional Catholics on Pentecostals and Pentecostal discourse on Catholics are constructed. It would also be interesting to study how the Russian Orthodox Church constructs its discourse about Protestants and Catholics in the context of ethno-nationalism. Ultimately, the underlying issue in ecumenism is something common to contemporary cultural issues: the question of how the "other" is constructed. Postcolonialism could lead us to a critical approach to the way the "other" churches, ecclesial groups, and denominations are constructed.[38]

Not unlike the case of Indian caste, each denomination has an ascriptive identity in the discourse of the "other." The "other" Church, denomination, or community is represented as something fixed and unchanging. Postcolonialism helps us read various Christian denominations as *different discursive practices* with their resources in history and tradition.

Closely connected with discourse analysis in ecumenical practice is the question of *representation*, which is again a very important theme in postcolonial theory. Representation is not only an epistemological issue but also a deeply political one and a platform for the play of power. Postcolonial theoretical forays have shown that stereotypical representation of the other is a strategy of power and control. This mechanism could be at play in the field of religion and among the Churches, too.

Postcolonialism has been critical of abstract universalism and moral globalism which want to transcend the particular and its historical and spatial situatedness. The standard ecumenical agenda has traits of theological universalism which the postcolonial approach could help to address, bringing ecumenism to the level of grassroots, everyday practices, habits, and behaviors. Fostering dialogue at the grassroots level would imply a

38. See Jahnel, "Vernacular Ecumenism and Transcultural Unity," 404–25.

deconstruction of the discourses about various denominations and the kind of language we use to describe the other in ecumenical circles.

Conclusion

The ecumenical landscape has been changing through developments in the Churches and in the situation of the world. We need to take this into account. We are in a situation which calls for a redefinition of ecumenism itself, thanks to the profound transformations that have taken place in the last couple of decades. What were once the defining characteristics of ecumenism are no longer such for the new generations. Let me quote, in conclusion, the words of Konrad Raiser in his foreword to the second edition of the *Dictionary of the Ecumenical Movement*:

> Now . . . many of the traditional orientations of ecumenism are challenged or called into question. A new generation has moved into the positions of leadership in the churches for whom the ecumenical struggles and advances of earlier periods are no longer part of their personal memory, but at best a significant feature of recent history.[39]

There were times when *unity* was thought of as an important contribution for peace and reconciliation. Times have changed, and generations have succeeded. I surmise that the future of ecumenism, and the ecumenism of the future generations, lie in *fostering pluralism* and in appreciating difference, which will define the mutual relationships of the Churches. Promoting pluralism jointly in the society and in the world would be a great contribution of the Churches to peace in the world.

Bibliography

Abraham, K. C. "An Ecological Perspective on Ecumenism." In *Theology Beyond Neutrality: Essays to Honour Wesley Ariarajah*, edited by Marshal Fernando and Robert Crusz, 193–204. Colombo, Sri Lanka: Ecumenical Institute for Study and Dialogue, 2011.

Achútegui, Pedro S. de. "Statement and Recommendations of the First Asian Congress of Jesuit Ecumenists Manila." *Philippine Studies* 23.4 (1975) 18–23.

Ariarajah, S. Wesley. "Contribution of Asian Participation to Edinburgh 1910 Conference." In *Power, Politics, and Plurality: An Exploration of the Impact of Interfaith Dialogue on Christian Faith and Practice*, edited by Marshal Fernando, 257–68. Colombo, Sri Lanka: Ecumenical Institute for Study and Dialogue, 2016.

39. Lossky et al., *Dictionary of the Ecumenical Movement*, xi.

———. "Wider Ecumenism: Some Theological Perspectives." In *Encounters with the Word: Essays to Honor Aloysius Pieris, SJ, on His 70th Birthday, 9 April 2004*, edited by Aloysius Pieris et al., 3–22. Colombo, Sri Lanka: Ecumenical Institute for Study and Dialogue, 2004.

Ashcroft, Bill, et al. *Key Concepts in Postcolonial Studies*. London: Routledge, 2004.

———. *The Postcolonial Studies Reader*. London: Routledge, 1995.

Barker, Francis, et al. *Colonial Discourse, Postcolonial Theory*. New Delhi: Viva, 2012.

Bhabha, Homi K. *The Location of Culture*. London: Routledge, 1994.

Bhakiaraj, Paul Joshua. "Forms of Asian Indigenous Christianities." In *The Oxford Handbook of Asian Christianity*, edited by Felix Wilfred, 171–81. New York: Oxford University Press, 2014.

Bilimoria, Purusottama, and Dina Al-Kassim, eds. *Postcolonial Reason and Its Critique: Deliberations on Gayatri Chakravorty Spivak's Thoughts*. New Delhi: Oxford University Press, 2014.

Chia, Edmund Kee-Fook. "Ecumenical Pilgrimage Toward World Christianity." *Theological Studies* 76.3 (2015) 503–30.

Chow, Alexander. "Protestant Ecumenism and Theology in China Since Edinburgh 1910." *Missiology* 42.2 (2014) 167–80.

Christian Conference of Asia, et al. *Living and Working Together with Sisters and Brothers of Other Faiths in Asia: An Ecumenical Consultation, Singapore, July 5–10, 1987*. Hong Kong: Christian Conference of Asia and Federation of Asian Bishops' Conferences, 1989.

Clifton, Shane. "Ecumenism from the Bottom Up: A Pentecostal Perspective." *Journal of Ecumenical Studies* 47.4 (2012) 576–92.

Congregation for the Doctrine of the Faith (CDF). *Dominus Iesus: On the Unicity and Salvific Universality of Jesus Christ and the Church*. Vatican City: Libreria Editrice Vaticana, 2000.

———. "Letter to the Bishops of the Catholic Church on Some Aspects of the Church as Communion." May 28, 1992. Online. http://www.vatican.va/roman_curia/congregations/cfaith/documents/rc_con_cfaith_doc_28051992_communionis-notio_en.html.

———. "Responses to Some Questions Regarding Certain Aspects of the Doctrine on the Church." June 29, 2007. Online. http://www.vatican.va/roman_curia/congregations/cfaith/documents/rc_con_cfaith_doc_20070629_responsa-quaestiones_en.html.

Daughrity, Dyron B. "South India: Ecumenism's One Solid Achievement? Reflections on the History of the Ecumenical Movement." *International Review of Mission* 99.1 (2010) 56–68.

Dirlik, Arif. "The Postcolonial Aura: Third World Criticism in the Age of Global Capitalism." *Critical Inquiry* 20.2 (1994) 328–56.

Eilers, Franz-Josef, and Federation of Asian Bishops Conferences. *For All the Peoples of Asia: Federation of Asian Bishops' Conference Documents from 2002–2006, 2007–2012*. Vols. 3–4. Quezon City: Claretian, 2002.

Fernando, Jude Lal. "Ecumenism in Modern and Postmodern Contexts: In Search for an Ethic of Unity and Identity." *Svensk Missionstidskrift* 100.1 (2012) 65–89.

Fey, Harold E., ed. *1948–1968*. Vol. 2 of *The Ecumenical Advance: A History of the Ecumenical Movement*. 2nd ed. Geneva: WCC, 1986.

Gandhi, Leela. *Postcolonial Theory: A Critical Introduction*. New Delhi: Oxford University Press, 1999.

Gnanadason, Aruna. "The Contributions of the Ecumenical Movement in Asia to World Ecumenism." In *The Oxford Handbook of Christianity in Asia*, edited by Felix Wilfred, 134–44. New York: Oxford University Press, 2014.

Hurley, Michael. *Christian Unity: An Ecumenical Second Spring?* Dublin: Veritas, 1998.

Jahnei, Claudia. "Vernacular Ecumenism and Transcultural Unity Rethinking Ecumenical Theology after the Cultural Turn." *The Ecumenical Review* 60.4 (2008) 404–25.

Jeyakumar, Arthur. *Christians and the National Movement: The Memoranda of 1919 and the National Movement*. Bangalore: Centre for Contemporary Christianity, 2009.

John, Mary. *Indian Catholic Christians and Nationalism: A Study Based on the Official Catholic Journals of the Period 1857–1947*. Delhi: ISPCK, 2011.

Kelly, James R. "Spirals Not Cycles: Towards an Analytic Approach to the Sources and Stages of Ecumenism." *Review of Religious Research* 32.1 (1990) 5–15.

Kilaini, Method. "Ecumenism in a Multi-Religious Context." *The Ecumenical Review* 53.3 (2001) 357–65.

Kinnamon, Michael, and Brian E. Cope, eds. *The Ecumenical Movement: An Anthology of Key Texts and Voices*. Geneva: WCC, 1997.

Kirchschläger, Peter G. "Human Rights and Canon Law." *Concilium* (2016) 65–77.

Koshy, Ninan, et al. *A History of the Ecumenical Movement in Asia*. Vols. 1–2. Hong Kong: Christian Conference of Asia, 2004.

Kumar Das, Bijay. *Critical Essays on Postcolonial Literature*. 3rd ed. New Delhi: Atlantic, 2012.

Lindbeck, George. "The Unity We Seek Setting the Agenda for Ecumenism." *Christian Century* 122 (2005) 28–31.

Loomba, Ania. *Colonialism/Postcolonialism*. New York: Routledge, 2015.

Lossky, Nicolas, et al. *Dictionary of the Ecumenical Movement*. 2nd ed. Geneva: WCC, 2002.

McLeod, John. *Beginning Postcolonialism*. New Delhi: Viva, 2012.

———. *The Routledge Companion to Postcolonial Studies*. New York: Routledge, 2007.

Mongia, Padmini, ed. *Contemporary Postcolonial Theory: A Reader*. New Delhi: Oxford University Press, 1996.

Mullins, Mark R. *Christianity Made in Japan: A Study of Indigenous Movements*. Honolulu: University of Hawaii Press, 1998.

Murray, Paul. "Receptive Ecumenism and Ecclesial Learning: Receiving Gifts for Our Needs." *Louvain Studies* 33 (2008) 30–45.

Murray, Paul, ed. *Receptive Ecumenism and the Call to Catholic Learning*. Oxford: Oxford University Press, 2008.

Nayar, Pramod K., ed. *Postcolonial Studies: An Anthology*. Oxford: Wiley Blackwell, 2016.

Nedungatt, George. "Ecumenism and Canon Law." In *Revision of Canon Law*, edited by Felix Wilfred et al., 53–62. London: SCM, 2016.

O'Grady, John, and Peter Scherle, eds. *Ecumenics from the Rim: Explorations in Honour of John D'Arcy May*. Berlin: LIT Verlag Dr. W. Hopf, 2007.

Parry, Benita. *Postcolonial Studies: A Materialist Critique*. New York: Routledge, 2005.

Paul VI. *Lumen Gentium: Dogmatic Constitution on the Church*. Boston: Pauline, 1965.

Pratt, Andrew. "Out of One, Many; Within One, Many: Religious Pluralism and Christian Ecumenism in the United States." *Perspectives in Religious Studies* 42.2 (2015) 143–57.

Radano, John A., ed. *Celebrating a Century of Ecumenism: Exploring the Achievements of International Dialogue, in Commemoration of the Centenary of the 1910 Edinburgh World Missionary Conference.* Grand Rapids, Ml: Eerdmans, 2012.

Raiser, Konrad. *To Be the Church: Challenges and Hopes for a New Millennium.* Geneva: WCC, 1997.

Rouse, Ruth, and Stephen Charles Neill, eds. *1517–1948.* Vol. 1 of *A History of the Ecumenical Movement.* 3rd ed. Geneva: WCC, 1986.

Said, Edward W. *Orientalism.* New York: Vintage, 1978.

Sawyer, Mary R. "Black Ecumenical Movements: Proponents of Social Change." *Review of Religious Research* 30.2 (1988) 151–61.

Second Vatican Council. *Unitatis Redintegratio: Decree on Ecumenism.* Boston: St. Paul, 1964.

Snaitang, O. L. *A History of Ecumenical Movement: An Introduction.* Bangalore: BTESSC/SATHRI, 2004.

Stanley, Brian. *The World Missionary Conference: Edinburgh 2011.* Grand Rapids: Eerdmans, 2009.

Vischer, Lukas. "Reform of Canon Law: An Ecumenical Problem." *The Jurist* 26 (1966) 395.

Vorgrimler, Herbert, ed. *Commentary on the Documents of Vatican II.* Vol. 1. New York: Herder and Herder, 1967.

Weingartner, Erich. *The Tozanso Process: Ecumenical Efforts for Korean Reconciliation and Reunification.* Maryknoll, NY: Orbis, 1997.

Wilfred, Felix. "Christianity and Religious Cosmopolitanism." In *The Past, Present, and Future of Theologies of Interreligious Dialogue,* edited by Terrence Merrigan and John Friday, 216–32. New York: Oxford University Press, 2017.

———. "Die Rezeption des II Vatikanums in Asien." In *Vaticanum 2: Die Bleibeneden Aufgaben des Zweiten Vatikanischen Konzils im 21. Jahrhundert,* edited by Christoph Böttigheimer and Rene Dausner, 426–46. Freiburg: Herder, 2016.

———. *The Oxford Handbook of Christianity in Asia.* New York: Oxford University Press, 2014.

Young, Robert J. C. *Postcolonialism: A Very Short Introduction.* New York: Oxford University Press, 2003.

13

"I Am with You Always" (Matt 28:20): Jesus' Perspective on Ecumenism in the World Church

Teresa Okure, SHCJ

THIS STUDY TAKES A close look at "ecumenism in the world church" from the perspective of Jesus, who alone builds his church (Matt 16:16). Is "ecumenism" in the world church related to "Christian unity" for which Christ prayed, died, and rose from the dead, and which he bequeathed to his followers of all times (his world church) as his last will and testament? Though this reflection uses the great commission in Matthew as its entry point, its scope is Jesus' view on the question of "ecumenism in the world church" as found in our primary biblical—especially Gospel and New Testament— sources. The approach is inspired by the spirit of jubilee (Lev 25) that calls for a return to the origins and the ancestral land in the search for sustainable renewal. Its ultimate aim is to gain insight that can motivate and move Christians together to rediscover and embrace that Christly authenticity which Jesus bequeathed to them, God's church.

Preliminaries

I sincerely thank the organizers of this year's conference on ecumenism in the world Church for inviting me. In particular, I thank God for making it possible for me to accept the invitation and actually be here against all odds. I am particularly grateful that the conference has a preference for a dialogical style (which, for me, means a life-centered style) and that it does not emphasize PowerPoint presentations, though it considers this very helpful. Both provisions fit in well with my natural way of reading Scripture. I thank you all who have come to listen to my presentation. Actually, as the conference theme states, we are gathered here in Jesus' name, not to listen to me or other presenters but to listen to Jesus, who has convoked us on this occasion and in everything we do in life.

God's word "increases" and "multiplies" through sharing and proclamation (Acts 6:7). Our Christian faith commits us to do whatever we do by word or deed "in the name of the Lord Jesus, giving thanks to God the Father through him" (Col 3:17; cf. 1 Cor 10:31),[1] empowered by the Spirit who leads us to "the complete truth" (John 16:12) about why and how we are to gather as church in Jesus' name.

Hermeneutical Principles Guiding This Reflection

Four basic hermeneutical principles guide and enrich my reading of Scripture, and I apply these to this current presentation as well. My approach is scriptural and narrative. To say that the approach is scriptural is to say that it is Jesus-centered.[2] These four hermeneutical principles are the hermeneutics of (1) self-inclusion; (2) life; (3) appropriation; and (4) re-framing the question, and these four are intertwined. My presentation's conversational and anecdotal style invites reflection by raising many questions. I urge you to enrich the examples of these principles with your own from Scripture and from life.

Hermeneutics of Self-Inclusion

I learned the hermeneutics of self-inclusion by listening to Luke the Evangelist. In the prologue of his Gospel, Luke states that, having carefully studied and investigated the records of the things that "happened among us from those who were eyewitnesses and ministers of the word," he, too, thought it necessary to write his own understanding (interpretation, hermeneutics) of these events to the most excellent Theophilus so that he might "know the truth concerning the things" about which he had been instructed. The goal of his writing was to enable him and Theophilus to understand better and

---

1. Scripture translations in this work are my own, unless otherwise stated.

2. Benedict XVI (*Verbum Domini*, 11–13, 31) urges that everything in the Church's life be done from the standpoint of Scripture which gets its full meaning from Jesus.

become part of the events which happened among them (Luke 1:1–4). Luke was not an eyewitness of the events in the lifetime of Jesus. But he considered these events as having relevance for him and Theophilus.

By adopting a hermeneutics of self-inclusion, Luke discovered new perspectives in the life of Jesus which the Jewish-centered Evangelists, Mark (Peter's Evangelist) and Matthew (Levi), did not include. It led him, a Gentile Christian from the margins, to discover and include stories of peoples from the margins in the life and ministry of Jesus set within the socio-cultural context in which Jesus was born, lived, ministered, and died. Two outstanding examples are the inclusion of the outcast Samaritans, even making them bearers of key gospel values,[3] and the high rate of inclusion of women (non-legal persons in Jewish society at Jesus' time) paired with men on equal footing. Stories that exemplify the latter are those of the owner of the lost sheep and the lost coin (Luke 15:4–10); of Simeon and Anna (Luke 2:25–38); and of Cornelius and Lydia (Acts 10; 16:1–15).[4] Additionally, Mary, the mother of Jesus, and Elizabeth are key figures in the event of the incarnation (Luke 1:26–56, 57–66). Comprehensively, Luke pushes the genealogy of Jesus from Matthew's "son of David, son of Abraham" (Matt 1:1) to "son of Adam, son of God" (Luke 3:38; cf. 3:23–38), at which stage no human being can be excluded from belonging to the genealogy of Jesus.

These select Lucan examples suffice for what I mean by the hermeneutics of self-inclusion. Applied to the issue of ecumenism in the world church, I need to ask, "How does this issue concern me, especially as I was not there when the problem started? Do I need to go back to Erfurt, where Martin Luther lived and was ordained as a monk before he posted his ninety-five theses that led to the split within the church, the body of Christ, five hundred years ago?[5] What is ecumenism? Ecumenism has existed and been voluminously elaborated in theological institutions, church and ecumenical documents, symposia, and the works of scholars.[6] Is it the same as Christian unity? The Greek *oikoumenē* signifies the entire inhabited world created, loved, and redeemed by God in Christ (cf. John 3:16). Can one put a handle on this world to dialogue about it?

3. In the parable of the Good Samaritan, the Lucan Jesus posits the Samaritan as an example of what it means to be a neighbor (Luke 10:29–37) and recounts that a Samaritan leper alone, out of ten, returned to give thanks (Luke 17:11–19); both are peculiar to Luke. The Samaritan woman appears in John 4:1–42.

4. For Luke's pairing of Cornelius and Lydia, see Okure, "Challenge of Lydia's Leadership," 327–53.

5. 2017 marks the five hundredth anniversary of Luther's split with the church.

6. A Google search for "ecumenism," a concept dating back to Edinburgh 1910, yields about 1,860,000 results. See Farrell, "Ecumenism Today."

"Christian unity," on the contrary, is more specific, with detailed, visible practices that mark the separation—for instance, the Eucharist, church leadership, devotion to Mary. Does ecumenism convey the same tangibility as does Christian unity or disunity? Does it challenge us to a personal active response the way Christian unity does? If not, how can I relate with it?

These questions do not imply that ecumenism has achieved nothing; otherwise, we would not be here. But why has it not achieved the full "visible unity in one faith and one eucharistic fellowship, expressed in worship and common life in Christ, through witness and service to the word,"[7] a unity for which Christ prayed (John 17:20–21) and which most, if not all, Christians desire? I cannot, for instance, translate ecumenism in my Ibibio language the way I can translate Christian unity (*edidiana kiet me Christians ke Christ*) or disunity (*unana edidiana kiet ke Christ*)? Viewed from the standpoint of Christian unity or disunity, ecumenism has concrete areas that all Christians have to work on collaboratively in order to make Christian unity happen.

Pope Francis is often quoted, rightly or wrongly, as saying that Christian unity will not happen until Jesus' second coming. If true, the pope may be voicing the basic problem surrounding Christian unity: our core unwillingness or unreadiness to make it happen. How does this stance square with Jesus' own intensive prayer and last will and testament for all his followers of all times—"that they may all be one"—even as he and the Father are one (John 17:21)? What has continually blocked the fulfillment of this prayer? Does the current state of division among Christians serve the evangelist's purpose that unity was to serve, "so that the world may believe that you sent me" (John 17:22)? Jesus' prayer is for here and now, not for his second coming. Do we have the right to directly or indirectly block God's answer to his prayer? Jesus not only prayed; he consecrated himself so that we might "be consecrated in the truth" (John 17:19), the truth being God's word about us and about creation, not our word about God.

These and more concrete questions arise and require active answers when I think of Christian unity or the lack of it for my hermeneutics of self-inclusion. I do not have the same handle on the discourse on ecumenism. Put this way, I can see that the issue of Christian unity concerns me because, by baptism, God has constituted me as a Christian and registered me as a firstborn "citizen" of heaven (cf. Heb 12:22–24). While people may deny their citizenship or adopt a new one, essentially, they can do nothing to change the fact that they were born as citizens of a given country. The same applies with regard to our citizenship of heaven. We may be good or bad

7. World Council of Churches, "Constitution and Rules of the WCC," 2.

citizens of heaven, but citizens we are. The hermeneutics of self-inclusion obligates me to see all Christians as sisters and brothers in Christ, irrespective of their denomination, because God has included them, too, in God's family, aware that Christ is among us and has commissioned us together to proclaim God's gospel to "all nations" (Matt 28:20).

Hermeneutics of Life

A hermeneutics of self-inclusion leads to the hermeneutics of life. The things "that were accomplished among us" are essentially about life. Friends and colleagues first described my hermeneutical approach as "a hermeneutics of life" before I became conscious of it myself.[8] The hermeneutics of life has two basic dimensions: firstly, Jesus is "the life" (John 14:6) and "in him was life" ($z\bar{o}\bar{e}$, absolutely; John 1:4); secondly, the gospels and all discourses of and about Jesus are about life. The life in him "was/is the light for all humans" in the entire inhabited earth. Jesus declares that he came to give "life in all its fullness" (John 10:10) and to impart knowledge of God which is not intellectual knowledge but "eternal [or enduring] life" for the receiver (John 17:3). The climactic bestowal of this life is the Eucharist, a sacrament of initiation, which one must eat to have eternal life.[9] It is the bond of unity. Jesus had a Eucharistic mindset and bequeathed the same to his followers.[10]

This is the core reality in which I include myself and in which I practice my hermeneutics of self-inclusion as a Catholic Christian in the world church. At every stage, I need to ask: how does my hermeneutics of life enable me personally to receive this life in its fullness and live it in the context of the world church? What are the perimeters of this life, and what blocks it from flowing fully into me and us since "we though many are one single body for we all share in the one loaf [the body of Christ]" (1 Cor 10:17)? To what extent am I Eucharist, breaking the bread of my life for others to eat and have life in its fullness, regardless of creed, denomination, gender, color, or race?

This life results in unity and reconciliation: the gathering together of all things to God in Christ. Scriptural examples abound. Jesus died in order "to gather together all God's scattered children," not only the Jewish nation

---

8. My sisters in my Society of the Holy Child Jesus call me "John 10:10." They say I hardly speak about Scriptures without quoting the text, "I have come that they may have life and have it more abundantly (or ever increasingly)." See also my interview by Mark Riedemann in Okure, "God Speaks to Africa."

9. The protracted discourse in John 6 illustrates this.

10. Okure, "Eucharist," 90–133.

(John 11:52). When "lifted up," he would, "draw all peoples to myself" (John 12:32). The Pauline letters declare that, in and through Jesus, God unites to the divine self "all things . . . in heaven and things on earth" (Col 1:20). Ephesians and Galatians celebrate God's breaking down of all anthropological and sociocultural barriers between Jews and Gentiles in Christ, making them one (cf. Eph 2:11–22; Gal 3:25–29), even "appealing to us" to be reconciled to God (2 Cor 5:16–21). Jesus inseparably reconciled humanity to the divine self by becoming a human being (cf. John 1:14), "like us in all things except sin" (Heb 4:15). Becoming is something physical, not abstract.[11]

The question arises: does the current division and disunity among Christians serve this comprehensive reconciling purpose of Jesus' mission? Christians are collectively "Christ's body" (1 Cor 12:27) and branches of his vine (John 15:5). No part of the body exists in function of itself. Branches exist to bear fruit; otherwise, they are useless. Are we true to our Christian identity if we fail to commit ourselves to be architects, evangelists, promoters of God's gathering and uniting of all things to him in Christ? We are expected to be the immune system of Christ's "body the church" (Col 1:24), not HIV viruses, inserting ourselves into the system, simulating this system while eating it away from within until it collapses.[12]

The Eucharist is the way of life for Jesus and the Christian, the bond of unity for all incorporated into his body by baptism. Ironically, the Eucharist constitutes one of the greatest, if not the greatest, divide among Christians constituted such by Christ's passion, death, and resurrection. Part of the problem is that we have grown comfortable with divisions within Christianity and have developed all kinds of reasons for remaining as we are. How do we live and practice ecumenism within Christ's one divided body? How do we receive the body of Christ divisively? Paul had severe words for the Corinthians whose reason for division during the Lord's Supper was nowhere near the divisions we have today (1 Cor 11:17–43).

Hermeneutics of Appropriation

The hermeneutics of appropriation takes its basic inspiration from Jesus' concluding advice in his Sermon on the Mount (Matt 5–7). The one who hears, keeps, appropriates, and puts into practice his teaching in this sermon (the charter of God's kingdom) is like one who "builds his/her house [*oikos*, a unit of the *oikoumene*] on rock" such that no force, such as a tsunami or

11. See further John 1:14; 1 John 1:1–3; 2 Pet 1:16–18.

12. AIDS results from the breakdown of the immune system by the HIV virus, which is why it is called *Acquired Immune Deficiency Syndrome*.

hurricanes Katrina, Harvey, or Irma, can destroy it (Matt 7:24). Again, he says, "Now that you know these things, happiness will be yours if you do them" (John 13:17). In other words, if you receive my teaching, appropriate, eat, digest, and make it the food that nourishes and sustains every aspect of your life and actions, you will find true happiness. Jesus himself made God's word and will "the food" that nourished and sustained his life and mission (John 4:34; 17:4), even when doing so meant drinking the bittersweet cup of his glorifying death (John 18:10–11). Deuteronomy 6:4–9 helps us to concretize the all-embracing nature of the hermeneutics of appropriation:

> Hear, O Israel, the Lord your God, the Lord is one. You shall love the Lord your God with all your heart, and with all your soul, and with all your might. Keep these words that I am commanding you today in your heart. Recite them to your children and talk about them when you are at home and when you are away, when you lie down and when you rise. Bind them as a sign on your hands. Fix them as an emblem on your forehead. And write them on the doorposts of your house and on your gates. (NRSV)

This passage counsels the appropriation of the Mosaic Law. Jesus has given us "a new commandment" with his new covenant: to love one another as he has loved us (John 13:34–35) by laying down our life for one another after his example (John 15:13). Do we make this commandment the organizing principle of our lives and ecumenical relations as counseled in Deut 6? The hermeneutics of appropriation obligates us to remember Jesus' fundamental assurance: when you are "gathered in my name" as church (ekklēsia) know, be aware, and never forget that "I am in the midst of you" (Matt 18:20). As you engage in my commission to evangelize all nations, know that "I am with you always" (Matt 28:20). Does remembrance of Jesus' presence in our midst govern how we relate to each other in the world church? Christians hardly see themselves as people gathered in Jesus' name, without boundaries of race, class, biological sex, and color (cf. Gal 3:28; Col 3:11).

Often, we gather not consciously in Jesus' name but in the name of our churches as Anglican, Roman Catholic, Orthodox, Lutheran, Methodist, and the plethora of Pentecostal Churches of our times. Religious congregations, too, define themselves more by their founders (Franciscans, Dominicans, Jesuits, Augustinians, etc.) than by Jesus. In Africa, Christian churches are more than legion; almost every other house along the street may be a church of its own, and the number increases almost daily. We received a divided Christianity and have unfortunately been excessively faithful in keeping and expanding that heritage. Who accepts responsibility for bringing this unfortunate heritage to Africa? It has triggered and promoted tribalism that was not there before (tribes, yes, but not tribalism); this, too, has entrenched itself inside the church and serves as an essential operating principle, whereby one is labeled "son/daughter of the soil." The recent crisis in Ahiara Diocese, Nigeria, is a case in point.[13]

Paul saw something akin to this when he asked the Corinthians who aligned themselves with their preachers—Peter, Paul, Apollos—whether "Christ has been dismembered" (*memeristai ho Christos*; 1 Cor 1:12–13): You take the head; I, the leg; another, the heart; and so forth. He reminds them that ministers and founders are but mere servants through whom they believed (1 Cor 3:5), as the Lord assigns to each but that everything belongs to them, and they to Christ, and Christ to God (1 Cor 3:22–23). Keen awareness that Jesus is with us "always" (Matt 18:20; 28:20) would commit us in turn to develop a deep consciousness to be with him always. It would help us to relate always with each other in his presence, even as he consciously lived and related with God, doing only as he saw the Father who was always with him doing (cf. John 5:19; 11:42; 17:32).

Hermeneutics of Reformulating the Question

Though put last, the hermeneutics of reformulating the question undergirds the other hermeneutics. When he was a student in Leuven in the early 1970s, Oscar Bimwenyi of Zaire (now, the Democratic Republic of Congo) discovered that he was learning answers to theological questions he never asked, while his own questions were not even asked, let alone answered. In liaison with fellow students from Latin America, he started the Ecumenical Association of Third World Theologians (EATWOT; notice the ecumenical dimension). The first conference of this new breed of seekers was held in Dar es Salaam, Tanzania, in 1979, and President Julius Nyerere of Tanzania (now a "Servant of God" heading for beatification) was present.

EATWOT works on a hermeneutics of suspicion of received questions and answers. It posits that theological questions and answers are not universal, suitable for all peoples of all times, devoid of context, independent of those who ask and give the answers. On the contrary, they are fundamentally subjective, subject to the humans who ask and give the answers

13. A Google search on "Ahiara diocese crisis" offers links to full details of the complicated story of Bishop Okpaleke, appointed by Pope Francis for the diocese but rejected for not being indigenous to the diocese.

in any given epoch.[14] Every theological question is *from* a context and *for* a context.[15] Experience—life—is the first school of theology (not "faith seeking understanding through philosophical discourse," which is the classic definition attributed to Anselm). When the local is genuinely true, the universal and ecumenical world perspective is genuinely true. The local is an integral building block of the universal.

A hermeneutics of self-inclusion, of life, and of appropriation necessarily involve a hermeneutics of asking the question anew from the standpoint and location of the inquirer. There is a story told of an African in a catechism class on original sin and the consequences of having eaten the forbidden fruit (labeled "apple," though not in the text) (Gen 3). The catechumen asked "Is this tree in our country?" "No," was the answer. He rejoined, "In that case, the problem does not concern us." In another class on the Blessed Trinity (Father, Son, and Holy Spirit), someone else asked, "Did you say the Second Person is truly God's Son and God is his Father?" "Yes," came the reply. "Then, where is the mother?" The missionary started giving a philosophical explanation about emanation, consubstantiality with the Father, and so forth. The catechumen got up and ceremoniously left, saying, "No one deceives an old man in his old age." These catechumens were doing theologies of self-inclusion, of life, and of reformulating the question aimed at better appropriating the teaching given to them.

True theologies in context need to be rooted in God's word about God, about us, about church, and about creation, not *a priori* rooted in our word about God, which is often crippled by questions born of past contexts (God and Jesus are with us always; so, too, the Spirit delights in renewing all things). John Paul II (now Saint) counsels this:

> The commitment to ecumenism must be based upon the conversion of hearts and upon prayer, which will also lead to the *necessary purification of past memories.* With the grace of the Holy Spirit, the Lord's disciples, inspired by love, by the power of the truth, and by a sincere desire for mutual forgiveness and reconciliation, are called to *re-examine together their painful past* and the hurt which that past regrettably continues to provoke even today. All together, they are invited by the ever fresh power of

14. For the first manifestos of EATWOT, see Appiah-Kubi and Torres, *African Theology en Route*; Fabella and Torres, *Irruption the Third World*; and *Voices*, the EATWOT journal, accessible online at http://eatwot.net/VOICES. (For a complete list of its issues, see http://internationaltheologicalcommission.org/files/EATWOTsBibliography.pdf.)

15. This view has inspired many contextual theologies, such as those found in Segovia and Tolbert, *Reading from This Place*, and lately, the Society of Biblical Literature's Bible commentary series, Texts@Contexts.

the Gospel to acknowledge with sincere and total objectivity the mistakes made and the contingent factors at work at the origins of their deplorable divisions.[16]

How do we today reset the question of ecumenism, the quest for Christian unity in God's world church? Do we need to keep struggling to find satisfactory answers to the same old questions, not asked by us? Are the ecumenical questions asked five hundred years ago and as individuals and groups have articulated them throughout history as relevant today as they were then? Are we asking the right questions? If not, can we get the right answers? Are we using the right language, images, and conceptions in our discussion of Christian unity? If not, will we ever get the correct answers, true answers, that propel us to full visible Christian unity? Where do we get pertinent questions and sustainable resources that can help us to be focused on the issue of full visible Christian unity for which Christ prayed?

Resources for Rethinking Ecumenism as Christian Unity

1. Recognition of Truths That Set Free

Christian unity and ecumenism are issues for the church, not for individuals. If ecumenism is difficult to grasp, even more so is the concept of church. When we add "world" to it ("world church"), the concept becomes vaster and more unmanageable.[17] We view the church variously as institution, bride of Christ, body of Christ, people of God, communion, mother, and so forth.[18] Most people, however, see the church as the hierarchy set to govern the laity. This emerges in such clauses as "the church teaches"; "the church says"; "holy mother church reminds us" and "gives us the sacraments." What readily comes to mind in each of us when we speak of the church and the world church? How do we live ecumenically in this church in a hermeneutics of life and self-inclusion?

Scripture views the church essentially as God's building, garden, and tilling (1 Cor 3:9; Eph 2:10) and as God's family (Eph 4:1–6). In the classic passage at Caesarea Philippi, Jesus told Peter (*Petros*, "rock") that he, not

16. John Paul II, *Ut Unum Sint*, 2. In many ways, this encyclical is a follow-up on the Second Vatican Ecumenical Council's *Unitatis Redintegratio: On Ecumenism*.

17. Okure, "Church in the World," 393–437.

18. For elaborations on the church by the Second Vatican Ecumenical Council, see *Lumen Gentium*, esp. chapter 2 (Flannery, *Vatican Council II*, 320–407).

Peter, would build his church on this rock (Matt 16:18). If the church is essentially God's work and establishment, planned "before the foundation of the world" (Eph 1:4), how can we humans claim it divisively as our corporate properties, aligned according to our human founders and patrimonies, at the expense of the visible unity of God's church? Could the basic problem be that we have developed our theologies and arguments (our right to worship as we believe, our patrimony, etc.) to benumb us into living comfortably with the divisions we are causing in Christ's body and dull our senses to the tragedy of disunity among Christians? How does Jesus feel about the enduring divisions in his body?

We need the shock therapy of the truth that sets free to help us abhor divisions among us. A first step is to humbly accept that the church is not our property; hence, we have no right to re-figure and reconstruct it to accommodate our inherited divisions. This truth helps us to face squarely, with deep humility, the tragedy of divisions within God's church. Earlier, I mentioned the HIV virus. The virus gets into the body's immune system and simulates the system (like a chameleon) such that the system thinks it is part of it. When medication is administered to destroy the virus, the system fights the medication, thinking it is attacking it. Meanwhile, the virus continues to eat away at the system until it is totally powerless to defend the body, which now collapses—hence the name "acquired immune deficiency syndrome" (AIDS). Fortunately, with regard to Christ's body, no virus can succeed in utterly destroying it. Jesus' resurrection from the dead—death being "the last enemy [virus] to be destroyed" (2 Cor 15:26)—guarantees against this. But that does not exonerate us.

Keen awareness of this truth impels each church to return to our inner rooms and to seriously ask ourselves whether we are part of the immune system of Christ's body (gathering with him) or whether we are inside the body calling ourselves Christians while our visible life and psychic self-identification lie in our diverse denominations. Pulling down other Christian denominations is common practice in many parts of the world church. Ironically, the early Christians, our ancestors in faith, started with sociocultural and religious divisions: Jew, Gentile, circumcised, uncircumcised, Greek, barbarian, Scythian, male, female (cf. Gal 3:28; Col 3:11). They accepted that Jesus had broken down their mutually dividing wall of the law by his body on the cross, forging them into a unity in the one family of God. Thus, they dropped their ingrained discriminatory and pejorative labels and accepted the name or called themselves "Christians." This name emanated from their first ever racially inclusive community in Antioch (Acts 11:19–26). Yet today, we identify ourselves by our denominations, not as Christians. This self-identification registers and continues to block our unity as Christians. Can we return to our common identity?

Through deep prayer and humility, we receive the grace to see the harm done in allowing our affiliations within the one filiation of God in Christ—our partisanship inside the one party of Christ, our different churches within the one church of God—to operate satisfactorily while we call ourselves Christians. Once we are genuinely dissatisfied with our divisions and are prepared to pay whatever price it takes to return to unity, God, who sees our genuine desire to let go what we hold dear that blocks the mutual flow of Christ's blood in us, will reward us.

Each year, we pray together for Christian unity for a week that culminates in the feast of the conversion of St. Paul (January 25). We earnestly ask God to unite us without being ready and willing to budge on what we consider as essentials. What are these essentials outside Christ? He is "the treasure hidden in the field," "the pearl of great price" (Matt 13:44–46); "all things and in all things is Christ" (Col 3:11). Can each church sacrifice, make a bonfire, of what it considers essential outside Christ in order "to gain Christ and be given a place in him" as Paul did in true conversion (Phil 3:3–9)? As a condition for discipleship, Jesus says that whoever loves father, mother, children, wife, husband, and even his/her own life (we add church here) more than him is unworthy of him (Matt 10:37; Luke 14:26). Like Paul, can every Christian church say, "All that previously mattered so much to me, I count as rubbish if only I can gain Christ and be given a place in him, no longer seeking for posts, places, position in my own church patrimony, at the expense of unity in Christ?" The Second Vatican Ecumenical Council and the Great Jubilee 2000 invite us to return to Scripture, to our roots, to rediscover our true identity as Christians in all we do. Viewed in our ecumenical context, this requires that we return to Jesus and commit ourselves to understudying and receiving from him sustainable solutions to our lack of unity.[19] Focused concentration on our one patrimony of Jesus' gospel and his traditions would lead us faster to that unity for which we have been intensely praying for over a century.

19. The key documents are too many to be listed. Perhaps lesser known is John Paul II's *Novo Millenio Ineunte*, in which he invites all Christians to engage in this reflection on the Great Jubilee with him to forge new ways forward. Benedict XVI, *Verbum Domini*, 31, gives a summary of the Catholic Church's slow return to Scripture and affirms with the Council that Scripture is "the soul of Theology" and of the life of the Church.

2. Jesus' Gospel-centered Resources for Effective Ecumenism

Matt 18: A Church "Gathered in My Name"

Scholars see Matthew 18, on which this conference theme is focused (v. 20), as a chapter about the church gathered in Jesus' name. The chapter addresses the issues of the greatest in God's kingdom ("church," in our context); leading others astray (vv. 5–10); seeking the lost sheep (vv. 12–14); brotherly/sisterly correction (vv. 15–18); effectiveness of prayer of agreement (vv. 19–20); and forgiveness, which is illustrated with a parable (vv. 1–35). What can we learn from Jesus in this chapter to move us forward in the quest for Christian unity?

The disciples asked Jesus who was the greatest in the kingdom of heaven. Jesus did not reject the concept of being the greatest. He simply gave them the criterion for such greatness—becoming like little children, a criterion which was radically countercultural. Children in the Jewish and Greco-Roman cultures, like women, were non-legal persons. Jesus taught this criterion graphically, with his own version of PowerPoint. He called a little child to him (the child would have been in the community of disciples), stood him in their midst (so they could all see), and told them "Amen, in truth, truly I say to you, unless you [plural] change and become like little children you [plural] will not enter into the kingdom of heaven. Whoever [singular] makes self as humble as this little child is the greatest in the kingdom of heaven." Jesus is here telling his disciples that whoever (individual or group) has a child-like self-conception is the greatest in God's kingdom.

What if we were to bring this home today and ask Jesus, "Which is the greatest of the churches in the world today?" He would likely give us the same answer as he gave his disciples. That, historically, the Catholic Church is the greatest is not in question; children are not existentially greater than their mothers. We cannot rewrite the truth of history. The question is whether, when the church split, we still had the same organic universality in the Catholic Church. We may cite, though imperfectly, the analogy of the creation of the man and woman in Genesis 2. Before the separation of the creature God formed from the dust of the earth, the creature was *adam* (*adamah*, "that taken from the earth"). Scholars believe the creature was androgynous, both male and female. Once God separated the creature into male and female, each received a new designation (Gen 2:23) as man (*ish*) and woman (*isshah*). So, a new relationship was developed in the one humanity, but they reunited as husband and wife in "one flesh" (Gen 2:24).

What is the message here? For us to return to unity, each church party must learn to *change* and become like a little child, not holding on to its having been right. The truth is each church erred. John Paul II apologized to Luther;[20] so, too, did Pope Francis, both verbally and in his presence at different celebrations of five hundred years of separation. Is it not strange that we should celebrate separation, what was essentially anti-gospel? The celebration has reminded us that we erred.

There is an important lesson not to be missed in the little child as a model for greatness in God's kingdom/church: children do not think within borders of any kind—race, sex, or color. I recall the story of a boy at the International School in Lagos. He asked his mother if he could invite his friend to his birthday party. The mother tried in vain to find out if the friend was Black or White. Finally, she called a domestic employee, placed her hand next to that of the worker and asked the child, "Has your friend the same color as mine and yours or that of the staff?" The child replied, "Mommy, I don't know; when I go tomorrow, I will look." The friend was a Nigerian. The mother told the story and was ashamed for teaching the child racism based on color differences. Children do not hold on to hurts that last five hundred years. They do not live that long as children. I personally have learned much from using children as a lens for reading Mark's Gospel.[21]

Comprehensively, Matthew 18 teaches that greatness in the kingdom of heaven is not earned. It is conveyed by God. And this applies to Jesus himself in the celebrated passage of Philippians 2:6–11. Because he humbled himself to the lowest rank, God raised him to the greatest and highest level. The verb to make oneself as humble as a little child—*tapeinosei* (v. 4)—is the same as Jesus uses when speaking of himself (Matt 11:29). His followers are to learn from him gentleness and lowliness of heart: "That I am gentle [*praus*] and humble [*tapeinos*] of heart [*tē kardia*]." In Jewish culture as in African, specifically Ibibio, culture, the heart is the seat of life. We think and store thoughts in the heart (*ekikere k'esit*), not in the mind or head [*iwuot*]. Disciples are to learn this humility as integral to their life of being church. In Jesus' conception of greatness, unlike in ours, all disciples receive the same stature and dignity in him of being the firstborn, since heaven is "the assembly of the firstborn" (Heb 12:23).

Together, we need to reflect further on how to carry this model of the child into our discourse and desire for full visible Christian unity which Christ bequeathed to us as his dying gift and for which he gave us the Holy Spirit, who "causes to live" (*to zōopoioun*; John 6:63), to bond us into unity.

20. See, for instance, Accattolli, *When a Pope Asks Forgiveness*; John Paul II, *Ut Unum Sint*, 2. The Anglican-Roman Catholic International Commission (ARCIC III), of which I am a member, is currently studying the history of apologies by the Anglican and Roman Catholic Churches.

21. Okure, "Children in Mark," 127–44.

What would each church need to do, visibly and concretely, for the unity to occur in the spirit and ways of the child? Jesus condemns in no uncertain terms any action that puts a stumbling block before any of the little ones who believe in him. He forbids us to nurture anything in us that is a stumbling block for our entry into life and that prevents us from becoming the greatest, be it the eye, the hand, or the foot (Matt 18:5–10). In short, Jesus counsels us not to allow anything to stand in the way of our entering into life in God's church.

Finally, Jesus concludes his teaching on not allowing anything to block our entering into life by saying that this life is not possible without forgiveness from the heart. God, the Shepherd, takes the initiative in seeking the lost sheep (18:12–20). This section ends with the text of the conference theme. Jesus counsels us that, in the ecclesial community, any common decision we reach concerning forgiveness will be sound, as long as we follow the criteria he has mapped out for us. Our prayer of agreement in his name—that is, as Jesus has directed, lived, and taught us—will be granted because "where two or three of you are gathered in my name, I am there in your midst" (Matt 18:20). In other words, we cannot lose sight of him, his instructions and criteria, and still hope to be whole.

Forgiveness is an indispensable condition for being church and for true Christian unity. It is our sure way forward to full visible Christian unity, as it was essential in our salvation: "Father, forgive them, they know not what they are doing" (Luke 23:34). God cancels our debts, knowing that we have no means of paying them back, so that we may do the same for one another. This is the point of the parable of the talents in Matt 18:23–35. If we are to move forward, the different Christian churches need to be ready to forgive and cancel each other's debts since there is no way of paying back the mutual wrongs done in the course of the past five hundred years.

"I Am with You Always" (Matt 28:20)

This passage moves us out of intra-ecclesial relationships in the church to missionary activity that transcends us and supposes our bonding together in a common mission; a common purpose or identity binds people together.[22] What is the purpose of Christian unity? To become one big mega-body, "a self-referential church," as Pope Francis puts it?[23] People from a given coun-

---

22. See Luke 17:11–19, which tells of the ten lepers, both Jews and Samaritans, who banded together, bonded by their common ailment and banishment from their respective communities.

23. On this issue, see, for instance, Mirus, "Spiritual Worldliness."

try may not relate and interact with one another at home. But once they meet outside their country, they instinctively bond and become friends.

This passage presents to us Jesus' post-resurrection commission, rooted in his conferral with "all authority in heaven and on earth." He commissions us to go and evangelize: "Make disciples of all nations" (*panta ta ethnē*), not simply individuals. This discipling of all recalls the last judgment (Matt 25:31–46). The son of man (this human being) will assemble "all the nations" (not just individuals) and judge them on their corporate response to human need. "I was hungry and you gave me to eat." Are we helping all the nations (ours included) to do this today? What difference would it make if, instead of focusing on what divides us, we together joined hands, heart, and souls, and, forgetting our churches, our patrimony, focused on our common mission given by Jesus? "Go out," do not stay put. Or look inwards or examine one another finding yourselves wanting, but go out to the whole world, proclaim the good news—Jesus of Nazareth—God's good news for all humanity, without exception.

The success of our mission and corporate witness to the world rests on our unity: "May they all be one so that the world may believe that you sent me" (John 17:20). Go, gather together all God's scattered children; break down the walls and barriers of hatred, racism, religious bigotries, and competition, as God's coworkers. Reconcile to God "all things" in heaven and on earth.

This commission is the climactic activity for the disciples in Matthew's Gospel as in all the gospels. In John, it takes the form of forgiving sin and also of Peter the leader, tending and feeding, not ruling over or dominating, the sheep—all sheep—with tender loving care. This mission lasts as long as the world lasts: "I am with you always till the end of the earth," til the gospel has been proclaimed to all peoples according to God's plan.

This corporate mission requires that we learn to befriend each other, as little children do, beyond and across denominational divides. We recall the boy who invited his friend to his birthday party. Today, we hear of Christian-Muslim conflicts in Nigeria often blown out of proportion by the media bent on seeing nothing good in the nation. In March this year, one of our SHCJ novices in Jos, northern Nigeria, was knocked down by a *keke* (a five-seater tricycle). The novice was crossing the highway after 6 a.m. Mass. The *keke* driver, eager to make as much money as possible before the end of the day, swerved round in the wrong direction to beat the traffic, and he very badly knocked down the novice (who, thank God, later recovered). He turned out to be a Muslim. His *keke* had a problem, so his fellow *keke* driver, a Christian, gave him his *keke* for the day (that being a Sunday, and the

Christian driver respecting the Day of the Lord) to help him make money for himself.

People responded to this grassroots friendship and bonding by observing how, at the mega level, we focus on the hatred and revenge between Christians and Muslims. Yet, the little people (the little children) know how to create friendship and help one another: "Unless you change and become like little children, you will not inherit God's kingdom, or be fully part of God's church." If we are to attain full visible Christian unity or communion, we need the spirit of little children and of forgiveness to move us forward and help us stop being "a self-referential church," refocusing on Christ and on the common mission he entrusted to us.

Towards Conclusion and a Prayer

This chapter has been non-conventional, raising questions for our common reflection and action and inviting each of us to engage in the hermeneutics of self-inclusion, life, appropriation, and reformulating the question of ecumenism and Christian unity. We need new wine and new wineskins if we are to live in the Spirit who makes us "a new creation" (2 Cor 5:17). This requires that we take seriously the contexts out of which quarrels emerged, hear the gospel afresh, and align ourselves with God's ecumenical ventures in service to his world church—all humanity.

In the spirit of jubilee, which calls for returning to our land and origins, we return to Jesus to hear his teaching about the essentiality of Christian unity and to put into practice what we learn from him, assured that he is with us always til the end of time. We ask him to help us to know/believe that he is with us always:

Give us, dear Jesus, listening ears and willing hearts to store and meditate on your living word and ever-active presence among us. Help us to embrace you in each other with joy, the joy of the gospel you spoke of, that comes to a woman in childbirth after she has given birth and forgets her birth pangs, "the missionary joy of sharing life with God's faithful people as we strive to light a fire in the heart of the world."[24] Empower us to share and spread this joy to all humanity. Help us to remove from our minds and psyche the barriers and boundaries we have erected for ourselves against one another, to our own impoverishment. Help us to be Eucharist with you, breaking the bread of our lives so that others, the world, may receive God's good news and have that fullness of life you came to give. May our united

24. Francis, *Evangelii Gaudium*, 271.

witness as members of your one body be the leaven that will transform and unite our war-driven and bigoted world. Amen.

Bibliography

Accattoli, Luigi. *When a Pope Asks Forgiveness: The Mea Culpas of John Paul II*. Boston: Pauline, 1998.

Appiah-Kubi, Kofi, and Sergio Torres, eds. *African Theology en Route: Papers from the Pan African Conference of Third World Theologians, December 17–23, 1977, Accra, Ghana*. Maryknoll, NY: Orbis, 1979.

Avis, Paul. *Reshaping Ecumenical Theology: The Church Made Whole?* New York: T. & T. Clark, 2010.

Benedict XVI. *Verbum Domini: The Word of God in the Life and Mission of the Church*. Vatican City: Libreria Editrice Vaticana, 2008.

Fabella, Virginia, and Sergio Torres, eds. *Irruption the Third World: Challenge to Theology, Papers from the Fifth International Conference of the Ecumenical Association of Third World Theologians, August 17–29, 1981, New Delhi, India*. Maryknoll, NY: Orbis, 1983.

Farrell, Brian. "Ecumenism Today: The Situation in the Catholic Church." November 21, 2004. Online. http://www.vatican.va/roman_curia/pontifical_councils/chrstuni/documents/rc_pc_chrstuni_doc_20041121_farrell-ecumenismo_en.html.

Flannery, Austin, ed. *Vatican Council II: The Conciliar and Post Conciliar Documents*. Mumbai: St. Paul's, 2007.

Francis. *Evangelii Gaudium: The Joy of the Gospel*. Vatican City: Libreria Editrice Vaticana, 2015.

John Paul II. *Novo Millenio Ineunte*. Vatican City: Libreria Editrice Vaticana, 2001.

———. *Ut Unum Sint: On Commitment to Ecumenism*. Vatican City: Libreria Editrice Vaticana, 1995.

Kasper, Karl. "The Ecumenical Movement in the Twenty-First Century." Presentation at the Fortieth Anniversary of the Joint Working Group between the Roman Catholic Church and the WCC, November 18, 2005. Online. https://www.oikoumene.org/en/resources/documents/commissions/jwg-rcc-wcc/the-ecumenical-movement-in-the-21st-century.

Kerr, David A., and Kenneth R. Ross, eds. *Edinburgh 2010: Mission Then and Now*. Regnum Studies in Mission 1. Oxford: Regnum, 2009.

Mirus, Jeff. "Spiritual Worldliness: Pope Francis's Critique of the Church." *Catholic Culture*, March 27, 2013. Online. http://www.catholicculture.org/commentary/otc.cfm?id=1066.

Okure, Teresa. "The Challenge of Lydia's Leadership (Acts 16:11–15) for the Contemporary Church." In *Bible and Leadership in Africa: Proceedings of the Seventeenth Congress of the Panafrican Association of Catholic Exegetes*, edited by Moise Adeniran Adekambi et al., 327–53. Abidjan: ITCJ, 2017.

———. "Children in Mark: A Lens for Reading Mark's Gospel." In *Mark*, edited by Nicole Durand et al., 127–46. Texts@Contexts Series. Minneapolis: Fortress, 2011.

———. "The Church in the World: A Dialogue in Ecclesiology." In *Theology and Conversation: Towards a Relational Theology*, edited by Jacques Haers and Peter de Mey, 393–438. Leuven: Peeters, 2003.

————. "The Eucharist: A Way of Life for Jesus and the Christian According to the Scriptures." In *Fiftieth International Eucharistic Congress: Proceedings of the International Symposium of Theology: The Ecclesiology of Communion Fifty Years after the Opening of the Second Vatican II, June 6–9, 2012*, edited by International Eucharistic Congress, 90–133. Dublin: Veritas, 2013.

————. "God Speaks to Africa." Interviewed by Mark Riedemann. YouTube video, 26:27. September 25, 2013. https://www.youtube.com/watch?v=ZdCNrZXUKTE.

Segovia, Fernando F., and Mary Ann Tolbert. *Reading from This Place*. Minneapolis: Fortress, 1995.

World Council of Churches. "Constitution and Rules of the World Council of Churches (WCC)." *Oikoumene*, February 14, 2006. Online. https://www.oikoumene.org/en/folder/documents-pdf/pb-02-constitution-rules.pdf.

Index